Hacking iPod® and iTunes®

Hacking iPod® and iTunes®

Scott Knaster

Wiley Publishing, Inc.

Hacking iPod and iTunes

Published by
Wiley Publishing, Inc.
10475 Crosspoint Boulevard
Indianapolis, IN 46256
www.wiley.com

Copyright © 2004 by Wiley Publishing, Inc., Indianapolis, Indiana

Published simultaneously in Canada

ISBN: 0-7645-6984-8

Manufactured in the United States of America

10 9 8 7 6 5 4 3 2 1

For general information on our other products and services or to obtain technical support, please contact our Customer Care Department within the U.S. at (800) 762-2974, outside the U.S. at (317) 572-3993 or fax (317) 572-4002.

Wiley also publishes its books in a variety of electronic formats. Some content that appears in print may not be available in electronic books.

Library of Congress Cataloging-in-Publication Data

For Timmy Thomas, wherever you are.

Credits

Executive Editor
Chris Webb

Development Editor
Scott Amerman

Production Editor
Angela M. Smith

Copy Editor
TechBooks

Editorial Manager
Kathryn A. Malm

Vice President & Executive Group Publisher
Richard Swadley

Vice President and Executive Publisher
Bob Ipsen

Vice President and Publisher
Joseph B. Wikert

Media Development Specialist
Angela Denny

Proofreading and Indexing
TechBooks

About the Author

Scott Knaster has been writing and hacking since way back when music came on LP-ROMs. His books were required reading for Mac programmers for more than a decade. Scott's most recent book was *Mac Toys* (with John Rizzo). Scott has every issue of *MAD* magazine, which explains a lot about his philosophy of life.

Acknowledgments

All the people in this list are true hackers: they bent reality to help me write this little book.

David Shayer, king of notes, supplied vast amounts of Note Reader information.

Keith Stattenfield helped with logistics and heuristics.

John Vink wrote the Celebrity Playlist application in Chapter 11 and provided lots of support and encouragement.

Greg Marriott, always helpful, delivered crucial info and a couple of great stories.

Tony Fadell, ringmaster, offered encouragement and insight.

Special thanks to the authors of shareware and scripts that greatly enhance what we can do with our iPods and iTunes.

Carole McClendon makes everything works smoothly, all the time.

Chris Webb gave me the chance to write about something I love, and he and Scott Amerman guided the project from start to finish.

Barbara Knaster was the Schwag Queen, in charge of getting samples of iPod accessories, and the Permit Person, making sure we had permission to use screen shots and product images.

The following companies kindly provided samples and support:

Arkon

ATI

Belkin

Griffin Technology

Marware

Sendstation Systems

Slim Devices

Ten Technology

Xtreme Mac

Most of all, thanks to Jess and Devi for living through yet another one of Dad's crunches.

Contents at a Glance

Contents

Part II: Hacking iTunes   101

Chapter 5: Play with Your Music 103

Part III: Appendices   247

Introduction

"A whole book about that?"

That was the reaction of a non-iPod-savvy friend when I told him I was writing a book about cool and wacky things you can do with your iPod and iTunes. He believed that when you get an iPod, you push a button and listen to music, period. He thought the iPod was simply a music player. He was misinformed.

The iPod is a digital music device—a wonderful and popular one. Playing music is what it was made for. If all you want to do is connect your iPod to your computer and transfer the music to it from CDs and the iTunes Music Store, you'll find all the information you need in the manual that comes in the box. But if you're curious about other stuff you can do with your iPod, you want to know more about the cool-but-obscure features inside iTunes, or you just want to spend a couple of hours exploring your iPod and iTunes, this book can help.

My skeptical friend would be surprised to learn that there are already a few good books about the iPod. This one is different. In this book, we spend most of our time on the fringes, outside the mainstream of features, focusing on the tricky, little-known, and unusual. A topic does not have to be useful to be included—it just has to be interesting. I tried to make this book a celebration and exploration of the iPod and iTunes. It's as if we sat down for coffee and I started showing you features and tweaks that I thought you might like to see.

Because this book exists out on the edges, there are plenty of topics we don't spend much time on. For example, we don't get into the basics of how to transfer songs to your iPod, but we do talk about how to transfer *weather forecasts* to your iPod.

I hope you have a good time and maybe even learn something useful as we wander around the iPod and iTunes for a few hours. If not, the book makes a great coaster to set your drink on while you're ripping CDs.

Digital Music

In 1975, I wanted an iPod.

I wasn't one of those creative kids who sat around with a notebook and made amazing drawings of space ships, monsters, and battles. Those kids went on to work on "*The Lord of the Rings*" and win Oscars. But I loved music, and I thought technology was incredibly cool. So one day I channeled my intense geekiness into "designing" the world's greatest jukebox.

This bookcase-sized magical device would hook up to my stereo, record all my vinyl records, and store the music somehow, probably on a library of very small tapes. There would be a keyboard and monitor attached. To listen to music, I would type commands like PLAY BAND "PINK FLOYD" or PLAY SONG "BALLROOM BLITZ". I could hear songs or albums in any order I wanted. Robotic arms might be involved in grabbing the right tape—being a software guy, I was vague on that part. I never tried to build my proto-iPod, which is probably a good thing.

Many years later, smart people had a simple, incredibly powerful idea that changed the world: media in the real world, like pictures and sound, could be digitized and manipulated by computers. Audio CDs were just giant disks filled with data. The invention of MP3 made it possible to cram music into one-tenth the space that it occupied on a CD, and the advent of MP3 encoders like SoundJam and Winamp made it real. No longer did we have to hand-encode our own MP3s by candlelight in unheated cabins.

Apple was late to this party, but eventually it figured out that a revolution was taking place and it started running faster than everyone else. The company absorbed SoundJam and transformed it into iTunes. Macs began shipping with drives that could burn CDs. And then, in October 2001, Apple introduced the iPod with iTunes 2. And it was about a million times better than what I had dreamed up 26 years earlier.

Getting thousands of songs into one box is a great achievement. Making the box small enough to fit in your hand is incredible. It's mind-boggling to look at an iPod in your hand and think that all your music is inside there.

About Hacking

The term *hacking* has gotten a bad reputation. Many people think of hacking as something evil, exploitive, and criminal. In recent years there has been a trend to reclaim the word and return it to its original, more noble meaning: creatively reshaping the world to make things better and more interesting. Hacking is about innovation, exploration, learning, and fun.

Hacking doesn't have to involve high technology. You can hack anything. My wife Barbara hacks her delicious pumpkin bread recipe by substituting applesauce for oil to make it more healthy. Holding a tiny nail in place with a pocket comb so you can hammer it is a classic hack. Heloise of *"Hints from Heloise"* fame was a household hacker. MacGyver was a famous hacker with a long-running TV show. When you figure out a secret route to the airport, you're hacking.

In this book, we hack iPod and iTunes by prodding, poking, and playing with them. Apple keeps iPod and iTunes locked up pretty tight, which eliminates the extreme hacks possible with more open system. So we won't be taking your iPod apart and turning it into a Pop-Tart toaster. Despite that, there's plenty of depth and power for curious folks to investigate in iPod and iTunes.

Who Is This Book for?

If you're comfortable with the basic features of your iPod and iTunes and you're interested in finding out more about what they can do, this book is for you. I don't assume any particular technical knowledge or geeky skill, although some topics are more challenging than others.

I tried to make this book as accessible as possible to both Macintosh and Windows users. Although most iPod and iTunes hacks work equally well on Macintosh and Windows, the iPod's Mac legacy means there are some tricks that only work on the Mac. These are noted with a "Mac-only" icon.

What's in This Book?

This book is divided into two parts: Part I for iPod and Part II for iTunes. Within each part, chapters divide the material into broad categories, although for some topics, the right chapter is not always clear, so I tried to make the most sensible guess for each hack.

Part I: Hacking iPod

This part focuses on special things you can do with your iPod. We start off gently by exploring some of the official but fringe iPod features and tricks, such as smart playlist updating and voice recording, and eventually end up way off in the fun zone talking about things like downloading driving directions to your iPod.

Part II: Hacking iTunes

In this part we spend time discussing our favorite music program, for Mac and Windows. We delve into topics that include getting album art, sneaking around the back rooms of the iTunes Music Store, playing with the psychedelic Visualizer, and broadcasting your tunes wirelessly to your stereo.

Appendixes

Our fact-filled appendixes provide thorough information about Note Reader, the iPod's best-kept secret, along with lists of links to more information, charts of iPod and iTunes versions, and an overview of the iTunes XML library format.

Compatibility and Conventions

The iPod hacks in this book assume you're running the latest version of iPod software for your model—as of this writing, that's 1.3 if your iPod doesn't have a dock connector, 2.1 if it does, and 1.0 if you have an iPod mini. The iTunes topics require iTunes 4 for Mac OS

X or Windows. Hacks that have special requirements are noted. For example, some tricks only work if you have iTunes 4.2 or later, which is the current version as of this writing.

Apple avoids model numbers in its product names and instead distinguishes between iPods by describing physical features. iPod fans outside Apple are more casual, calling them first, second, and third generation, or 1G, 2G, and 3G. Here's a translation between the official and unofficial terms:

iPod Models	
Official Apple designation	**Unofficial terms**
iPod (5GB) and iPod (10GB)	Original iPod; first generation; 1G
iPod (Touch Wheel)	Second generation; 2G
iPod (with Dock Connector)	Third generation; 3G
iPod mini	iPod mini or just mini

For information on newer iPods and software, see this book's companion Web site at www.wiley.com/compbooks/extremetech.

All iPod models have the same buttons:

iPod Buttons		
Official name	**Legend printed on button**	**Unofficial terms**
Play/Pause	>||	Play
Previous/Rewind	|<<	previous, prev
Next/Fast forward	>>|	next
Menu	MENU	menu
Select	(blank)	select, center button

When using your computer, some instructions in this book ask you to Control-click on a Mac with a one-button mouse, or right-click on Windows or on a Mac that has a two-button mouse. On a Mac, Control-click and right-click are the same.

Keeping Up-to-Date

One of the quirks of modern technology is that it often takes longer to make a book than it does to turn around a new generation of iPod. There's a good chance that by the time you read this, Apple will have new iPod or iTunes announcements that didn't make it into the book. That's why we have the Internet. You can always check this book's companion Web site at `www.wiley.com/compbooks/extremetech` to get the latest scoop on new goodies from Apple. If you want to let me know about mistakes in the book or cool new iPod stuff, please send me e-mail at `hackingipod@papercar.com`.

Listen Up!

I hope this book makes your relationship with your iPod and iTunes even better than it is, and you find many new and wonderful ways to get more out of your gadgets as you peruse the hacks. I also hope the book inspires you to explore and find your own nifty tricks and tips for improving your digital life. Have fun with the book, enjoy your music, and happy hacking.

Conventions Used in This Book

Throughout the book, you'll find highlighted text where I point out cautions, cross-references, notes of interest, and helpful recommendations. Specifically, four types of highlighted pointers appear:

 Gives you valuable information that will help you avoid disaster. Read all of these carefully!

 These are pointers to other areas in the book or on the Internet where you can find more information on the subject at hand.

 A recommendation of best-practice methods and superior products or tools to use.

 Pertains to items of interest related to the subject at hand.

Hacking iPod

part

Sounds Awesome: Music on Your iPod

This is a book about a music player and music software, so I think it's reasonable to start off with a chapter about music before we get into the wackier stuff. A beginning is a delicate time—let's begin our adventure with some delicate, friendly hacks.

Share Your iPod

Apple has always focused on making products for individuals: One of the company's early slogans was "one person, one computer", which was a radical thought in the early 1980s. After all, that's why they called it *a personal* computer. But the reality is that as much as you want to keep your beautiful iMac, PowerBook, or iPod to yourself, sometimes you just have to share. The folks at Apple acknowledge this with features like multiple-user accounts and printer sharing in Mac OS X, although they would probably be happier if we all went out and got one of each, for everybody: one person, lots of computers.

You might not feel like sharing your iPod, but there are times when it's just too valuable to keep to yourself. For example, if you're about to take a long family road trip, having everybody's tunes in the car is a great way to make the ride go faster, especially when you're in unknown radio territory.

Using your iPod to please all members of the family probably means loading it with some music you don't usually carry around, unless you share the same taste in songs as your teenage son (maybe) and nine-year-old daughter (less likely).

Create a portable family jukebox

Assuming you have your iPod all filled up with your favorite music, how do you go about temporarily transforming it into the portable family jukebox? If you have everybody's music you want collected together on one computer, you simply need to make sure your iPod is set up to automatically synchronize songs and playlists with iTunes. You can check your setting in iTunes by connecting the iPod to your computer,

FIGURE **1-1: The iPod Preferences dialog box lets you decide how music will be copied from iTunes to iPod.**

selecting the iPod in the column at the left, and then clicking the tiny iPod button near the lower-right corner of the iTunes window. That will bring up the iPod Preferences dialog box (Figure 1-1).

In the Preferences dialog box, choose the second option, "Automatically update selected playlists only." Then, go through the playlists and check the ones you want to copy to your iPod. If you have more than a few playlists, you'll have to scroll to see them all. And if you don't have enough to make the list scroll, you'll probably enjoy beefing up your playlist collection when you get to Chapter 5.

Tip

If you think you might have enough space on the iPod for all your music and all of everyone else's, you should just copy all the playlists to the iPod. See the sidebar *Sink the iPod* for more information.

When you're done picking playlists for the iPod, click OK. As soon as you do, iTunes empties out your iPod, then starts copying the music and playlists over there. You can keep an eye on copying progress in the status display. When it's all done, the display will say "iPod update is complete," and you're ready to go.

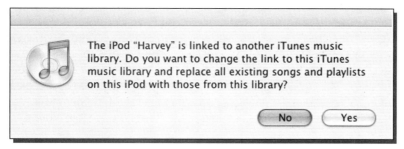

The iPod "Harvey" is linked to another iTunes music library. Do you want to change the link to this iTunes music library and replace all existing songs and playlists on this iPod with those from this library?

No   Yes

FIGURE 1-2: The iPod tells you if it's linked to another computer.

Music, music, everywhere

What if you don't have all your family's tunes on one computer? In that case, you need to grab your iPod and cable and walk around the house from computer to computer, like Johnny Appleseed. Except instead of planting trees, you'll be gathering music. Connect your iPod to each computer in turn. After you connect, go to iTunes, if the computer doesn't take you there automatically. If you have music on computers that can't run iTunes or can't connect to an iPod, you need to copy the songs to one that can.

When you hook up the iPod, you'll probably get a message like the one in Figure 1-2, pointing out that your iPod is in alien territory. Just click "No" to indicate that you don't want to move the iPod permanently to this computer. Then, click the tiny iPod button on the lower right to open iPod Preferences again. But this time, you should select "Manually manage songs and playlists," then click OK. You can now drag songs and playlists directly to the iPod, even dropping them inside playlists that are already on the iPod.

Caution

Using the "Manually manage songs and playlists" can be dangerous. By messing directly with music on the iPod, you can make changes that are out of sync with the songs and playlists you're keeping in iTunes. You can lose songs and playlist changes when you return to automatic updating. For more information about this, see the sidebar *"Sink the iPod"*.

When you get your iPod back to your own computer, you'll find that it remembers the "Manually manage" setting. You should keep it on that setting until you return from the trip and you're ready to restore your iPod to your exclusive control, when you'll probably want to go back to automatic updates.

Sink the iPod

On that happy day when you brought home and set up your iPod, you got to decide how music was to flow into it from iTunes. You picked from three options for how to sync your iPod with your computer. The first, "Automatically update all songs and playlists," is useful only if you have enough room on your iPod to hold all the music you have in iTunes. If you think that describes you, iTunes can check your assumption. Choose that option, then click OK. Immediately, if not sooner, iTunes starts thinking very hard, adding up the space used by all your music in iTunes, and comparing that sum to the room you have on your iPod. If you have enough space on the iPod, then you've got it easy. All your music and playlists get copied over, so you can grab your iPod, round up the family, and jump in the car. (If all your music fits on an iPod, Apple would probably like you to consider visiting the iTunes Music Store more often.)

If you're a master manipulator, you might have picked the option, "Manually manage songs and playlists". This setting gives you dictatorial control over the music on your iPod. With this option, the only way to get music onto the iPod is to drag it over there with your bare mouse. Once a track is on the iPod, you can have your way with it: change tag information like name and artist, choose an equalizer preset, or even delete the poor thing. But watch out: changes you make to songs and playlists on the iPod are *never* copied back to iTunes on your computer.

Obviously, you have to be very careful with this option, and I recommend you avoid using it, except in specialized situations, such as collecting music from several computers for our family road trip. It's too easy to get confused and inadvertently delete music from the iPod that you don't have anywhere else. (Well, it was too easy for *me*, anyway.) If you must use this setting, make sure you don't make changes to songs and playlists directly on the iPod while you're working in iTunes. And please drive safely!

Update Your iPod without Replugging

As an iPod owner, you get to experience frequent cool moments as you come across its niftier features. One of those moments happens whenever you simply connect your iPod to your computer. If you're using automatic updating (see the hack *Share Your iPod*), you watch as the computer feels that the iPod is there, starts iTunes, and begins updating the music on the iPod.

Sometimes you find yourself messing around with playlists while the iPod is connected. If you open iPod Preferences and make any changes to the set of playlists you want to put on the iPod, then click OK, iTunes automatically updates what's on the iPod to match your new set of playlists.

But there is a case when automatic updating isn't fully automatic. If you change a song in a playlist in iTunes, and that playlist is synched with the iPod, the change isn't immediately copied to the iPod. Instead, the update happens when you eject the iPod, right before the computer lets go. But you might want the iPod to update right away, for example, if you're on the edge of running out of iPod space and you're watching carefully as you try to tweak your playlists to use up every last ounce of iPod disk storage.

One way to force an update is to eject the iPod and disconnect it, then immediately plug it back in so you can keep working on it. But that would be wrong. There's a much easier way lurking in iTunes: the "Update Songs on iPod" item at the bottom of the File menu. Just choose that item, and your iPod will be updated at once. This also saves wear on your iPod's connectors and cables, not to mention your fingers.

Use Smart Playlists to Keep Your iPod Fresh

The iTunes Smart Playlists feature seems merely interesting at first glance, but there's far more to it than meets the eye, like an iceberg or the One Ring. Smart Playlists provide easy and powerful ways to create lists of songs, and you can teach them to update themselves automatically, based on rules you devise. By combining Smart Playlists with the automatic update that happens when you connect your iPod to your computer, you get an almost magical combination that can deliver fresh music every time.

There are a few Smart Playlist properties that are especially useful in ensuring an ever-changing supply of tunes:

- Play Count keeps track of how many times you've listened to a particular song.
- Date Added tells when you put the song in the iTunes library.
- Last Played is the date of the most recent time iTunes or the iPod played the tune.

Play Count and Last Played are especially supercool, because they keep track of your listening whether it's on the iPod or in iTunes. So, if you listen to "Father of Mine" by Everclear on your iPod, the next time you connect to your computer, the Play Count and Last Played values for that song will know that it was played.

By using these three properties, you can easily build Smart Playlists that bring fresh stuff to your iPod. For example, if you want to grab music that you haven't heard in a couple of months, you can make a Smart Playlist like the one shown under construction in Figure 1-3.

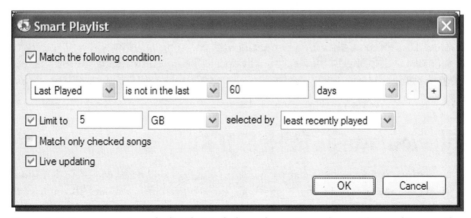

FIGURE 1-3: You can create a playlist that includes only music you haven't listened to recently.

With the settings shown in Figure 1-3, you'll get a playlist made of songs that haven't been played for at least 60 days. By using the "Limit" setting, you can make sure this playlist doesn't take over your whole iPod. This example uses a 5GB limit—you can adjust that to your taste. The "Live updating" checkbox is essential. It ensures the playlist refreshes itself every time a song is played. Without that box checked, the Smart Playlist essentially becomes frozen as soon as it's created, which can be useful, but right now we want fresh, not frozen.

Here's another way to load new tunes into your iPod: make a Smart Playlist with settings "Date Added is in the last 30 days". This will give you a list of the stuff you've bought or ripped in the past month.

Do you ever get so busy that you buy music and then forget to listen to it? D'oh! Create a Smart Playlist to overcome that problem forever. Just choose the condition "Play count is 0" and your music will no longer be able to hide from you.

Of course, listening to new music requires that you pay attention, at least a little, and sometimes you're just not in the mood for that much cogitation. A good antidote for that is a set of songs you like to listen to over and over. You can use Smart Playlists to construct a set of the 100 songs you play the most. First, turn off the "Match the following condition" checkbox at the top of the dialog box. Then, choose "Limit to 100 songs selected by most often played". Click OK, and there you go—musical comfort food.

Cross-Reference Smart Playlists are cool enough that we devote a big chunk of space to them later, in Chapter 5.

This Is the End

If you start to fool around with the Play Count and Last Played values, you might notice that you remember hearing a song, but iTunes doesn't think it was played. That could be. The Play Count and Last Played values aren't adjusted until the song plays all the way through to the end. And no fair skipping to the next song, either—the end of the song must be played. You can cheat a little by fast-forwarding through the song until the end, then letting the very last part play.

Shuffle Your Music to Hear It All

Sometimes you know just what you want to hear, and sometimes you don't. For those moments when you're feeling suggestible, your iPod can help you out. All you have to do is use the Shuffle setting. If you're already familiar with Shuffle, you might not have tried its little-known third option, which we'll discuss here.

Located in the iPod Settings menu, Shuffle has three options: Off, Songs, and Albums. When it's Off, all playlists and albums are played in their "natural" order. When you set Shuffle to Songs, the order of songs within a playlist or album is random. The third Shuffle setting, Albums, is useful if you like to listen to whole albums, one after another, on your iPod. With this setting, the iPod will choose a random album, play it all the way through in order, then continue to choose random albums and play their songs in order.

Random Difference

The iPod and iTunes deal with random play in subtly different ways. In iTunes, each playlist remembers its own Shuffle setting. On the iPod, the global Shuffle setting affects all the music you're playing. This leads to much consternation if you sometimes listen to a "Favorites" playlist on your iPod, which is best played at random, while other times you like to hear albums all the way through: you're constantly turning Shuffle on and off to make it work the way you want. And the Shuffle Album setting doesn't really help in this case. If you use Shuffle Album when playing your Favorites, the iPod picks off and plays all the Favorites that happen to be on the same album before it continues on.

Use Repeat, Use Repeat

Once you've mastered the Shuffle setting, which is not really very hard, you should also take a look at its close relative, Repeat. Like Shuffle, you'll find Repeat in the iPod's Settings menu. There are three settings for Repeat: Off, One, and All. If you leave it set to Off, your lists will play all the way through to the end, and then the iPod will simply stop playing, return to the main screen, and politely wait for you to decide what you want to do next.

If you're going to use Repeat, you'll probably want the All setting. This one plays the current playlist, album, or artist to the end of the list, then starts over again and keeps going until you change the setting, your battery runs out, or the sun goes supernova.

The final and quirkiest Repeat setting, One, simply repeats the same song over and over. Why would you want to do this? Maybe you really love a song—I mean, *really, really* love it—or you need to keep repeating a song for some public performance, such as playing the title theme music to *Beetlejuice* out your window on Halloween.

You get some interesting interactions when you turn on both Repeat All and Shuffle Songs. With this combo, you'll get the same playlist repeated endlessly, but the songs will be in a different order every time. That's kind of cool.

Note that unlike Shuffle, the Repeat settings work the same way in both iTunes and iPod.

Hacking the Culture: How to Win Friends

When Steve Jobs introduced the iTunes Music Store at a presentation on April 28, 2003, some experts said Apple was doing nothing less than saving the music industry from itself. Apple worked for 18 months to convince the major music labels that making songs available for purchase online was a good idea. Since then, the iTunes Music Store has been very successful and widely imitated. But one of the richest moments of that introduction came when Jobs displayed a quote he attributed to Hunter S. Thompson: "The music business is a cruel and shallow money trench, a long plastic hallway where thieves and pimps run free, and good men die like dogs. There's also a negative side."

When the quote appeared on the screen, the crowd applauded wildly, except for some of the music industry executives in the room.

Get Sound Check to Work

Ever notice how some CDs are REALLY LOUD and others are very quiet? The sound level is built into the way the CDs were recorded and mastered—the volume changes without you wanting it to. In particular, older CDs often seem to be mastered at low volume levels compared to recent music. This is really annoying when you're listening to a playlist with songs from various eras.

Luckily, iPod and iTunes have a magic trick that cures this problem: Sound Check. This feature analyzes the volume of songs and adjusts it so that they're all in the same range. When you play songs with Sound Check, your personal volume choice becomes the way to turn it up or down.

Unfortunately, Sound Check is a little trickier than it needs to be. You have to turn it on both in iTunes and on the iPod. Here are the steps:

1. (Here's the part most everyone remembers to do.) Turn on Sound Check in iTunes. Choose iTunes ➪ Preferences on the Mac, or Edit ➪ Preferences on Windows. Click the Audio tab, then make sure the Sound Check box is on. After you click OK, iTunes starts rummaging through your music and leveling the volume. iTunes displays its progress in the status area (see Figure 1-4). Connect your iPod to update its music.

2. (Here's the step people often forget.) On the iPod, go to the Settings screen and turn Sound Check on.

That's it. If you don't turn on Sound Check on the iPod, your songs won't be played at the leveled volume when you hear them on the iPod, and you'll wonder what the heck is going on.

FIGURE 1-4: Sound Check makes the volume levels similar on all your music.

Use the Equalizer to Get Terrific Sound

Modern music playback equipment uses a technique called *equalization* to modify the way audio information is reproduced. An equalizer splits the music into its component frequencies, then makes some of the frequencies louder and others less loud. The idea is to reduce the sounds that are harsh or not appropriate to the music, while emphasizing the sounds that are most important.

To produce the best results, equalizer settings vary depending on the type of music that's playing. For thumping dance music, a good equalizer setting would emphasize the lower range of frequencies, while a setting for music with more delicate vocals would enhance the middle-to-high ranges of the human voice

You probably know that your iPod and iTunes have equalizers built in. If you love music but you don't consider yourself an audiophile, you might not have explored the equalizer. If that's the case, you should give it a try. It's very easy to use, and it makes a remarkable difference in how your music sounds.

The easiest way to use the equalizer on your iPod is to pick a setting and turn it on. Go to the Settings menu and choose the Equalizer. On this screen it's the setting that starts with "EQ", such as "EQ-Off" or "EQ-Rock". After you choose it, you'll see a list of more than 20 settings for the equalizer, including Off. Pick the setting that matches the type of music you usually listen to and click the Select button. Now you'll get to hear lovely equalized music.

There are more advanced ways to use the equalizer. For example, each song can carry its own equalizer setting. This trick requires iTunes. To pick an equalizer setting for a song in iTunes, click a song and choose File ➪ Get Info. Click the Options tab. Choose a setting from the Equalizer Preset pop-up. Any songs that have their own equalizer preset will now be played using that setting, in iTunes and on the iPod.

Don't Be Denied

When you start playing with the equalizer on your iPod, you might want to go to the EQ menu while a song is playing to find out what its equalizer preset is. Unfortunately, there's no way to tell what preset a song has on the iPod. The setting shown in the EQ menu is the current global setting, not the preset for the current song.

Just to make things more useful, not to say more confusing, you can override the current song's (invisible) preset by choosing a different setting from the EQ menu while the song is playing. When you do this, the song continues to play but instantly switches to the new setting. The next time the song plays, it reverts to its preset.

Scrub Your Songs to Hear What You Want

Everybody is in a hurry nowadays, even us iPod owners. The original iPod software included a way to fast-forward or rewind through the current song by holding down ▷▷| or |◁◁. That was fast, but not fast enough, and a later version of iPod software added the ability to zip through songs just as fast as you can turn the scroll wheel. To use this handy feature, press the Select button when you're on the Now Playing screen. The progress bar gets a little diamond that shows the current spot in the song. When you see that, you can use the scroll wheel to move back and forth quickly through the current song, a technique called *scrubbing*. After you leave the wheel alone for a few seconds, the iPod figures you're done, and the regular progress bar comes back. You can also get it back right away by pressing Select again (you have to press it an extra time with a 2003 iPod in order to get past the "rate my song" screen).

Summary

Hacking isn't the exclusive domain of evil geniuses, master programmers, and those who own the big box of Craftsman tools. We can all hack our worlds to make them fit better. As promised, this chapter provides iPod music hacks that are simple, straightforward, and in many cases, even useful—hacks for everybody.

Your iPod might be the world's greatest music player, but that's not all it knows how to do—far from it. Coming up in Chapter 2, we'll move beyond the music as we delve into other iPod features.

More Than Music

The world at large thinks of the iPod as a supercool music player and a snappy fashion statement. But one of the reasons for the iPod's success is that it does much more than just store and play music while looking good, and it keeps gaining new features all the time, both from Apple and from others.

In this chapter, we'll start to explore some of the non-musical tricks you can pull with your iPod. A few of these require additional hardware, so I'll introduce you to those toys, while others work with the stock iPod and some additional (usually free) software.

Hardware Accessories

Apple keeps the iPod hardware locked up pretty tight, but there are definitely ways to expand your iPod's abilities with additional gadgets. In this section, you'll find out some of the basic ways you can add features and convenience to your iPod.

Use standard FireWire cables

The original iPod worked only with Macs. It wasn't long before Apple figured out that it was a bad idea to shut out the many millions of Windows users in the world who might want an iPod, so changes were made. With each update, the iPod became friendlier to Windows users. By 2003, two major obstacles stood in the way of Windows users becoming full iPod citizens: there was no Windows version of iTunes, and most Windows computers were equipped with USB 2.0 for connecting peripherals, instead of the FireWire connection required by the iPod.

Apple solved both these problems by the end of 2003. First, the company shipped iTunes for Windows, which is practically a clone of the Mac version. Once this happened—an event that Apple billed as "Hell freezing over" because of the unlikeliness of the company shipping a Windows-based application—all iPod users had the same software. New dock-connector iPods (often called third-generation, or 3G iPods by the cool kids) can connect to USB 2.0 as well as FireWire, and because most new PCs have USB 2.0, this levels the hardware playing field, too.

Unfortunately, in order to make iPods work with both FireWire and USB 2.0, Apple created the dreaded custom connector. Unlike their ancestors, 3G iPods don't have FireWire connectors. The wide, flat custom connector allows 3G iPods and iPod Minis to fit into their dock. Apple supplies a cable you can use to connect your iPod directly to your computer's FireWire port. But the drawback to this design is that you can no longer hook up with any plain old FireWire cable that's also used for connecting other FireWire devices, such as external hard disks. If you're on the road with your computer, you have to schlep Apple's special cable.

This is where the $19 PocketDock from SendStation comes in. (For more information about PocketDock, see www.sendstation.com.) PocketDock is a tiny cable adapter that lets you use your 3G iPod or iPod Mini with any standard FireWire cable. Figure 2-1 shows how it works. Just plug the PocketDock into your iPod's dock connector, and you then have an iPod with a FireWire port, ready to use any FireWire cable. SendStation calls PocketDock "essential", and that seems pretty close to the truth. This is the kind of product you would expect to find in the iPod box as a nice freebie, because it's extremely useful.

Record voice memos

Belkin's Voice Recorder for iPod is a cool accessory that turns your iPod into a traveling digital recorder. You can use it for speaking notes to yourself or recording one-on-one conversations. The Voice Recorder is a small iPod-white box that plugs neatly into the iPod's headphone jack. You don't have to install any software—the iPod already knows all about it. Once the Voice Recorder is connected, the Extras menu grows a new item, Voice Memos.

FIGURE 2-1: PocketDock from SendStation. Courtesy of SendStation.

From this menu, you can choose Record Now to start recording your monumental thoughts.

While you're recording, the screen displays a large timer so you know how long it's been listening, the word "Recording" flashes on the screen, and the Voice Recorder itself lights up a very subtle green LED. Recordings are stored as WAV files at 128K bits per second, which means you'll use up 16K bytes every second.

The best hidden cool hack in the Voice Recorder is the built-in speaker. When the recorder is plugged in, your iPod suddenly has an external speaker—a small, quiet speaker, but a speaker nonetheless. This is handy for a number of uses:

- Listening to voice recordings you've made, which is the intended use.

- Sharing a bit of music or other sound with a friend, without the sanitary nightmare of lending out your ear buds.

- Using the iPod as a music-playing alarm clock. (For details, see the section *Go to sleep and wake to your iPod* in this chapter.)

You can move voice recordings from the iPod to your computer. The next time you connect the iPod to your computer, iTunes will put up a dialog box asking if you want to add the voice recordings to your music library. If you say yes, the voice memos will be copied to your computer and added to your iTunes library.

If adding your intimate personal notes to your music library isn't exactly what you had in mind, you can copy voice recordings to your hard disk without putting them into iTunes. To do this, open your iPod in the Finder or Windows Explorer. You'll see that you have a new Recordings folder. Open Recordings to see your voice memos. Their names correspond to the date and time they were recorded. So, for example, a memo named "20040715 131522" was recorded on July 15th, 2004, at 1:15:22 p.m. You can copy these files just like any others.

Belkin's Voice Recorder for iPod costs about $50 and is widely available, including at Apple stores, and the online store. You need a 3G iPod to use the Voice Recorder.

In the summer of 2004, Griffin Technology added to its impressive product lineup by shipping iTalk (Figure 2-2). This product is very similar to Belkin's, differing only slightly in the physical design.

The iTalk has the same cool look as the rest of Griffin's products. You can get one from the Apple store or directly from Griffin for about $40.

Store digital photos

If you're a digital photographer, you probably know the hassle of running out of space for pictures on your camera. It's not like you can just carry a few extra rolls of film around with you—CompactFlash, SmartMedia, and the like are too expensive for that. Off-loading

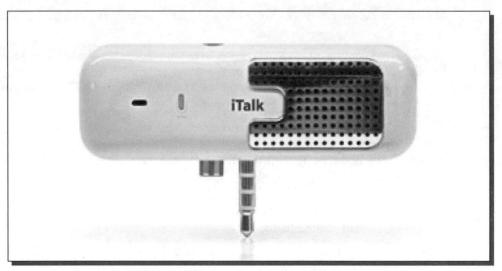

FIGURE 2-2: iTalk from Griffin Technology. Courtesy of Griffin Technology.

your photos to a computer is one solution, but you probably don't want to drag a laptop around with you when you're out taking pictures.

To solve this problem, you can get various portable hard disk solutions for storing your photos. But you already have a portable hard disk with abundant space—it just happens to be a music player too. So the folks at Belkin have given your iPod yet another job: digital photo storage. All you need is a box to read the photos and move them to your iPod. Belkin offers two products that can help: Media Reader for iPod, shown in Figure 2-3, and Digital Camera Link for iPod (Figure 2-4). I'll describe both of them here.

Belkin Media Reader for iPod

The Media Reader is a little bigger than a standard iPod and has slots for six different media types:

- CompactFlash types 1 and 2
- SmartMedia
- Secure Digital (SD)
- Memory Stick
- Multimedia Card (MMC)

If you have a digital camera, it almost certainly uses one of the media types accepted by the Belkin Media Reader. That's one of the great features of this product: you don't have

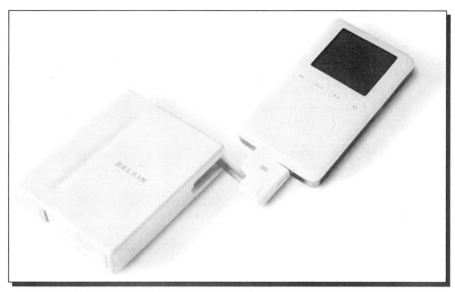

FIGURE 2-3: Belkin Media Reader connected to iPod. Courtesy of Belkin.

to worry about the competing standards when deciding whether this reader will work for you. Just make sure your camera uses one of the six supported types, which is nearly a sure thing, and you'll be compatible.

To use the Media Reader, you open the nifty sliding door that protects the media slots, then put in your card. Connect the reader to the iPod's dock connector. The iPod reacts by asking if you want to import photos from the media card. If you say you do, the photos are copied over while you watch a progress screen on the iPod. Copied photos are stored by roll number. Once the photos are copied over, you can delete them from the media card so you can go take more award-winning photos of rocks and dirt.

Once the photos are in the iPod, what can you do with them? You can get information about them, such as the number of pictures in a roll and the type of media they were stored on. Once you reconnect to your computer, you can copy the photos over by using any software that imports digital photos, such as iPhoto, or you can copy them manually by looking in the cryptically named DCIM (digital camera images) folder on the iPod.

One thing you can't do with the photos, unfortunately, is look at them on your iPod. The iPod screen graphics capability is limited, and there's no software support for showing images on the screen. Maybe this feature will show up in a future iPod.

The Belkin Media Reader for iPod works with 3G iPods. It's sold at Apple stores, including the online store (www.apple.com/store), and many other places for about $100.

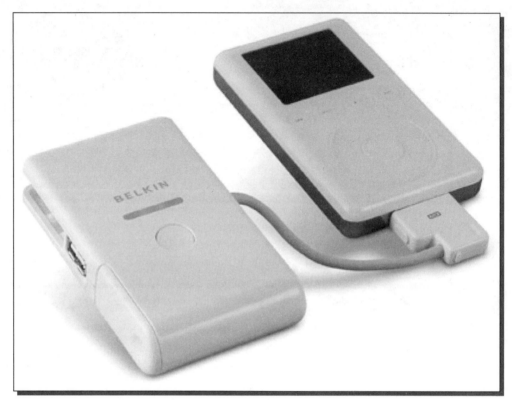

FIGURE 2-4: Belkin Digital Camera Link. Courtesy of Belkin.

Belkin Digital Camera Link for iPod

Belkin's second product for off-loading digital photos works in a different way, without having to use storage cards. To use the Digital Camera Link (Figure 2-4), you connect it directly to your camera's USB port, then hook the Digital Camera Link to the iPod's dock connector. Your photos will magically flow to the iPod. Then, when you get back to your computer, you can transfer the photos over from the iPod.

Belkin Digital Camera Link for iPod requires a 3G iPod and costs about $90 at Apple stores or directly from Belkin.

How can you decide which Belkin photo device to use with your iPod? Here are some guidelines. Choose the Media Reader for maximum flexibility and storage, because you can transfer photos from an unlimited number of cards. However, the Camera Link is smaller and uses just two AA batteries instead of four AAA required by the Media Reader. The Camera Link is also about $10 less expensive, so if you don't need to transfer more than one card's worth of photos, the Camera Link is a good pick.

Use external batteries

You can never be too rich, too thin, or have too much battery power, as the old saying (almost) goes. The iPod's built-in rechargeable battery gives you up to 8 hours of musical joy. That's usually long enough to get back to a safe haven so you can recharge. But what about those times when you need more power? Because the iPod's battery is built in, you can't simply carry around an extra battery, as you can with laptops and many other electronic devices.

The Backup Battery Pack from Belkin lets you use standard AA batteries to add up to 20 hours of playing time to your iPod. The Backup Battery looks like a backpack for your iPod. It attaches to the shiny iPod back with two handy suction cups. A cable plugs the backpack into the dock connector on the bottom—the Backup Battery only works with 3G iPods. When you attach the Backup Battery, the iPod draws power from it instead of the built-in battery, so you shouldn't plug it in until your main battery is dead or moribund.

The Backup Battery includes a nifty set of green LEDs that show you how much battery power is remaining, just like Apple's laptop batteries. When you need to remove the backpack, the suction cups have handy little pull tabs at the top to help pry them loose, a nice touch.

For those with big battery requirements, the Backup Battery for iPod sells for about $59 and you can get it from most places that sell iPod stuff, including the Apple store.

| Cross-Reference | For information on how to replace your iPod's internal battery—it can be done!—see the section *Replace Your iPod's Battery* in Chapter 3. |

Use your iPod as a light

You might have noticed that your iPod's backlight is very bright. In fact, it's vivid enough that ingenious iPod owners have devised clever ways to use the backlight, such as these:

- *Flashlight.* If you're going to the movies, you can use your iPod backlight to help you find your seat or that dropped box of Raisinets.

- *Safety light.* The iPod team reports hearing from joggers who keep their backlights burning as a safety device when running at night.

- *Book light.* In a pinch, use your iPod to illuminate a book or map in a darkened room, as shown in Figure 2-5.

- *Night light.* During a hotel stay in Philadelphia with my family, I used the iPod as a night light by plugging it into the wall on the bathroom counter and setting the backlight to stay on all the time.

FIGURE 2-5: iPod as book light.

You can set the backlight to stay on all the time by going to Settings ⇨ Backlight Timer and choosing "Always On". Of course, this uses plenty of battery power, but you should be fine for the length of a jog, unless you're an all-night marathoner. For night light duty, just be sure your iPod is connected to AC power.

Use Your iPod as an External Disk Drive

You can use your iPod as a highly portable, large-capacity external disk drive. Make sure the "Enable disk use" box is checked in iPod Preferences in iTunes, and your iPod will show up as just another disk in the Finder or Windows Explorer. Once you've done that, you can use its excess capacity to store any files you want.

There is one drawback to using your iPod this way, or for any other purpose than simply getting music from iTunes. When your iPod is purely for music, and you're using the automatic update feature, the iPod gets its songs from iTunes every time you connect to the computer. All the tunes are stored on the computer and copied over to the iPod when you sync. This means, in effect, that the iPod is just a backup device for songs on your computer. If that's all you use your iPod for, the iPod's contents are completely disposable: you can reformat it, lose it, or cast it into the fires of Mount Doom without losing any data. Once you start keeping other information on your iPod, you have to be aware of what you've stored there, even backing up those files if you want to be sure not to lose them. Because the iPod acts just like a standard external disk drive, you can back it up with any backup program, such as Retrospect from Dantz (www.dantz.com).

Boot from your iPod

Note This hack works on Macintosh computers only.

When you get in the habit of using your iPod as an external drive, you might wish you could turn the iPod into a portable startup disk for Mac OS X. That way, you can carry it with you on the road, to the office, or to a friend's house, and have your system, settings, passwords, and other vital info with you all the time. Making an iPod bootable is incredibly easy. All you have to do is run the Mac OS X Installer with the iPod attached, and select it as the target volume for the installation. Once you've installed Mac OS X, the iPod will appear as an option in the Startup Disk preference panel, as shown in Figure 2-6.

Another handy tool when using your iPod as an external drive is the popular donation-ware utility Carbon Copy Cloner, available from Mike Bombich at www.bombich.com/software/ccc.html. Carbon Copy Cloner lets you duplicate one existing disk volume to

FIGURE 2-6: iPod is a valid startup disk after running Mac OS X Installer.

another. You can use this program to back up all your precious stuff to an iPod, and even make the iPod bootable if you're copying from a bootable source.

Caution

Apple designed the iPod primarily for use as a music player. In that mode, the iPod software works hard to minimize wear and tear on the disk. It spins the disk up infrequently, reads off a bunch of music, turns the disk off, then keeps the music around in a RAM buffer to play it. If you make heavy use of your iPod as an external disk drive, especially as the volume you boot from, you might find Apple unwilling to perform a warranty repair if your iPod should break down.

Hacking the Culture: Theft by iPod

When you opened your new iPod, you certainly noticed the sticker on the screen that said "Don't Steal Music." Based on reports that began appearing shortly after the original iPod began shipping, these stickers might not have gone far enough, because apparently at least one malicious person decided to use an iPod for stealing more than music.

In February 2002, a CompUSA customer in Texas reported seeing a man produce an iPod from his pocket, connect it to a Macintosh on display, copy commercial software to the iPod, then disconnect the iPod and walk away. Although the iPod is best known as a music player, the thief exploited the iPod's ability to act as a capable external disk drive. While this is definitely an example of an iPod hack, it's not one I'm going to encourage.

Software

Groovy hardware isn't the only way to add features to your iPod. You can also change your iPod's life simply by taking advantage of cool software out in the world. In this section, we'll discuss software tricks that help your iPod manage your contacts, act like an alarm clock, and more.

Import your contacts and calendar

Your iPod has the innate ability to keep track of contacts and calendar events. If you have a Macintosh, you can use excellent free software from Apple to get your contacts and calendar info onto your iPod: Address Book, iCal, and iSync. Apple doesn't provide Windows versions of these programs, but there are other companies that supply their equivalent. Address Book, iCal, and iSync are installed on most Macs—check your Applications folder to find out for sure. If you don't have them, go right now and download them at www.apple.com/support/downloads/. And if you have Windows, just skip down to the section *Use Contacts and Calendar with Windows*.

Like most Apple gear, this set of programs is easy to use. If you keep your contacts in Address Book, and you use iCal to keep track of your appointments, you can easily sync your information to your iPod by following these steps:

1. Make sure your iPod is connected to your computer. Unfortunately, wireless iPods haven't been invented yet.

2. Run iSync. You should see the iSync window, listing all the devices it knows about.

3. Choose Devices ⇨ Add Device. You should see your iPod listed in the window that appears. Double-click it to sign your iPod up for synchronizing. Your iPod should appear in the iSync window.

4. Check the settings for your iPod in the iSync window. The first checkbox, "Turn on synchronization," should be on, and the boxes for Contacts and Calendars should be checked, as shown in Figure 2-7.

5. Click Sync Now to move your data to the iPod.

FIGURE 2-7: iSync window ready to synchronize with iPod.

Now you have your Address Book and Calendar info ready to go anywhere your iPod goes. Address Book and iCal entries are stored on the iPod under Extras, in the Contacts and Calendar lists, respectively.

For more ways to sync information between your Mac and iPod, see Chapter 4, especially the section *Get News, Weather, Movie Listings, and More.*

Where Have All the Contacts Gone?

Most of the information stored on your iPod is kept in simple, open formats. Contacts are stored in a standard format called vCard, then simply placed in the Contacts folder on the iPod. Similarly, Calendar entries on the iPod are files that use the standard iCalendar or vCalendar format, stored in the Calendar folder. Most address book and calendar programs, on both Mac OS X and Windows, can produce vCard, iCalendar, and vCalendar files. Once your data is in those formats, you can simply copy it to the right folder on your iPod and it will appear when you choose Contacts or Calendar.

Use Contacts and Calendar with Outlook

This hack is for Windows computers only.

Apple is very magnanimous to Windows users when it comes to iTunes, providing Windows and Mac versions that are nearly identical. But that cross-platform policy does not extend to Address Book, iCal, or iSync, programs that Mac users have for managing their contacts and calendar info, and then flowing that information to their iPods.

However, because the iPod uses standard formats—vCard for contacts, iCalendar and vCalendar for appointments—you're in luck no matter which program you use to manage your personal information. In this section, we'll discuss the most basic tricks for getting contacts and calendar data to your iPod from the most popular Windows personal information manager: Microsoft Outlook.

You can get vCards and iCalendars out of Outlook, but it's not particularly easy or obvious. There are separate procedures depending on whether you want to export just a couple of items, or a whole bunch. Here's how to put a single Outlook contact onto your iPod:

1. Connect your iPod to your computer. Choose Start ➪ My Computer to make sure your iPod is visible.

2. In Outlook, find the contact you want to move to your iPod and open it.

3. Choose File ⇨ Export to vCard file.

4. In the "File name:" box, type the name you want the contact to have.

5. In the "Save as type:" box, choose "VCARD Files" from the pop-up list. Don't click Save yet!

6. In the "Save in:" pop-up at the top of the dialog box, navigate to your iPod, as shown in Figure 2-8.

7. In the file window, which now shows the iPod's contents, double-click the Contacts folder.

8. Click Save.

The next time you disconnect the iPod, the contact you saved will appear in the iPod's contacts folder.

The procedure for putting an Outlook calendar event on the iPod is similar. It goes like this:

1. Connect your iPod to your computer. Choose Start ⇨ My Computer to make sure your PC can see your iPod.

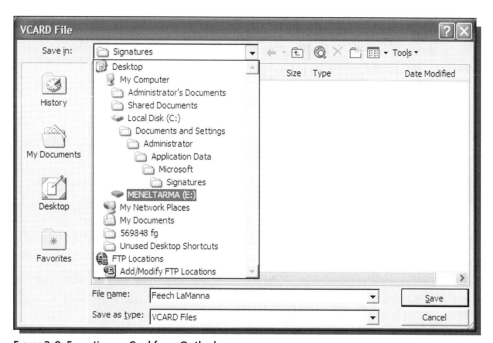

FIGURE 2-8: Exporting a vCard from Outlook.

2. In Outlook, go to the Calendar, find the item you want to move to your iPod, and open it.

3. Choose File ➪ Save As.

4. In the "File name:" box, type the name you want the calendar event to have.

5. In the "Save as type:" box, choose "iCalendar Format" from the pop-up list. Don't click Save yet!

6. In the "Save in:" pop-up at the top of the dialog box, navigate to your iPod.

7. In the file window, which should be showing the iPod's contents, double-click the Calendars folder.

8. At last, click Save.

You have now stored a single calendar event on your iPod. When you disconnect the iPod, go to Calendar and you should see your event on the appointed date.

This one-at-a-time stuff is OK for limited use. But what if you want to put a whole bunch of Outlook items onto your iPod at once? Luckily, you're not doomed to repeating this procedure over and over again for each item. Instead, there's a hack for exporting multiple items all at once. This procedure works for both Contacts and Calendar items, although you can't mix the two types in one export. Here are the steps for Contacts:

1. As before, be sure your iPod is connected, and that your PC knows it's connected.

2. In Outlook, go to Contacts and select all the items you want. You can use Shift-click and Control-click to choose multiple items.

3. Choose Actions ➪ Forward as vCard. This creates a new e-mail message with all the Contacts you selected converted to vCard format.

4. Address and send the e-mail to a trusted friend—like yourself. Although all the vCards are right there for the taking, there's apparently no way to access them all at once except as a received e-mail.

5. Collect your e-mail in Outlook. When you look at the received message, you should see all the vCards as attachments.

6. Select the message that you sent with all the vCards. Choose File ➪ Save Attachments ➪ All Attachments. Note: if you use an e-mail program other than Outlook to collect your mail, it might not have the Save All Attachments feature.

7. In the Save All Attachments dialog box that appears, click OK.

8. Next, you'll see a Save All Attachments file list. Navigate to your iPod's contacts folder and click OK.

You're done—the contacts have been shipped off to your iPod.

If you want to export multiple Calendar items, Microsoft makes the steps very similar, yet subtly different, just to keep us entertained:

1. Verify that your iPod is connected and visible under My Computer.

2. Go to the Outlook Calendar.

3. Most people have their Outlook calendars set up to display a graphical view, like the one in Figure 2-9. It's easier to select and export multiple calendar items if you display your calendar in a list view. To see your calendar in a list view, choose View ⇨ Current View ⇨ Active Appointments. Now your calendar will look something like Figure 2-10.

4. Use Shift+click and Ctrl+click to select multiple calendar items. Pick all the ones you want to export to your iPod.

5. Choose Actions ⇨ Forward as iCalendar. You'll get a new e-mail message with all the appointments converted to iCalendar files.

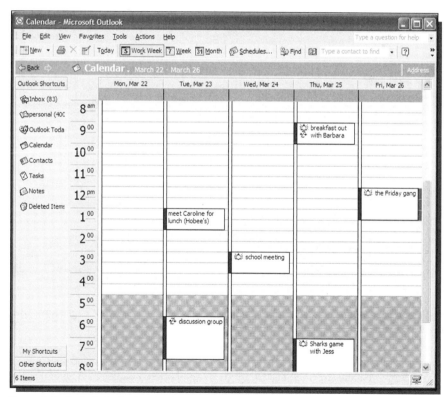

FIGURE 2-9: Typical Outlook calendar view.

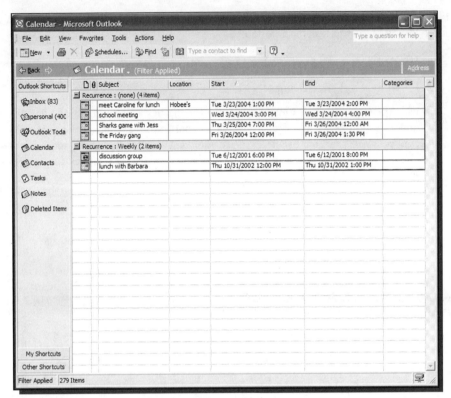

FIGURE 2-10: Calendar list view for multiple selections.

6. Address the e-mail message to yourself and send it.

7. Collect your e-mail. Select the message you sent and nod knowingly at all the iCalendar attachments.

8. Choose File ➪ Save Attachments ➪ All Attachments.

9. In the Save All Attachments dialog box, click OK.

10. You'll see a file list for Save All Attachments. Find your iPod, then its Calendars folder, and click OK.

That's it! You have now transported the appointments you selected in Outlook to the iPod's Calendar.

Cross-Reference

While these procedures can be used to put Contact and Calendar information on your iPod, they are definitely not a long-term solution for synchronizing between Outlook and your iPod every day. For slicker, automated techniques, see the Chapter 4 section *Synchronize Your iPod with Microsoft Outlook.*

Go to sleep and wake to your iPod

After a long night of dancing to the music in your iPod, you can use the same music and the same iPod as an alarm clock to wake you the next morning (or afternoon). The iPod includes an alarm clock feature you can use to play music at a specified time. To set it up:

1. From the main iPod menu, go to Extras ➪ Clock.

2. When you get to the screen that shows the current time, go to Alarm Clock.

3. From the Alarm Clock screen, choose Alarm and press the iPod's Select button (the one in the middle) until Alarm is set to "On." Your screen should look like the one in Figure 2-11.

4. Choose Time and press Select. Use the wheel to specify the time for your alarm. Press Menu when you're done.

5. Choose Sound and pick a playlist to be the soundtrack for your wakeup call. This only works if you're going to have an external speaker attached to your iPod when it attempts to wake you up. Otherwise, it will start playing, but you won't hear anything, which greatly reduces the alarm's effectiveness. If you're not going to have speakers attached, choose the Beep sound, which comes out of the iPod's built-in speaker.

 Cross-Reference The Belkin Voice Recorder and Griffin iTalk have a small built-in speaker you can use for making sure your alarm is actually alarming to you. If you need something more powerful but still compact and inexpensive, check out SimpleSpeaker, described in Chapter 3.

Not only can you use your iPod to wake you up, it's also handy for helping you get to sleep. The iPod includes a sleep timer feature that plays for a specified length of time before shutting down. To set the sleep timer, go back to the Clock screen and choose Sleep Timer. You can then choose from sleepy times ranging from 15 to 120 minutes before having your iPod shut itself off.

FIGURE 2-11: Setting the iPod's Alarm Clock.

iPod to bed and iPod to rise—there must be a poem in there somewhere, or at least an Apple commercial. Pleasant dreams!

For a more powerful alarm clock, but one that requires an entire Macintosh, see Chapter 6, "Make iTunes an Alarm Clock."

Use Apple's iPod scripts

This hack works on Macintosh computers only.

Mac OS X includes a cool technology called AppleScript that lets you automate common tasks in programs. Scripts written in AppleScript are little programs that you run by picking them out of the script menu in iTunes and other applications. We'll talk about AppleScript much more in Chapter 6, in the iTunes part of this book. But there are some nifty AppleScript features for iPods also, which is the focus of this section.

Apple provides the iPod scripts on its AppleScript site at www.apple.com/applescript/ipod. To use these scripts, download them from that address and put them in the Scripts folder, using the following steps:

1. In the Finder, open your Home directory. If you're not sure how to do that, a foolproof technique is to choose Go ➪ Home.

2. In your Home directory, find the Library folder, and inside Library, find Scripts.

3. Drag the scripts you downloaded into Scripts.

Most of Apple's iPod scripts perform cool tricks with Notes. Here's a description of what the scripts do:

■ *Eject iPod*. No, it doesn't make your iPod physically fly through the air—it just unmounts the iPod so you can disconnect it. This one is especially useful when you hook it up to a keyboard shortcut, which you can do with the Keyboard & Mouse panel in System Preferences.

To find out how to create keyboard shortcuts, see the section *Turn On AppleScript in iTunes* in Chapter 6.

- *Clipboard to Note.* This is a super-simple, really quick way to add a note to your iPod. To use it, select the text you want and copy it, then switch to iTunes and run this script. The copied text turns into a note and goes onto the iPod. If your copied text is longer than the 4K limit imposed by iPod notes, no worries: the script will automatically chop up your text in multiple notes that are linked together.

- *Clear All Notes.* Use this script to clear out all your notes in a hurry. The script also offers to remove all Notes subfolders.

- *List Notes.* Run this script when you want to see a list of all your notes. You can select one and click Open to see the note's text displayed in the TextEdit application. If you have a lot of notes, this can take a while. Figure 2-12 shows an example of how this works.

- *MacCentral.* This script opens the MacCentral Web site using Safari and copies the first article into an iPod note. Because you get the source listing for the script, you can modify it for other sites too.

- *Printer Friendly.* This one is useful, but kind of oddly titled. It grabs the text from the front window in Safari and makes a note out of it. It's called "Printer Friendly" because it works best with pages that have few graphics or links, but you can use it with any page you point it at.

FIGURE 2-12: List Notes displays its results.

> ### Scripted success
>
> If you're interested in learning more about how AppleScript can help you do cool things with your iPod, be sure to visit Doug's AppleScripts for iTunes at www.malcolmadams.com/itunes, and don't miss the exploration of some of Doug's scripts in Chapter 6.

Use WinAmp with Your iPod

Note   This hack is for Windows computers only.

You probably know that iTunes is not the only music player in the universe. Other programs, such as MusicMatch Jukebox and WinAmp, are found on the hard disks of millions of happy users. When the iPod first appeared, there was no iTunes for Windows. Instead, Apple worked with MusicMatch to make MusicMatch Jukebox the official iPod software for Windows. Although that designation ended abruptly in October 2003, when Apple introduced the Windows version of iTunes, you're still free to use MusicMatch with your iPod.

The millions of WinAmp users, however, have not been so lucky. WinAmp was one of the first digital music applications, and it includes nifty features like games and skinnable looks. However, WinAmp didn't provide support for the iPod. But in February 2004, Christophe Thibault released iPod Support Plug-in for WinAmp. This little bit of code allows WinAmp users to hook up their iPods and transfer music to them. When you install the iPod Support Plug-in, your iPod appears in WinAmp's device list, as shown in Figure 2-13.

The iPod Support Plug-in provides basic features, such as the ability to copy music to the iPod and to play music stored on the iPod while in WinAmp. But the plug-in lacks features that iTunes provides, most notably support for iTunes-managed playlists. Still, devoted fans of WinAmp can now stick with their favorite digital music program and manage music on their iPods.

To download WinAmp, go to www.winamp.com/player/. The basic version of WinAmp is free—for $15, you get more features, including MP3 ripping and fast CD burning. The iPod Support Plug-in is free at www.winamp.com/plugins/details.php?id=138888.

Connect your iPod to Macs and Windows PCs

If you have both a Mac and a PC, you might find it handy to use your iPod with both computers. There's an easy way to do it. First, make sure there's nothing on your iPod you need, because you're going to reformat it. To do that, run the Windows version of the iPod Updater and click Restore (see Figure 2-14). This formats the iPod using the FAT32 file

FIGURE 2-13: iPod appears in WinAmp when you install iPod Support Plug-in.

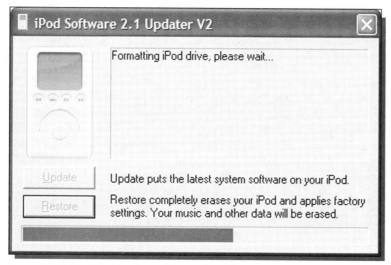

FIGURE 2-14: iPod Updater formatting an iPod for Windows.

system, which is native to Windows but is also supported by Mac OS X. You can then talk to the iPod with iTunes on either operating system, and from the Mac OS X Finder as well as Windows Explorer.

If you decide later that you want your iPod to be formatted exclusively for Macs, you can reverse the process by running the Mac version of iPod Updater. Once again, just make sure there's nothing on the iPod you want to keep before paving over the disk contents with iPod Updater.

You can tell if an iPod is formatted for Windows by choosing Settings ➪ About and scrolling all the way to the bottom. If you see "Format Windows", then the iPod is formatted with the FAT32 file system.

Download Audio Books

Music is not the only kind of content you can listen to on your iPod. Audio books and other spoken word recordings provide a great way to pass the time when you're commuting on the train, driving cross-country, or waiting for the dentist.

The main source of audio books and similar recordings is Audible (`audible.com`). When you visit the Audible home page (Figure 2-15), you can search from a vast library of recordings that include novels, non-fiction books, magazines, radio shows, and more, You can subscribe to an abridged audio edition of the *New York Times*, available each day at 6:00 a.m. You can even get language lessons, so you can learn to complain in Italian while you're stuck in traffic.

Because audio books are usually much longer than mere songs, the iPod has custom features for audio books. When you listen to an audio book, then take a break, the iPod places a bookmark where you stopped listening. The next time you return to the book, you can pick up right where you left off. This trick works even when you synchronize your iPod with iTunes—the bookmark travels across the sync.

Another cool audio book feature on your iPod is chapter marks. When you're listening to your iPod and looking at the Now Playing screen, you can press the Select button to get into an enhanced fast forward and reverse mode in which you can zoom forward or back in seconds by using the scroll wheel—a feature called *scrubbing*. When you do this while listening to an audio book, you'll see vertical marks on the timeline that indicate the start of chapters. You can use these chapter marks to jump directly to the part of the book you want to hear.

For more on audio books and how to find them in the iTunes Music Store, including free 90-second previews, see the section *Listen to Audio Books* in Chapter 11.

FIGURE 2-15: `Audible.com` **home page.**
Courtesy of Audible.

See Outlines from OmniOutliner

| Note | This hack works on Macintosh computers only. |

OmniOutliner from Omni Development, Inc. is a superb tool for working with any kind of hierarchy, such as brainstorming ideas, outlines, tables of contents, and organization charts. Some Macs come with OmniOutliner preinstalled. If you don't have it already, you can download a free trial version or buy it at `www.omnigroup.com/applications/omnioutliner`.

You can get an add-on script from Omni that lets you export outlines to your iPod and view them there. This is great way to outline a speech, then have the outline in front of you on your iPod while you're speaking. You can download the free script at www.omnigroup.com/applications/omnioutliner/extras/. There are two versions: one exports to an iPod note, which requires a 3G iPod, and the other exports to a contact, which will work with any iPod (see Figure 2-16).

Once you download the scripts from the Omni Web site, you can open the disk image and double-click the installer to get the scripts into the OmniOutliner scripts folder. After they're installed, start OmniOutliner, select an outline, and choose a script from the Scripts menu to do your export (see Figure 2-17). That's it—you've got an outline to go!

Read and Write iPod "books"

Yes, it's true that you're reading an iPod book, and there are several other iPod books out there for your enjoyment. But the folks at iPodLibrary.com are talking about a different kind of iPod book: the kind that lives on your iPod. The creators of iPodLibrary.com are looking for people to create and submit what they call "funky little podBooks": collections of interesting content that you can carry around with you on your favorite music player (see Figure 2-18).

Putting "books" of information on iPods is another step in making your iPod indispensible If you think of your iPod as a portable reference library, the potential for these podBooks is enormous. Imagine the possibilities:

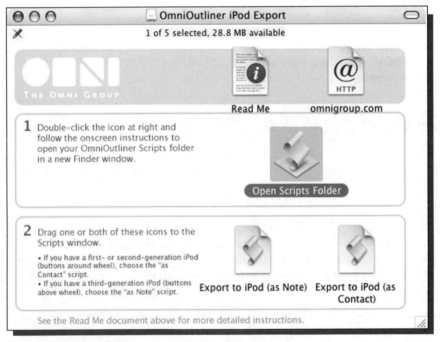

FIGURE 2-16: OmniOutliner export to iPod includes two scripts.

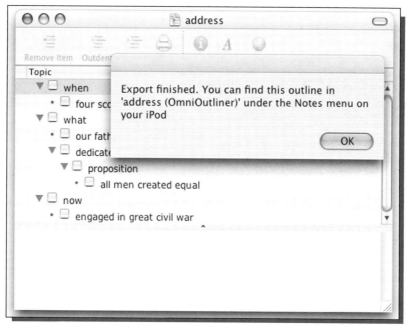

FIGURE 2-17: Outline has been exported.

- *Official Rules of Baseball.* Hard-core baseball fans like to go to the ballpark with a copy of the rulebook for helping to figure out weird plays. Rather than schlepping the physical rule book, a podBook of baseball rules could supply the necessary information.

- *Collector's info.* The next time you go to a convention or collector's shop looking for stamps, coins, Lord of the Rings toys, comic books, bobbleheads, matchbook covers, or other precious hobby item, just think how handy it would be to have a price guide in your iPod.

- *Movie guide.* A list of movies, with star ratings and genre information, can come in handy the next time you find yourself at the video store wandering around like a zombie trying to find something good that you haven't already seen 3 times.

- *Discography.* If you have decided to dedicate your life to collecting (for example) all music recorded by Crosby, Stills, Nash, *or* Young, you have a lot of vinyl and CD gathering to do. A definitive discography stored in your iPod can come in handy as you haunt the used record stores.

- *Astronomical data.* If you're from space, get out your favorite astronomical guidebook and create a podBook full of info about the planets, stars, asteroids, space missions, and other cool heavenly stuff.

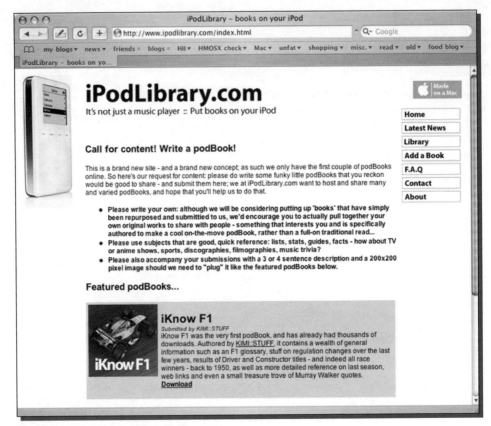

FIGURE 2-18: Home page for iPodLibrary.com.

To help get the library started, iPodLibrary.com already offers a couple of podBooks for downloading:

- *iKnow F1*. This book provides all kinds of info about Formula One racing, including historical rules changes, listings of race winners and other title holders, and even a Formula One glossary.

- *Apple_Bytes*. If you're a fan of Apple history and trivia, you'll get a kick out of this book. It offers a vast array of info, useful and otherwise about Apple, including listings of code names, product timelines, and even the legendary story of the Dogcow.

For another example of a great document on your iPod, see the section *Read the United States Constitution* in Chapter 4.

Summary

This chapter explores stuff your iPod can do that has little or no relationship to playing music. You found out about a few Apple-sanctioned accessories, as well as some handy ways to use your iPod with the addition of some free and inexpensive software.

In the next chapter, you'll get the opportunity to expand your iPod worldview with a look at more esoteric ways to use your iPod's hardware and add-ons. In Chapter 3, you'll stray a little farther from the mainstream, which should be lots of fun.

Way Beyond the Music: Hardware

Right after Apple introduced the iPod in late 2001, enterprising companies started producing iPod accessories. As the iPod's popularity grew, more cool gear started showing up—everything from cases to power adapters to car stuff. In time, some of the iPod's internal secrets spilled out as well, discovered by iPod owners who were inspired to keep pushing buttons until they found something.

This chapter is dedicated to cool hardware you can get to enhance your iPod, along with nifty stuff that's inside every iPod, such as semi-documented button combinations and diagnostic mode. We'll also discuss how you can give new life to an iPod with a battery that won't charge any more.

Check Out Built-in Secrets

The iPod is stingy with its secrets, as I've discussed in previous chapters. In this section, you'll explore what is known about the wacky stuff built into your iPod.

Use button combinations

There is a subset of iPod users who are fairly obsessive about their music players—maybe you're one of us. When Apple ships a new iPod model, these folks start pressing buttons in all combinations, hoping to find cool hidden stuff. It's sort of like reading tea leaves or looking for meaning in ancient ruins. The following are the extra features you can get by using various buttons on your iPod, original or 3G:

- *Power off—Hold down Play until the iPod goes off.* This actually shuts off the display and puts the iPod to sleep, rather than powering the player down entirely.

in this chapter

- ☑ Use Button Combinations

- ☑ Run iPod Diagnostics

- ☑ Hear Sounds from the iPod Speaker

- ☑ See a Numeric Battery Display

- ☑ Get a Wireless Remote for Your iPod

- ☑ Listen to Your iPod in Your Car

- *Reset*—*Hold down Play and Menu at the same time until you see the Apple logo.* This is useful for restarting an iPod that seems to be stuck.

- *Enable disk mode*—*Reset the iPod.* When you see the Apple logo, hold down *Previous* and *Next* at the same time until you see the "OK to disconnect" screen. To get out of disk mode, reset the iPod.

- *Run a disk scan*—*Reset the iPod.* When you see the Apple logo, hold *Menu*, *Next*, *Previous*, and *Select* at the same time (whew). This instructs your iPod to scan its hard disk for bad areas. You'll see a picture of a magnifying glass going over your disk, and a progress bar at the bottom. The scan can take a long time, especially for bigger hard disks. If your iPod fails the scan, there will be additional info on the screen, and you should probably get service for your iPod.

- *Enter diagnostic mode*—*Reset the iPod.* When you see the Apple logo, hold down *Next*, *Previous*, and *Select*. When the Apple logo goes away, release the buttons. You'll see the coolest thing ever: a backwards Apple logo, as if you were inside the iPod looking out. If it's a 3G, you'll hear the iPod emit a little squeal, like you were pinching it. Diagnostic mode contains stuff used by engineers, technicians, and factory folks to test out the iPod. You can find out much more about it in this chapter's *Run iPod Diagnostics* section.

iPod mini

Some of the button presses are a little different for the iPod mini, although the results are the same. Here are the buttons you use on the mini:

- *Power off*—Hold down *Play* (same as regular iPods).

- *Reset*—Hold down *Select* and *Menu* at the same time until you see the Apple logo.

- *Enable diagnostic mode*—Reset the iPod. When you see the Apple logo, hold down *Select* and *Back*. When the Apple logo goes away, release the buttons to see the famous backward Apple and get into diagnostic mode.

There are no button combos that enable disk mode or disk scan on a mini, but you can get to those features from the menus in diagnostic mode.

Run iPod diagnostics

When you enter diagnostic mode, you get an ugly, non-iPod-looking screen with a list of eight diagnostic tests. Each test is marked with a letter, A through H. You might expect to use the wheel to select the tests, but it doesn't work. Instead, use the Next and Previous buttons to move up and down the list. Press *Select* to run the highlighted test. While a test is running, press *Play* to return to the menu. If you scroll down past test H (or up past test A), you'll see a second screen, items I through P.

Table 3-1   iPod Diagnostics

Test letter and name	Description
A. 5 IN 1	This runs several tests in a row: LCM, RTC, SDRAM, FLASH/CHECKSUM, and FIREWIRE/FW ID. (See the following to find out what they do. Note that you have to press *Play* twice to get through LCM.) But the real cool stuff comes after the tests finish. On a 3G iPod, you can press buttons to make noises come out of the built-in speaker. Press *Previous* to hear the wheel's clicking sound, Menu and Select to get two different long beeps, and Next for an effect that sounds a little like a Star Wars blaster. You can have a lot of fun walking around with your iPod, pressing buttons and staring intently at the screen as if you were doing something serious. The clicking sound makes a great fake radiation detector. Press *Play* to return to the Diagnostics menu.
B. RESET	This resets the iPod, just like pressing *Menu* and *Play* together, but slightly easier on your fingers.
C. KEY	This test is actually sort of a video game. You have to press all five buttons on the iPod within about 5 seconds. As you press each one, its name appears on the screen. If you get them all in time, you see KEY PASS. If you're too slow, you're humiliated with KEY FAIL.
D. AUDIO	When you run this test on a 3G iPod, you'll hear a Pac Man-like drumming noise if you have an external speaker connected. On an older iPod, the screen will display AUDIO 0X00000001 DONE.
E. REMOTE	This one tests the iPod remote. It's another game: you get a few seconds to press all the buttons on the remote. As you press each button, a rectangle appears on the screen in a position that corresponds to the location of the button you pressed. If you don't press them all in time, or you don't have a remote connected, you'll see RMT FAIL.
F. FIREWIRE/FW ID	This test checks out the iPod's FireWire port to make sure it's working OK. If it is, you get the comforting FW PASS message.

(continued)

Table 3-1 iPod Diagnostics (Continued)

Test letter and name	Description
G. SLEEP	When you run this test, your iPod drops off to sleep. When you try to wake it, you might see the low battery icon, and the iPod might refuse to come back to life. If this happens, try resetting the iPod or connecting it to power. That should jolt it awake.
H. A2D	This one checks out the iPod's analog to digital components. The test lists sometimes-cryptic names and results for several parts, which vary depending on the particular iPod model.
I. OTPO CNT	Run this test to play with the scroll wheel. "OTPO" is engineering-ese for the wheel —it was supposed to be "opto", but the misspelling is charming, so why fix it now? When you run this test, move the wheel and you'll see the iPod react by changing the big hexadecimal number on the screen.
J. LCM	This tests the iPod's display. LCM probably stands for "liquid crystal monitor". Run the test, then press *Select* to see a gradient pattern on the screen. Press *Select* again to see a giant plus sign. This plus sign refers to the positive effect the iPod has had on Apple's bottom line.
K. RTC/CHG STUS	On older iPods, RTC tests something related to the iPod's real-time clock, the one that knows the time of day. The value sometimes changes a little, but is always small. Is it related to the clock "drift", as described in *Scary Time* in this chapter? I don't know. It's one of those iPod mysteries. This test is replaced by CHG STUS (charge status) on 3G iPods. CHG STUS displays values indicating whether there's anything connected via USB, FireWire, or the headphone port. It also appears to show if charging power is available.
L. SDRAM/USB DISK	SDRAM tests the iPod's synchronous dynamic RAM. That's the magic ingredient that fights skip protection and prolongs battery life: music is preloaded into RAM and the disk drive spins down. USB DISK tests something unknown and reboots the iPod into disk mode.

Table 3-1   iPod Diagnostics   (Continued)

M. FLASH/CHK SUM	The FLASH test, called CHK SUM (checksum) on 3G iPods, examines the iPod's flash ROM. The test finishes by displaying a hexadecimal number, probably a checksum to verify the ROM.
N. OPTO/CONTRAST	The OPTO test, on older iPods only, doesn't seem to do anything at all. CONTRAST lets you fine-tune the screen contrast with the wheel, but any changes you make go away when you leave diagnostic mode.
O. HDD SCAN	This item runs the hard drive test, without the cool animation you get for a disk scan, as described in the section *Use Button Combinations*. Scanning the disk takes many minutes. When the scan is done, you'll see either HDD PASS or HDD FAIL. HDD means "hard disk drive". "FAIL" means "Go get it fixed."
P. RUN IN	This last item runs a series of tests over and over, until you press and hold *Play*. It seems designed to make sure the iPod is ready to go after it's manufactured or repaired.

Hear sounds from the iPod speaker

Grab your iPod and take a good look at it. See the speaker? No, of course you don't. The speaker is well-hidden, apparently near the FireWire or dock connector, because that's where the sound seems to emanate from. The iPod doesn't play music through its internal speaker. It's limited to clicks, pops, and other gadget-type noises the iPod has to make during its usual duties. Even when you have headphones or an external speaker connected, these sounds come out of the internal speaker. Just for fun, here's a list of the standard sounds you'll hear from the iPod speaker:

- *Clicks*—When your move the wheel, you hear a click. You can turn this off by going to Settings ➪ Clicker.

- *More clicks*—Pressing a button also produces a click from the built-in speaker. If you have Settings ➪ Clicker turned off, this won't make a sound either.

- *Buzzes*—When you plug your 3G iPod or mini into its dock, you have certainly noticed the electronic buzzer noise that tells you it's connected.

- *Beeps*—If you turn on your iPod's alarm clock feature and you don't have an external speaker or headphones attached (it's unlikely you would be sleeping with headphones), you can set the iPod to blast out a jaunty little series of beeps in order to wake you up. If you set the alarm to a playlist instead, and you don't have an external speaker connected, the iPod still tries to play the music, but you won't be able to hear it.

- *Chirps*—If you have an iPod connected to USB or unpowered FireWire, the iPod will start chirping at you when it has just a few minutes of power left. If you have a 3G iPod, it will also display a low battery message on the screen.

- *Squeals and other sounds*—As you found out earlier, diagnostic mode produces a whole collection of cool sounds from the internal speaker on a 3G iPod, including the squeal you get when you enter diagnostic mode and the sounds you can generate by pressing buttons after running the 5 IN 1 test. It's practically like having your own tricorder.

Scary Time

Every iPod has a clock that knows the time of day. But no iPod keeps perfect time: the clock circuit in every iPod runs a little bit fast or slow by a matter of milliseconds. This seems terrible, but the good news is that although the clocks aren't perfectly accurate, they are perfectly predictable: they run fast or slow by the same amount every day.

The iPod uses an ingenious scheme to prevent this error from adding up. Every iPod is measured at production time to determine how fast or slow its clock runs. That value is stored in the iPod's ROM. At the start of every day, the iPod uses this stored value to adjust its clock and correct for the error. If the iPod is asleep, it wakes up very quietly, without putting anything on the screen or making any sound, fixes the clock, then quietly goes back to sleep. Shhh.

When Apple first added the alarm clock feature to the iPod, the company began receiving bug reports that sounded like ghost stories. At midnight, iPod screens would suddenly light up for no apparent reason, then turn off a moment later. It turned out that Apple's clock-correction code forgot to check whether the user had turned on the iPod's backlight timer. If the backlight was not set to "Off", it would come on when the clock was corrected. Only the light came on—nothing appeared on the screen, giving the iPod a haunted look. One user reported being awakened by the light of his zombie iPod. By the time he looked around, the light was out, leaving the guy unnerved and perhaps wondering about his sanity.

Apple fixed the bug in the next release of iPod Updater, and no more ghost stories were reported.

Use a Tiny External Speaker

For $10, you can't go wrong with the SimpleSpeaker, a neat gadget made by Higoto and distributed by Madsonline (www.madsonline.com). SimpleSpeaker is just that: you plug it into the top of your iPod to get reasonable external sound. SimpleSpeaker provides stereo sound and doesn't need batteries to operate. This is useful when you're traveling and you want to use your iPod as an alarm clock, or just listen to music without having to use your ear buds or headphones. When you plug a SimpleSpeaker into your iPod, the whole apparatus takes on a kind of top-heavy Mickey Mouse look, as you can see in Figure 3-1. But it's not about looks—SimpleSpeaker is a convenient and inexpensive addition to your iPod travel kit.

Share Your iPod with a Splitter

If you're traveling with friends or family, or you have two children who actually like the same music, you can look into getting a special plug that lets you connect your iPod's headphone jack to more than one set of headphones or ear buds. These devices are called splitters or Y-connectors. XtremeMac makes one, the iShare Earbud Splitter, that comes in iPod white. The iShare has a well-made look, with gold connectors for good sound quality. See www.xtrememac.com for more information. The iShare sells for about $13.

FIGURE 3-1: SimpleSpeaker attached to iPod.
Courtesy of Apple.

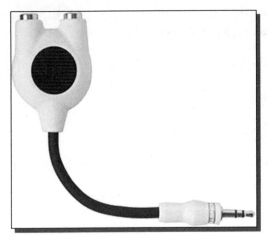

FIGURE 3-2: Monster iSplitter lets you share your iPod.
Courtesy of Monster.

Monster makes a similar product, called iSplitter, for about the same price. Apple carries the Monster iSplitter in its retail and online stores. Figure 3-2 shows what it looks like.

If you're willing to compromise style and premium brands, you can save money by getting a no-name splitter from your local electronics store. You should be able to find one at Radio Shack or Fry's for about $6, but you can be sure it won't be iPod white.

If more than two people want to listen, you can connect a series of splitters together, plugging one into the next. If you keep splitting the signal, it will degrade eventually and you won't be able to hear it any more, but the iPod puts out plenty of oomph, so you should be able to supply sound to at least three or four listeners successfully.

You can get other uses out of your splitter. For example, you and a friend can share the audio output from a laptop or portable DVD player on a plane, or two people can hook into the audio from a portable video game.

 Cross-Reference A more advanced way to share your iPod or other audio output is by using cordless headphones. Check out Chapter 7, "Broadcast Your iTunes."

See a Numeric Battery Display

Third-generation iPods and iPod minis include a cool hack that's practically useless— that's the fun kind! This hack changes the battery display on your iPod from the familiar reclining battery icon to a numeric view. Here's how it works: the iPod looks for a file named _show_voltage in a particular place on its disk. If that file is present, the iPod uses the numerical battery meter.

This hack is only applicable when the iPod is running on battery power. When it's connected to a powered cable, the iconic battery meter reappears.

To turn on this hack, you simply need to create the magic file (its contents don't matter) in the iPod's iPod_Control/Device directory. The tricky part is that iPod_Control is hidden from the Finder and from Windows Explorer. I'll describe how to accomplish this on both Mac OS X and Windows.

Mac OS X

There are a couple of different ways to perform this hack with Mac OS X. The first requires a third-party utility program, but it's pretty easy. The second uses standard software only, but it's a little trickier.

Use the Finder and a utility program

The easiest way to do this hack is with a program like TinkerTool (available at www.bresink.com/osx/TinkerTool.html and described in more detail in the next chapter), which lets you make all the files on your iPod visible. Here's how:

1. Make sure your iPod is connected to your Mac.

2. In TinkerTool, click the Finder tab and check "Show hidden and system files".

3. Click "Relaunch Finder".

4. In the Finder, choose Go ⇨ Computer to see your iPod and other volumes.

5. Still in the Finder, open your iPod, then the iPod_Control folder, then the Device folder (see Figure 3-3).

6. Click the SysInfo file and choose File ⇨ Duplicate.

7. Click once on the SysInfo Copy file to select it. Wait a second or so. Then click its name once to select it for renaming.

   If you click twice on SysInfo Copy too quickly, the Finder will open the file in TextEdit. If that happens, calmly return to the Finder and repeat step 6, waiting a second between clicks.

8. Change the name of SysInfo Copy to _show_voltage. Note that there's an underscore before "show" and another before "voltage".

This works because the iPod only cares that there's a file named _show_voltage—its contents are never examined. It doesn't matter how you create the file or what's in it. SysInfo is simply a small file that's conveniently there for the copying.

When you disconnect your iPod, the battery meter will be replaced by a number indicating the battery charge, with 500 or so as the maximum value. Neat!

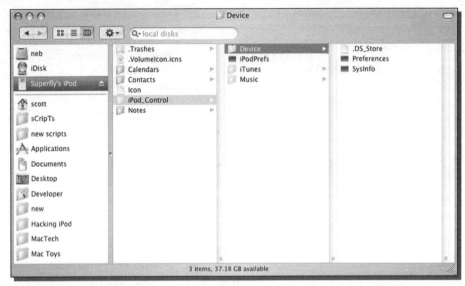

FIGURE 3-3: Device folder contents shown in Finder.

Use Terminal

You can accomplish this hack without TinkerTool or any other third-party software, as long as you don't mind using Terminal to get down in the command line a bit.

Caution

Terminal provides a command-line interface to your Macintosh. If you make a mistake or start playing "I wonder what happens if I do this", all sorts of bad results are possible, including deleting files and messing up the system. If you're not used to fooling around with this stuff, please exercise extreme caution.

1. Make sure your iPod is connected to your Mac.

2. In the Finder, choose Go ➪ Computer.

   You should now see a window that includes hard disks connected to your Mac, including your iPod (Figure 3-4).

3. Run Terminal. If you have never used Terminal, you'll find it in the Utilities folder inside your Applications folder.

4. In Terminal, type the word **touch**, with a space following it. Don't press *Return*.

5. In the Finder window that includes your iPod, drag the iPod icon to the Terminal window and drop it there (Figure 3-5).

FIGURE 3-4: Finder window showing iPod and other volumes.

Getting the iPod Name Right

Dragging the iPod and dropping it into the Terminal window copies the pathname of the iPod for you. This is a shortcut that's easier than typing the iPod name, and it also makes sure the name is in the proper format for Terminal. This is important if your iPod name includes certain non-alphanumeric characters, such as spaces and apostrophes. For Terminal to recognize these characters properly, they have to be preceded by backslashes. Otherwise, Terminal or a shell command might treat them as characters with a special meaning. For example, if the name of the iPod is "Superfly's iPod", dragging and dropping it into Terminal adds this text:

```
/Volumes/Superfly\'s\ iPod
```

Each backslash indicates to the shell that the character following it is simply part of a name and doesn't have special meaning.

1. Click in the Terminal window and press Delete once to remove the blank space after the name of the iPod, but don't press Return yet.

2. Still in Terminal, type the following text: **/iPod_Control/Device/_show_voltage**. (Don't forget the slash at the start or the three underscores.) The whole command line in Terminal now reads as follows:

```
[neb:~] scott% touch /Volumes/Superfly\'s\
iPod/iPod_Control/Device/_show_voltage
```

(Instead of "neb", "scott", and "Superfly's iPod", you'll see your disk, user, and iPod names.)

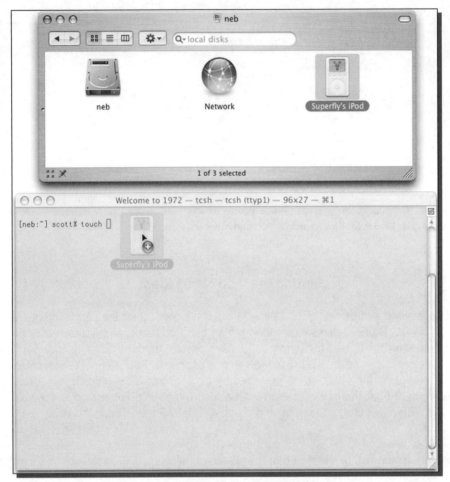

FIGURE 3-5: Drag the iPod and drop it into the Terminal window.

3. Make sure your command line looks like the one in step 7 (except with your disk, user, and iPod names), then, finally, you can press *Return*.

The touch command creates an empty file on your iPod with the magic name. That's all you need to get the voltage number to appear. You'll see it the next time you disconnect your iPod from your Mac.

Windows XP

Windows XP has a built-in feature for displaying hidden files. Once you turn it on, you can add the magic file:

1. Make sure your iPod is connected to your computer.

2. Click Start. On the Start menu, click My Computer.

3. Find your iPod in the My Computer window and double-click it to open it.

4. Take a look in the window that opens. If you see a folder named iPod_Control, go ahead to step 8. If you don't see iPod_Control, continue with the next step.

5. Choose Tools ⇨ Folder Options.

6. Click the View tab.

7. Look for the setting "Hidden files and folders". It's near the bottom of the window. Click "Show hidden files and folders". Click OK. The iPod_Control folder is now ghostly, but visible.

8. Double-click the iPod_Control folder.

9. Double-click the Device folder.

10. Click the SysInfo file and choose Edit ⇨ Copy.

11. Choose Edit ⇨ Paste.

12. Right-click Copy of SysInfo and choose Rename.

13. Change the name of SysInfo Copy to _show_voltage. Note that there's an underscore before "show" and another before "voltage".

This works because the iPod only cares that there's a file named _show_voltage—its contents are never examined. It doesn't matter how you create the file or what's in it. SysInfo is simply a small file that's conveniently there for the copying.

When you disconnect your iPod, the battery meter will be replaced by a number indicating the battery charge, with 500 or so as the maximum value.

Restore the battery icon

Once you're bored with the numeric indicator, you can restore the battery image simply by deleting (or even renaming) the magic file. On the Mac, if you have TinkerTool or the like, you can do that in the Finder. If you don't have a utility that lets you see invisible files in the Finder, you can use the Terminal to remove the file. On Windows, just make sure you have hidden files and folders enabled, then trash the _show_voltage file.

Get a Wireless Remote for Your iPod

The NaviPod from TEN Technology gives you wireless access to your iPod. This is ideal when you have your iPod connected to a stereo system across the room: you don't even have to rise from your couch or chair in order to control your tunes. Plug the infrared receiver into your iPod, then use the NaviPod's stylish round remote control to play, pause, change the volume, or move through your songs.

The NaviPod comes with a cool minimalist chrome stand you can use to prop up your iPod so it's better able to receive commands from the remote. This stand is a handy addition to your iPod repertoire, whether you use the remote or not. If you don't have a NaviPod, you can buy a stand for about $10 at www.tentechnology.com. The company will also sell you an extra (or replacement) remote for $10.

There are two NaviPod models, one for older iPods, the other for 3G iPods. NaviPod sells for about $50, and you can get it at Apple's retail and online stores.

Put Your iPod in a Case

iPods are known for their glamour and utility, but not their ruggedness. The shiny chrome back of an iPod never looks quite the same as it did the day you took it out of the box—it's hard to avoid fingerprints and scratches. Plus, iPods get handled a lot, and many of them spend a considerable amount of time outside. And with a hard disk inside, iPods were never designed to live through being dropped or tossed around.

Apple provides a carrying case and belt clip to help keep your iPod happy and healthy. The case is included with some models, and is a $40 option with others. It's a decent case, but it looks a little corporate, and as an iPod owner, you probably want more choices. Fortunately, independent vendors have stepped in to provide a huge variety of iPod cases for you to choose from. In this section, we'll discuss a few of the best and most wacky cases available. You can find plenty more by checking out the back pages of any Macintosh magazine or by visiting an Apple store in your town or in cyberspace.

SportSuit Convertible

The SportSuit Convertible from Marware is sturdy and stylish, and it costs about the same as Apple's ($40). You can remove the lid from this two-piece case to make it a little more portable. There's easy access to all the controls, and the padded lid includes a compartment to stash your ear buds, scraps of paper, or tiny pets. The case comes with an arm band and belt clip. You can buy other accessories, including a bike holder and lanyard. The SportSuit Convertible comes in six lovely colors. For more information, check them out at www.marware.com or at an Apple store.

Groove Purse Triplet

The Groove Purse Triplet (Figure 3-6) from felicidade is possibly the world's coolest iPod case. It's a white synthetic leather purse that turns into a boom box when you slide your iPod into it. The Groove Purse includes built-in speakers to help you impose your musical

FIGURE 3-6: Groove Purse Triplet makes your iPod a stylish portable stereo.
Courtesy of felicidade.

will on those around you. You can get your Groove Purse Triplet for about $145 from Dr.
Bott at www.drbott.com.

Vaja Leather

Vaja Leather Products makes gorgeous leather cases for all iPods. These semi-rigid cases
come in several models, and you can get them in 20 different colors. You can even have
your name laser-engraved on the back of your case. Vaja cases start at about $50, depend-
ing on the model. You can find out more at www.vajacases.com.

Icewear for iPod mini

Icewear is one of the first cases built to fit the iPod mini's stylish form (Figure 3-7).
Icewear uses the same material found in diving masks to protect the mini while still
allowing Apple's cool design to show through. The Icewear case leaves all controls and

Figure 3-7: Icewear case for iPod mini,
from Tunewear. Courtesy of Tunewear.

connectors accessible, so you can get full usage of your iPod without taking it out of the case. The back of the case includes slots for passing a belt through. Unlike many other iPod cases, Icewear leaves the screen uncovered, so readability isn't reduced. As of this writing, the Icewear case was not yet available, and no price was set. For more information, see www.tunewear.com/english/product/index.html.

Listen to Your iPod in Your Car

iPods and cars go together like apples and pie. You can find plenty of equipment to help make your iPod into a wonderful source of music for the road. In this section, we'll cover some of the ways to play iPod tunes in your car, truck, RV, or stagecoach.

Connect to your car stereo

The fundamental problem to solve when you want to use your iPod in the car is how to get the music from the iPod to your car stereo. If you have a cool stereo that allows for external input from a CD player or similar device, you can just run a cable from the iPod's headphone jack to the stereo input, and you're in business. Hooking up this way is simple and it provides a good, reliable connection to your stereo.

If your stereo doesn't have external input, you'll need another way to connect. If your stereo has a cassette player, consider getting a cassette adapter. This device plugs into your iPod's headphone jack and fools your cassette player into thinking there's a tape in there. There isn't: instead, there's a plastic shell of a cassette that transmits the iPod's sound through the stereo's speakers. This low-tech solution works pretty well, except that you might be annoyed by the transport noise as the fake cassette's wheels turn in the player. You can get one of these at the Apple store or any electronics or stereo shop for under $20.

The hackiest solution comes from using an adapter with an FM transmitter. These gizmos employ a low-power transmitter to broadcast your tunes wirelessly onto an unused FM frequency that you pick from among several choices. By tuning your car radio to the same frequency, you've created your own personal iPod radio station. Because the transmitter is low-power, the broadcast only goes for a few feet, which makes it useful within the confines of your car. One drawback to FM adapters is that they're prone to interference from other radio broadcasts at or near the same frequency. Here's some info on a few of the cooler FM adapters:

- The Arkon SoundFeeder SF250 is a general-purpose FM transmitter that uses a pair of slider switches to choose its frequency and sports a unique egg-shaped design (see Figure 3-8). The sliders glow green when the device is on. The SoundFeeder takes two AAA batteries and costs about $30. Read more about it at www.arkon.com/sf.html.

FIGURE 3-8: Arkon SoundFeeder FM adapter. Courtesy of Arkon.

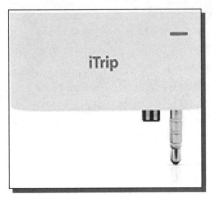

FIGURE 3-9: iTrip mini from Griffin Technology.
Courtesy of Griffin Technology.

- iTrip from Griffin Technology (www.griffintechnology.com) is unique in that it uses the iPod itself to change frequencies. The tuning commands are actually little song files that you load into the iPod via your computer. When you want to set the frequency, you play the corresponding song file: 87.9, 88.1, 88.3, and so on. That's pretty cool, but you won't want to accidentally play these boops and beeps through your car stereo unless your musical tastes are extremely eclectic. The iTrip draws its power from the iPod, so there are no batteries to worry about. iTrip sells for about $35 at Apple stores.

- In June 2004, Griffin shipped the iTrip mini, a new version specifically adapted to fit atop the iPod mini. The iTrip mini performs the same basic functions as its big sibling, but it snaps neatly into an iPod mini, as you can see in Figure 3-9. The iTrip mini sells for about $39, and it's available from Apple stores as well as the manufacturer.

- The irock 400FM Wireless Music Adapter will draw power either from the car's 12V DC plug (formerly known as the "cigarette lighter") or from two AAA batteries. This one costs about $30 and you can see it at www.myirock.com.

- Belkin makes the TuneCast Mobile Transmitter series of products. These compact adapters run on batteries and use buttons to select their frequency. Go to www.belkin.com for more info.

- Monster's iCarPlay Wireless plugs into your iPod's dock connector and charges its battery while you listen to tunes. This adapter plugs into the 12V outlet. You can get more information at www.monstercable.com. iCarPlay sells for about $70.

- TransPod from Digital Lifestyle Outfitters is an FM adapter that charges your iPod while it plays music, and it comes with a cool mounting unit (see Figure 3-10). TransPod is available at www.everythingipod.com for about $100.

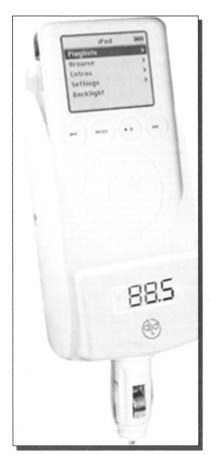

FIGURE 3-10: TransPod FM adapter.
Courtesy of Digital Lifestyle.

Really Reaching

FM adapters such as iTrip and SoundFeeder turn your iPod into a little mobile radio station, broadcasting a signal at low power on the FM dial. In the summer of 2004, a few clever hackers decided to see what would happen if they enhanced the power of their FM transmitters a little. According to the Endgadget web site at www.engadget.com/entry/3597373383872462/, some FM adaptors have antennas wound up inside. By opening the case (which voids the warranty) and pulling out the antenna, you can increase the range of the transmitter somewhat.

Once you've improved your transmitter, you can use your iPod as a tiny radio station. Engadget suggests several semi-joking uses for this, including broadcasting silence at your hard-rocking neighbor, playing gentle ocean waves over the eardrum-destroying car next to you at a red light, and taking over wireless receivers used by people exercising at the gym to listen to TV broadcasts.

Because FM adapters broadcast on specific frequencies, the tricky part of this hack is figuring out which frequency your intended victim is tuned to. For that reason, this hack probably works best when you try it on your friends and family. That would also be a good strategy for avoiding lawsuits and fistfights that might otherwise result.

Power your iPod in the car

You'll need a power source if you're going road tripping with your iPod. Some of the FM adapters listed earlier (iCarPlay and TransPod) charge your iPod while you're playing music. In addition to those, here are a few of the better iPod chargers available:

- PowerPod from Griffin Technology (www.griffintechnology.com) is cool because it works with all generations of iPods. Griffin pulls this trick by making the iPod-to-charger cable separate from the charger part that plugs into the 12v socket. PowerPod costs about $20.

- SiK makes the imp, a $30 charger with a replaceable fuse and line level audio output. Check it out at www.sik.com.

- Dr. Bott's Auto Charger for iPod costs $25 and comes with a SendStation PocketDock so that it can connect to any iPod. This model includes a replaceable fuse. See www.drbott.com to examine it in more detail.

Get the ultimate iPod car kit

The ICE-Link from Dension USA, which was a big hit at Macworld Expo in January 2004, allows your iPod to take the place of a CD changer in your car stereo. Your iPod plays when you select CD as the input source. If you have one of those cool controls that lets you select tracks from your steering wheel, ICE-Link makes it work with your iPod. When you select a different input, such as radio, the iPod pauses. ICE-Link includes mounting hardware and power and audio cables.

ICE-Link is custom fitted to various car models and costs about $200. For more information, visit icelink.densionusa.com.

The Ultimate Listening Machine

Apple has certainly noticed that lots of folks like listening to iPods in their cars. To help appease those customers, Apple is starting to team up with car manufacturers to fully integrate iPods into car stereos. According to reports available at the time of this writing, Apple and BMW will offer a campaign called "iPod Your BMW". Some BMW owners will have the option of getting an iPod that docks inside the glove box, with the controls on the steering wheel and a digital display on the dash. So if you're saving up for a new iPod, you might have to bank a little extra cash so you can buy a new BMW, too.

Replace Your iPod's Battery

iPod batteries are designed to withstand several thousand cycles of charging and discharging. Eventually, you might end up with a battery that will no longer hold a charge. But although the battery is built-in, all is not lost. When the battery conks out, you have four options:

- If you've managed to wear out your battery while your iPod is less than a year old, it's still under warranty, and Apple will fix or replace it for free. The full warranty statement is available at `store.apple.com/Catalog/US/Images/ipodwarranty.html`.

- If your iPod is out of warranty, Apple will replace it for about $100. You fill out a form, ship the iPod to Apple, and a new one (same model you sent in, sorry) comes back. See `www.apple.com/support/ipod/service/battery.html` to start the process.

- You can buy a replacement battery for about $60 or less and install it yourself. iPod replacement batteries are available from various sources, including `www.ipodbattery.com`, `www.pdasmart.com`, and smalldog.com.

- Your final option is to go back in time and buy AppleCare Protection when you get your new iPod. For $59, AppleCare extends your warranty from one year to two. AppleCare also covers the accessories that came with your iPod, such as the dock and remote, but it probably won't help you if your dog eats your ear buds. Read all about AppleCare at `www.apple.com/support/products/applecareipod.html`.

Battery replacement surgery

If your iPod needs a new battery, should you attempt to replace it yourself? If you have an earlier iPod, you will probably be OK, even if you don't have a lot of experience taking things apart. I'm mainly a software guy, and I had no trouble with the operation because I took it slowly and carefully.

If you have a 3G iPod, my advice is not to open it if you want it to work right again. These newer, thinner iPods are much more delicately put together. You stand a good chance of breaking something when you take it apart. In any case, if you would rather not operate on your precious music player just to fix a dead battery, remember that Apple will replace the iPod for $100.

 Apple's offer to replace your out-of-warranty iPod for $100 specifically states that a worn-out battery must be the only thing wrong with the iPod. If you try to replace the battery yourself, and break the Hold switch (or cause other damage), you're no longer qualified for the $100 repair. And if your iPod is in warranty, opening it voids the warranty, needless to say.

If you decide to go ahead and replace the battery yourself, good for you! Here are the steps you need to follow:

1. The best tool for opening your iPod is a thin, laminated card, like a driver's license or video store membership card. Find one of these. (You can also use a very small flat-blade screwdriver, but if you do, it's easy to scratch the iPod, or, if you're like me, you're likely to dig a small, painful hole in your hand when the screwdriver slips.)

2. Make sure the iPod is turned off. Just to be sure it stays off, turn on the Hold switch.

3. Hold the iPod in one hand and the plastic card in the other.

4. You're going to separate the white part of the case from the silver part. (Second- and third-generation iPods are more difficult to open because the case wraps around the connectors.) Put the corner of the card between the two parts of the case on one of the top corners. Wedge the card in until the case comes apart slightly.

5. Keeping the card wedged between the parts of the case, work the card around the side of the iPod. The case is held together by plastic clips, which you have to pry apart as you go.

6. When you have separated all the clips, pull the case apart. Pause to admire your handiwork.

7. The battery is glued to the hard drive. Hold the hard drive part down on the table with one hand, and use the other hand to pull the battery off. You might need to use the plastic card or a screwdriver to help pry the battery loose.

8. The battery is still connected to the circuit board. To detach it, gently (GENTLY!) pull the cable that connects it.

9. Plug in your new battery, taking care to orient it the same way as the old one.

10. Stick the battery to the hard disk, just where the old one was. Make sure you line it up correctly the first time – that glue is very sticky, as you have discovered by now.

11. Make sure that the battery cable is tucked in, and snap the case back together.

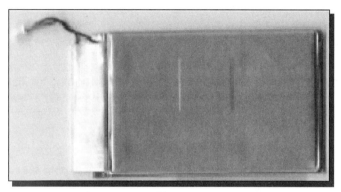

FIGURE **3-11: High-capacity iPod battery.**

Anxiously fire up your iPod to make sure it still works. Note: new batteries usually require charging, so don't freak out if it won't turn on without external power at first.

Advanced battery info

Now that we've discussed the basics of iPod battery knowledge, here are a couple of extra tips and tricks you might want to mess around with—if you dare.

- If you have a thick (pre-3rd generation) iPod, you can try wiring two batteries together in series. Of course, this will void your warranty, but it should work and will give you double the battery life in your iPod.

- Some manufacturers offer higher capacity batteries for iPods. For example, PDASmart.com sells a 2000mAh battery, which the company claims provides 60% more power than Apple's battery (see Figure 3-11). You can order yours from `www.pdasmart.com/products/AP17ipodpartscenter.htm` for about $90.

Battery Assault

In November 2003, Casey Neistat's iPod battery died after only 18 months of use. According to Neistat, when he asked Apple to fix it, Apple's response was that he buy a new iPod as a replacement. This incensed him so much that he and his brother Van created a documentary film, iPod's Dirty Secret, to tell the story. The Neistat brothers released their film on the Web, and all sorts of craziness broke loose. Many iPod users agreed with the film's premise, while others came to Apple's defense. Casey Neistat was quoted on the subject in an article in the Washington Post:

"We got close to 1,000 e-mails the first couple of days, a lot of people were in my exact position and had to buy the new iPod. Eighty percent of our mail was positive, people saying that they liked the sardonically irreverent way we did it. But there were die-hard Mac fans who were mad at us, who were panicking because they feel like we might cause somebody to not buy a Macintosh."

Less than two weeks after the movie was posted, Apple announced a new policy for iPod battery warranty and replacement: $59 for an extended warranty, and $99 to swap for a new iPod, as described earlier in this section. Was there a connection between the release of the movie and Apple's new policy? Apple says no: the new policy was being crafted for months before the movie was released.

For more information about this saga, see www.ipodhacks.com/article.php?sid=516. And if you want to look at the film itself, check out www.ipodsdirtysecret.com.

Summary

It's easy to spend hundreds of dollars accessorizing your iPod to make it more useful when you fly, in your car, or while you go for a run. But you can also be an iPod explorer just by messing around with the built-in diagnostic mode, a "feature" that comes free with every iPod. Diagnostic mode is a perfect iPod hack—it's not particularly useful, but it's pretty cool to show to your friends, especially when you get the iPod to start making those videogame noises.

In our next chapter, we'll continue to look at fun, weird, and occasionally useful tricks you can do with your iPod, this time focusing on software additions. Although Apple didn't intend for the iPod to be a software development platform, a robust collection of programs has sprung up to help you get more from your iPod and your computer.

Way Beyond the Music: Software

Computers are cursed with high expectations and amazing flexibility. A toaster is built to toast, and a refrigerator keeps things cold, but a computer is a general-purpose machine that can be made to perform an incredible variety of tasks. Because computer designers and engineers are creative people, it practically hurts them to put limits on what a computer or a program can do. But it's those limits, artfully applied, that define great digital products by focusing the attention of the designers and the users on the product's goal.

No product illustrates this principle of focus better than the iPod. In general terms, the iPod is not a music player: it's a computer. But when the original iPod appeared, Apple chose to limit its applications to music. Apple pointedly decided not to make the iPod into a platform for outside software developers.

But nerds are clever, and people quickly found ways to sneak extra features into their iPods. Determined iPod fans figured out how to disguise data as songs, and soon names and phone numbers started showing up on iPods alongside the music. Apple noticed this trend and began adding features of its own to the basic iPod software. Every iPod now has the native ability to hold contacts and calendars, and newer iPods (those with dock connectors) let you store notes.

Naturally, when people got hold of these additions, they built additional additions on top of them. Using the Contacts, Calendar, and Notes features, you can find software that lets you load up your iPod with all sorts of information, including movie listings, long text files, weather forecasts, and even Shakespearean sonnets. In this chapter, we explore how you can teach your iPod these new tricks.

Another neat tweak we'll discuss in this chapter is the ability to copy songs from your iPod. Although iTunes prevents this form of copying as an impediment to song piracy, there are plenty of legitimate reasons to move your music from your iPod, and lots of easy ways to do it.

See and Copy Your Songs

The joke is that while Microsoft invested millions of dollars developing digital rights management (DRM) software for Windows Media Audio to restrict what users could do with music, Apple spent a fraction of a penny per iPod on little stickers that say "Don't steal music". The truth is more complex. Apple has always walked a tightrope between the rights and desires of two very important groups: customers and music publishers.

When the original iPod appeared in 2001, some folks at Apple wanted the "Don't steal music" admonition to appear on the screen every time users turned their iPods on, but that point of view lost out. Instead, Apple decided late in the iPod's development to adopt a DRM strategy nicknamed "roach motel", after the bug control product and its slogan "Roaches check in, but they don't check out". In the iPod's case, it was the songs that were going in, but not out. As you know, iTunes only provides a way for you to copy songs from your computer to your iPod—it won't move them in the other direction.

If you go to the Finder or Windows Explorer and look at your iPod, you won't see your songs anywhere. That's because Apple has taken simple steps to hide them. It's more of a social copy protection system than a technological one. But the way they're hidden is an open secret, and it's easy to work around. Every iPod book and Web site explains how to see your hidden songs, and I'm going to do it, too—I'll just be a little nerdier about it than most other folks, in keeping with the hack spirit of this book.

The iTunes Music Store adds a twist to this story. When you buy songs from the Store, they're wrapped in a real DRM scheme, called FairPlay, that limits what you can do with them. The hacks in this section simply make the songs visible and let you move them around. Nothing here will help you get around FairPlay. If you copy a Store-bought song from an iPod to a computer that's not authorized to play that song, it still won't play.

Good and Evil

I'm not going to present a big legal or moral lecture here—I'm just a geek, not an expert in either of those areas—but there are plenty of legitimate uses for copying music from your iPod to your computer. For example, let's say you have music you've ripped from CD into iTunes, then copied to your iPod, and your hard disk dies. The music you bought is still on your iPod, and it would be handy to copy it back to your computer where it used to be. On the other hand, it's definitely uncool, not to mention illegal, to copy commercial, pay-for music from your friend's iPod to your computer. So it's a good idea to follow the advice printed on that little sticker: don't steal music.

There are three elements to Apple's gentle anti-copying scheme:

- In iTunes, if you drag a track from an iPod to the Library, or to a playlist on the computer, you won't be able to drop it there—it just zips back where it came from. Apple built this limitation into iTunes to prevent easy copying. There is no way to overcome it.

- In the Finder or Windows Explorer, your iPod appears as a hard disk, but the songs are nowhere in sight. That's because Apple has used an operating system feature to hide the files from view. Otherwise, they're normal, copyable files.

- The music files are arranged in folders that are not organized by any obvious scheme. That makes it more difficult to use clues like artist or album name to find the particular songs you want.

Let's discuss a few different ways to see and fool around with your iPod files. The tricks and tools vary depending on which operating system you're using.

Mac OS X

You can find and copy any song from your iPod with nothing more than the Finder, as long as you're using Mac OS X 10.2 or later. Here's how:

1. In the Finder, choose Go ➪ Go to Folder.

2. In the sheet that appears, type **/Volumes/iPodName/iPod_Control/Music**. (Instead of "iPodName", type the actual name of your iPod.) Click Go. Your iPod's music folder should appear in the Finder, but its contents are invisible.

3. Choose File ➪ Find. Click the "Search in:" pop-up, and choose "Specific places".

4. Drag the iPod music folder from the Finder window to the list at the top of the Find window. You should see the iPod Music folder added as another place to search. Make sure the Music folder is the only item checked.

5. Click the first pop-up in the "Search for items whose:" area and choose "Visibility". Click the second pop-up and choose "Visible and invisible items".

6. Click the plus sign at the right to add another search criterion. Choose "Name" and "Contains" from the two pop-ups. Type all or part of the song's file name into the text box at the right.

   Note that you're searching for a file name, which might not be the same as the name of the song. Your best bet is to search for words from the first part of the song title, as file names tend to get chopped when you rip CDs. So, for example, if you're looking for the song "Dead Leaves and the Dirty Ground", search for "Dead Leaves", not "Dirty Ground". You'll figure it out—you're smart.

Note If you're using Mac OS X 10.2, the way to choose search criteria is a tiny bit different. Use the "Add criteria" pop-up to make sure you end up with two criteria, one for "visibility" set to "all", the other for "file name" and "contains".

7. Click Search in the Find window. You'll get a Search Results window that shows the song you're looking for. See Figure 4-1 for an example of what that looks like.

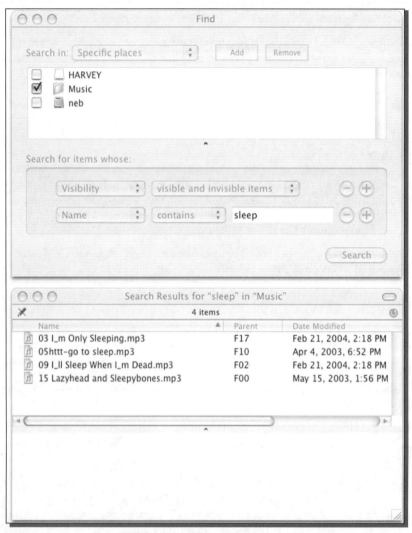

FIGURE 4-1: You can use the Find feature in Mac OS X to locate a particular song on your iPod. Courtesy of Apple.

Once you see the song in Search Results, you can simply drag it to another location, such as your hard disk, and the Finder will happily copy it over. If it's a song that you bought from the iTunes Music Store, the restrictions on playing the song come right along, so you can't use this technique as a way of breaking Apple's digital rights management.

This is a handy technique for finding and copying a single song. What if you want to simply move *all* the songs from your iPod to your hard disk? Start by doing the preceding steps 1 through 5 to get ready to search your iPod's music. Then continue with these steps:

1. Make the first search criterion "Visibility" for "Visible and invisible items", and be sure it's the only criterion listed. If you have another criterion there, maybe left over from a previous search, click the minus sign next to it to delete it.

2. Click Search to uncover everything in the Music folder. You'll get a Search Results window like the one in Figure 4-2.

3. Scroll the Search Results window to the right until you see the "Size" column. Click that column's header (where it says "Size"). You'll get a list of files in the iPod's Music folder in order from the largest to the smallest. This has the side effect of putting all the songs at the top, and the wacky folders that the iPod uses to organize your music (with names like F00, F01, and so on) at the bottom.

4. Click the first song in the Search Results window. Scroll down until you can see the last song, just above the parade of folders (F00, and so on). Shift-click the last song. This will select all the songs in the window.

5. Open a Finder window and create a new folder (File ➪ New Folder) on your hard disk to hold your iPod music. Name it "my iPod music".

6. Drag the song files from the Search Results window to the "My iPod music" folder. The Finder will copy your songs from the iPod to your hard disk.

Note After you drop the songs in the destination folder, you might get an error message from the Finder saying something like "The selected items cannot all be put into the same location, because at least one of them is busy." The problem here is that you have two (or more) song files with the same name. On the iPod, they're in different folders, but now you're putting them all into the same folder on your hard disk. The solution is to find the offending files in the Search Results window—you can click the "Name" column to help track them down-and then Command-click one of them to remove it from the selection. Try dragging and dropping again. You might have to repeat this process if you have more than one set of same-named files.

The same thing, only hackier

If you're happier typing at a command line than doing all that fancy-pants dragging and dropping, here's a way you can use Terminal to copy songs from your iPod.

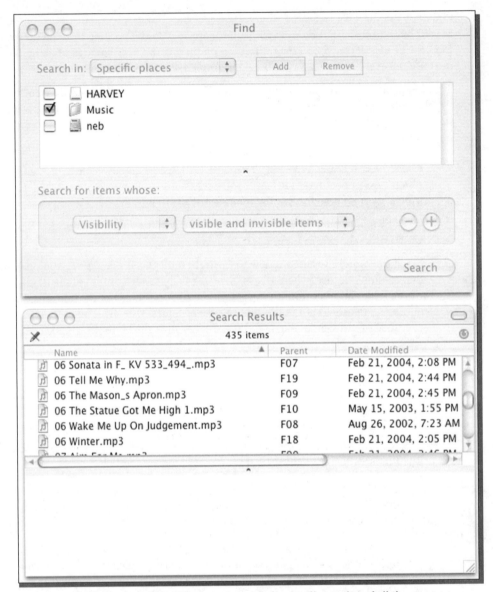

FIGURE 4-2: If you don't specify a file name to search for, you'll get a list of all the songs on your iPod. Courtesy of Apple.

Be careful with Terminal. You get to mess with your computer and iPod from a real Unix shell. The civilized veneer of the Finder and the Aqua user interface are stripped away, and you can do unwanted nasty things like using the cp command in step 4 to accidentally delete files. If you're not comfortable with this stuff, you might want to consider this section read-only for now.

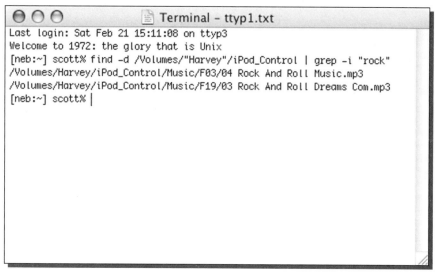

```
Last login: Sat Feb 21 15:11:08 on ttyp3
Welcome to 1972: the glory that is Unix
[neb:~] scott% find -d /Volumes/"Harvey"/iPod_Control | grep -i "rock"
/Volumes/Harvey/iPod_Control/Music/F03/04 Rock And Roll Music.mp3
/Volumes/Harvey/iPod_Control/Music/F19/03 Rock And Roll Dreams Com.mp3
[neb:~] scott% |
```

FIGURE 4-3: You can search for songs on your iPod with the Find command in Terminal.

1. Go to Terminal. For those not in the know, but eager to learn, it's an application, usually located in the Applications/Utilities folder.

2. Type this command into the Terminal window:

   ```
   find -d /Volumes/"my iPod"/iPod_Control | grep -i "part of
   name"
   ```

   Instead of "my iPod", use the name of your iPod. In place of "part of name", type any part of the file name you're looking for. Remember that you're searching for a file name, which might not be the same as the name of the song, and you should try to search for words from the first part of the song title. After typing this command, you'll get a list of songs, if any, that match your search request. See Figure 4-3 for an example.

3. The output in Terminal includes complete pathnames for all the files it found. In Terminal, look through the output for the song you want to copy.

4. With the file path you got from step 3, use the cp command in Terminal to copy the song, as in this example:

   ```
   cp /Volumes/"my iPod"/iPod_Control/Music/F16/"01 Dead Leaves
   And The Dirt.wav" ~/Documents/"my iPod music"/
   ```

   (The command is wrapped on two lines in this book, but it should be all one line when you type it into Terminal.) Note that you have to put quotation marks around the names of iPods, files, or folders that have spaces or non-alphanumeric characters in them.

Ceci est une pipe

In case you're curious, here's a little explanation of the two simple commands you typed in Terminal. The first:

```
find -d /Volumes/"my iPod"/iPod_Control | grep -i "part of name"
```

The find command simply finds files in a directory (folder). The "-d" option asks Find to look recursively inside any directories it sees. "/Volumes/"my iPod"/iPod_Control" tells Find where to start looking. The vertical bar after that is called a *pipe*. It tells find to send its output, which will be a list of all files in the iPod_Control folder, to another command—in this case, a command called grep, which is a Unix tool for finding text. The grep tool looks for the text we want, and the "-i" option tells grep not to worry about whether the text is upper or lower case.

Here's the command we used to copy the song:

```
cp /Volumes/"my iPod"/iPod_Control/Music/F16/"01 Dead Leaves
And The Dirt.wav" ~/Documents/"my iPod music"/
```

This one is very simple, too. The cp command copies files. The first item is the file to be copied, and it's followed by the directory that tells where we want the copy to go.

That's it. If you're keen on learning more about the deep world of Unix shells and commands, there are many books, magazine articles, and Web sites available to teach you more about Unix in Mac OS X. Have fun, and be careful out there.

Automatic for the pod people

Now that you're an expert in built-in ways to uncover hidden iPod songs, you might want to check out some utility programs that make it easier to see what's really on your iPod. In this section, I'll write about a couple of the most popular of these programs, TinkerTool and iPod Viewer, and I'll provide pointers to more utilities.

TinkerTool

Marcel Bresink's TinkerTool (www.bresink.de/osx/TinkerTool.html) is a free utility with a switch that lets you see, find, and copy all invisible files and folders in Mac OS X, whether on the iPod or anywhere else. TinkerTool lets you mess with lots of other settings too, but if all you want to do is see the hidden music on your iPod when using the Finder, you only have to turn on one checkbox. Go to the Finder screen in TinkerTool and click "Show hidden and system files". Instantly you'll see . . . well, it doesn't happen instantly. To make the change take effect, you have to click Relaunch Finder at the bottom of the window (see Figure 4-4).

After you change the setting and relaunch the Finder, it won't take long for the Finder to come back, new and improved. Now, when you open your iPod in the Finder, the

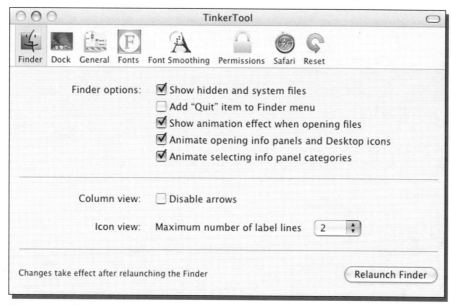

FIGURE 4-4: TinkerTool Finder settings screen.

iPod_Control folder will be visible, along with all the folders and songs inside. Of course, you shouldn't move or delete files on the iPod itself, as that would certainly annoy the iPod.Note

TinkerTool is worthy of much more investigation. Although a full discussion of its features is outside the modest scope of this book, here are just a few of the cool hacks you can accomplish with TinkerTool:

- Change system fonts and font smoothing settings.

- Make icons for hidden applications appear transparent in the dock (see Figure 4-5).

- Put single or double scroll arrows in windows, at either end of the scroll bar, or both ends.

iPod Viewer

iPod Viewer (`homepage.mac.com/initgraf/iPodViewer/frameset.html`) is a slick tool available free from InitGraf Software. iPod Viewer examines the contents of

FIGURE 4-5: Dock with hidden application icons transparent.

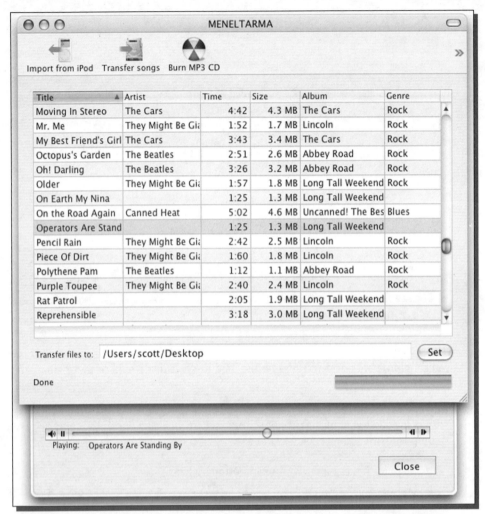

FIGURE 4-6: iPod Viewer lists the songs on your iPod and lets you play them on your Mac.

your iPod and lists them for you in its window (see Figure 4-6). You can click a column header to sort the songs any way you like, just as in iTunes. And iPod Viewer is not just a viewer—it's a player. If you double-click a song, a little drawer appears at the bottom of the window and your song starts playing.

From iPod Viewer, you can copy any or all songs to your Mac by selecting the ones you want and clicking "Transfer songs". You can even burn a CD full of MP3s directly from iPod Viewer, without having to copy the files to your Mac first. Just pick the songs you want and click "Burn MP3 CD" in the toolbar. That's really neat!

Other programs

One more program worth mentioning is PodMaster 1000, available for a shareware fee of $8 at `homepage.mac.com/podmaster/FileSharing1.html`. You can use PodMaster 1000 to copy songs from your iPod, play tunes through the Mac's speakers, and change tag information. PodMaster even has a window that makes it look like an iPod on your screen.

You might also want to try out an AppleScript called "iPod Tracks ➾ Desktop". To use this free goodie, you select songs you want to copy in iTunes. Then, you just run the script, and the songs show up on your Desktop. Neat! You can find this script by searching for it at `www.versiontracker.com`.

I have described some great utilities in this section, but there are many more tools for managing tracks on your iPod. If you go to `www.versiontracker.com` and search for "iPod", you'll find a bunch of them.

Windows XP

Seeing your iPod's songs in Windows XP is even easier than on the Mac. That's because Windows Explorer has a built-in feature for displaying hidden files. Here's how to do it:

1. Click Start. On the Start menu, click My Computer.

2. Find your iPod in the My Computer window and double-click it to open it.

3. Take a look in the window that opens. If you see a folder named iPod_Control, you're done. You or somebody else has already set up Windows Explorer to show hidden files on the iPod. If you don't see iPod_Control, continue to the next step.

4. Choose Tools ➾ Folder Options.

5. Click the View tab.

6. Look for the setting "Hidden files and folders". It's near the bottom of the window (see Figure 4-7). Click "Show hidden files and folders". Click OK. The iPod_Control folder is now ghostly, but visible.

7. Double-click the iPod_Control folder, then double-click the Music folder inside it. You'll see all the "F" folders that contain your iPod's music. Open them up to view the music inside (see Figure 4-8).

Once the scales have fallen from your eyes and you can see hidden files on your iPod, just go ahead and drag them to your hard disk. What if you're looking for a particular file? You can use the Search feature in Windows Explorer, but you have to change a setting first:

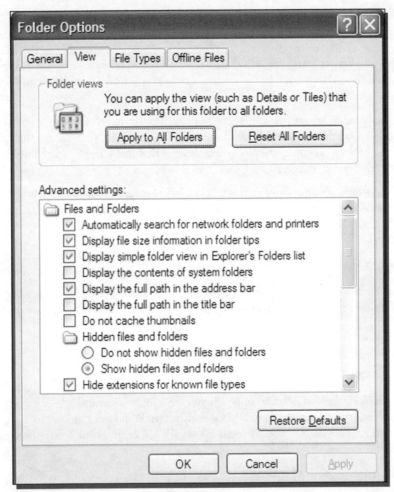

FIGURE 4-7: The option you're looking for is near the bottom of the Advanced settings list.

1. Click the Search button in the toolbar. The Search Companion appears on the left side of the window, usually accompanied by that eager dog (which you can change to a woman in a hovercar, by the way, but that's a hack for a different book).

2. Near the bottom of the Search Companion area, click "Change preferences".

3. Click "Change files and folders search behavior".

4. Click the "Advanced" button, and then click OK. This will take you back to the main Search screen.

FIGURE 4-8: Typical iPod contents as they appear in Windows Explorer.

5. Click "More advanced options". Some new options will appear. You might have to scroll down to see them.

6. Make sure "Search subfolders" and "Search hidden files and folders" are checked.

7. Scroll the search area back to the top, and type part of the song's name in the first text box. Your screen should now look like Figure 4-9. Click Search.

When you click Search, the puppy will quickly find the files you're looking for on your iPod. You can then drag any or all of them to your hard disk. Woof!

Cool tools

Apple sold iPods for Windows for a long time before it shipped iTunes for Windows. One result of this was a bunch of applications that help you monkey around with your iPod on

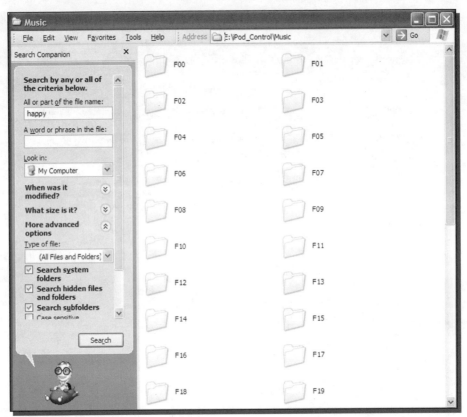

FIGURE 4-9: Typical iPod contents as they appear in Windows Explorer.

your PC, including some that help you see and copy music from your iPod back to your hard disk.

EphPod

EphPod (www.ephpod.com) is a program created by Joe Masters that lets you see and copy files, and do much more besides. You can get a look at EphPod in Figure 4-10. When you run EphPod, you get a list of all the usual iPod stuff: playlists, artists, genres, and songs. To copy a song to your hard disk with EphPod, find the song and right-click it, then choose "Copy Songs to Directory" from the shortcut menu. Pick the place where you want the songs to go, and you're done.

EphPod is a handy program with many more features for helping you manage your iPod, so be sure to check it out. EphPod is "donationware"—if you like it, the author asks you to give money to his beer fund (which doesn't really all go to beer).

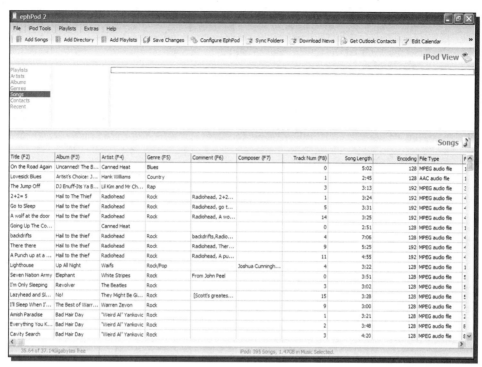

FIGURE 4-10: EphPod is an excellent program for helping manage your iPod on Windows, and it's free. Courtesy of EphPod.

XPlay

Another neat program for Windows users is XPlay, from Mediafour Corporation (www.mediafour.com/products/xplay/). XPlay has the extra added wrinkle of working with Mac-formatted iPods as well as those connected to Windows computers. XPlay has a "Copy To" button in its toolbar that lets you move music from your iPod to your hard disk. XPlay sells for $30, and there's a free test drive version available.

Put Large Text Documents on Your iPod

Note

This hack works on Macintosh computers only.

The iPods introduced by Apple in 2003 and later, including the iPod mini, featured a new button layout and docking connector. The software changed too, and Note Reader was one of the biggest new features. Note Reader provides a way to put general text documents

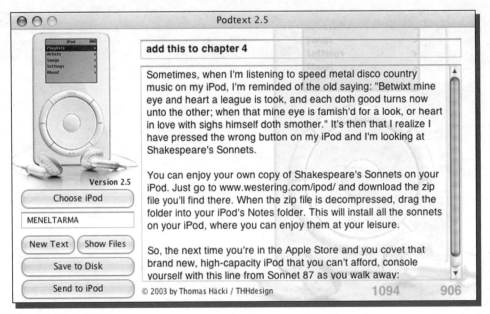

add this to chapter 4

Sometimes, when I'm listening to speed metal disco country music on my iPod, I'm reminded of the old saying: "Betwixt mine eye and heart a league is took, and each doth good turns now unto the other; when that mine eye is famish'd for a look, or heart in love with sighs himself doth smother." It's then that I realize I have pressed the wrong button on my iPod and I'm looking at Shakespeare's Sonnets.

You can enjoy your own copy of Shakespeare's Sonnets on your iPod. Just go to www.westering.com/ipod/ and download the zip file you'll find there. When the zip file is decompressed, drag the folder into your iPod's Notes folder. This will install all the sonnets on your iPod, where you can enjoy them at your leisure.

So, the next time you're in the Apple Store and you covet that brand new, high-capacity iPod that you can't afford, console yourself with this line from Sonnet 87 as you walk away:

© 2003 by Thomas Häcki / THHdesign   1094   906

FIGURE 4-11: Podtext.

on your iPod so you can check them out whenever you have time. Getting notes into Note Reader is easy: just drag text files into the Notes folder, using the Finder or Windows Explorer. It's very cool.

However, Apple decided to limit Notes and Note Reader to new iPods only. Unlike many other new features, you couldn't get Notes by upgrading the software of your pre-2003 iPod. Bummer.

Luckily, the iPod universe is filled with clever programmers who help us get around problems like this. Podtext by Thomas Häcki is an example of this phenomenon. Podtext lets you store notes in your Contacts folder, which every iPod has, regardless of vintage. You can use Podtext itself to type notes, then save them directly to the iPod or to your hard disk. You can open these Contacts-Notes directly in Podtext and edit them, but you can't open a file from the Mac's hard disk. Instead, you can open the file with another program, such as TextEdit, select text there, then drag it into Podtext. Figure 4-11 shows you what Podtext looks like.

If your text file is too big to fit into a contact on the iPod (more than 2,000 characters), Podtext will automatically split it into multiple files for storage, then stitch it together again when you edit it.

You can get Podtext for free at www.podtext.thhdesign.com.

If you have a Notes-capable iPod and you want to know more about cool stuff you can do with Note Reader, see Appendix A.

> ### Free Reading
>
> You can track down lots of great, free reading material on the Web that's available as text. One excellent source is the Internet Archive at `archive.org`. This fabulous site has thousands of freely available texts, mostly from books whose copyright has expired. You'll find *Moby Dick*, *Alice in Wonderland*, *The Art of War*, and various bibles among the collection here. Although most of these texts are too long to fit into a single iPod note, Podtext automatically splits them up for you.

Read the United States Constitution

When you visit the National Archives in Washington, D.C., you can see the documents known as the Charters of Freedom of the United States: the Declaration of Independence, the Constitution, and the Bill of Rights. These documents, now more than 200 years old, are preserved in containers filled with inert gas and covered with thick bulletproof glass. At night, the documents are sealed in a vault of reinforced concrete and steel weighing 55 tons. And while it's important to protect the original editions of these documents, it's no less important to note that you can have your very own copy of the U.S. Constitution stored on your iPod (Figure 4-12).

Thanks to the American Constitution Society, you can download the Constitution and put it into your iPod's Notes folder. To get your iPod Constitution, go to www.acslaw.org/misc/iPoddl.htm and download it. Follow the instructions on the download page (which simply tell you to drag the files to the Notes folder on your iPod), and you have your Constitution. It's not exactly a 55-ton vault, but it's highly portable.

Once you have the Constitution on your iPod, you can read it by looking under Notes on the iPod's main screen, just as you do with all iPod notes. For more information on the Charters of Freedom exhibit, see the National Archives web site at `www.archives.gov/national_archives_experience/charters.html`.

Read Shakespeare's Sonnets

Sometimes, when I'm listening to speed metal disco country music on my iPod, I'm reminded of the old saying: "Betwixt mine eye and heart a league is took, and each doth good turns now unto the other; when that mine eye is famish'd for a look, or heart in love with sighs himself doth smother." It's then that I realize I have pressed the wrong button on my iPod and I'm looking at Shakespeare's Sonnets.

You can enjoy your own copy of Shakespeare's Sonnets on your iPod. Just go to `www.westering.com/ipod/` and download the zip file you'll find there. When the zip file is decompressed, drag the folder into your iPod's Notes folder. This will install all the sonnets on your iPod, where you can enjoy them at your leisure.

FIGURE 4-12: Preamble to the Constitution.

So, the next time you're in the Apple Store and you covet that brand new, high-capacity iPod that you can't afford, console yourself with this line from Sonnet 87 as you walk away:

Farewell! thou art too dear for my possessing.

Get News, Weather, Movie Listings and More

Note This hack works on Macintosh computers only.

Pod2Go by Kevin Wojniak (`kainjow.com/pod2go/website/`) is a brilliant gem of a program for your iPod. iPod2Go grabs news and other information from the Internet and your Mac and copies it to your iPod. Then, when you're on the train, sitting at lunch, or waiting for your bail bondsman to arrive, you can read what you've downloaded.

Pod2Go gets information in a bunch of categories: news, weather, movies, stock quotes, horoscopes, text, and driving directions. The news info comes in a format called RSS (Really Simple Syndication) that's supported by thousands of Web sites. Pod2Go is preloaded with a long list of news sources you can sign up for, but you can add any RSS feed you want. Pod2Go works with any iPod. If you have a 3G iPod, Pod2Go will store information as iPod notes or contacts, your choice; on earlier iPods, Pod2Go uses contacts,

Cross-Reference Although Pod2Go is Mac-only, Windows users can get some of the same news and weather information by using iPodSync, described in this chapter under *Synchronize Your iPod with Microsoft Outlook*.

Setting Your Sites

If you have a favorite news site or Web log that's not on the built-in list, the site still might provide a news feed that you can read with Pod2Go. To find out, go to the site and look for an icon reading "XML" or "RSS", or a link that says something like "Syndicate this site". Click the icon or link. You'll go to a Web page that seems to be filled with gibberish text: that's the RSS feed. Go to your browser's address bar, select the URL, and copy it. Over in Pod2Go, on the News screen, click Custom Feed, select the "Enter URL" box at the top, and paste. Select a category and click OK, and Pod2Go will add your site's RSS feed to your iPod for more fun reading.

You can use Pod2Go to collect weather conditions and forecasts for any cities in the world. The method for finding cities is very flexible: just enter a city, state, country, or ZIP code, and Pod2Go will present you with a list of possible matches to choose from. You can add as many cities as you want, and they're easy to remove from the list if you change your mind or move off-planet.

Pod2Go's movie feature gets showtimes for movie theatres in the U.S. and Canada. You just enter a city or ZIP code and Pod2Go grabs today's listings from the Web and copies them to your iPod. This is great for those occasions when you find yourself in the car and looking for a movie to see on a whim (not applicable for people who have children). See Figure 4-13 to get an idea of what this looks like.

If you always need to know the prices of your favorite stocks so you can evaluate your portfolio, use Pod2Go's stock quote feature. However, this feature is less valuable than many of the others, because old stock quotes grow stale quickly after you download them to your iPod.

Speaking of features and their value, Pod2Go can get your horoscope. You might not be interested in this, but if you plan your life by the stars, or you use horoscopes for amusement

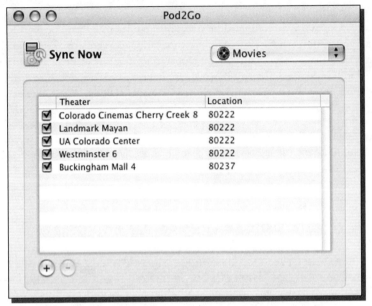

FIGURE 4-13. Pod2Go provides a way to collect information from the Web, such as movie times, and copy it to your iPod. Courtesy of Pod2Go.

purposes, you can enjoy reading the astrological advice and predictions for your birth sign and any others you care to download to your iPod.

Pod2Go includes a really cool feature that lets you copy any text to a note on your iPod, including text from a Web page or Word document. Just click the "New from" button and point Pod2Go at a document on your hard disk, or type a URL. When you download a Web page like this, the iPod won't display the page the way it looks in a Web browser —it just gets the text for the page. You can also use this feature to type a note directly into Pod2Go, which will then sync it to the iPod.

The driving directions feature in Pod2Go is a great way to save paper. Now, when you get directions to that intriguing party out on the edge of town, you can simply carry them along on your iPod instead of printing them out. Just be careful not to actually read directions off the iPod while you're driving.

By default, Pod2Go copies information to the iPod whenever you connect it to your Mac. There's a preference for turning this off, as well as a setting that ejects the iPod as soon as its done being synchronized.

Pod2Go's interface is clean and easy to figure out. To add an item to be synched, go to the appropriate page (News, Weather, Text, etc.) and click the plus sign. There's a minus sign you can use to get rid of items you don't want any more.

More than just information

Pod2Go excels at collecting stuff from the Web and putting it on your iPod, but that's not all it does. You can use Pod2Go to synchronize various information between your Mac and iPod, including your address book, iCal calendars, Stickies notes, and Safari bookmarks. But wait—isn't that some of the work usually handled by Apple's free iSync program? Yes, it is, but the idea here is that as long as you're synchronizing info between your Mac and iPod with Pod2Go, it's easier to handle with one program than with two. You'll still need to run iSync if you want its additional features, such as synching with Mac or with other devices.

When you connect your iPod to your Mac, iTunes starts up or comes to the front. With Pod2Go, you can set other applications to start up when the iPod is connected.

Pod2Go comes with its own global menu, a tiny iPod that appears on the right side of the menu bar. You can use this menu for quick access to features including performing a sync, going to Pod2Go, or ejecting the iPod.

Pod2Go is powerful, easy to use, and free. If you have a Mac and an iPod, you should have Pod2Go.

Tip   Another quick way to eject the iPod is to control-click (or right-click) the iTunes icon in the dock, then choose Eject iPod (your iPod's name will appear in place of "iPod").

Synchronize Your iPod with Microsoft Outlook

Note   This hack works on Windows computers only.

Back in Chapter 2, I described the most basic ways of saving contacts and calendar items from Microsoft Outlook to your iPod (*Use Contacts and Calendar with Microsoft Outlook*). Those techniques are OK for transferring one or two items to your iPod, but if you're really going to live the iPod dream of having a portable address book and calendar, you need automatic synchronization.

Macintosh users get iSync, Address Book, and iCal, Apple's free software for managing personal information and flowing it between the Mac and mobile devices. As a Windows user who runs Microsoft Outlook, what can you do? By adding some third-party software, you can have a synchronizing experience that rivals what Mac users get.

In this section, we'll take a look at a couple of inexpensive pro solutions, and one excellent free hack.

PocketMac

PocketMac iPod Edition (about $23 at www.pocketmac.net/products/pmipodmac/ ipodmac.html; free trial version available) beefs up the features of your iPod by connecting it to data from Microsoft Outlook and other programs on your Windows computer. PocketMac grabs contacts, calendar items, tasks, notes, and e-mail from Outlook, then moves them to your iPod. You can set PocketMac to fire up automatically whenever you connect your iPod, or you can give it a manual command when you want it to sync.

When you install and run PocketMac, you see the main screen, as shown in Figure 4-14. By clicking the button with a gear on it, you see the sync settings and choose which data you want automatically copied to your iPod.

You can fine-tune exactly which data you want synchronized. For example, if you get a lot of e-mail and you don't want to wait while it copies to your iPod, you can turn of e-mail sync. Along with the Outlook preferences, note that there are some other interesting settings:

- If you check "Word Documents", PocketMac iPod Edition will convert Word documents to iPod notes and file them in the Notes folder. If a document is too big to fit into a single note, PocketMac will split it into multiple notes and connect them together for convenient reading.

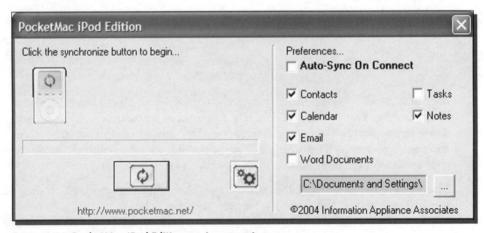

FIGURE 4-14: PocketMac iPod Edition: main screen turn on.

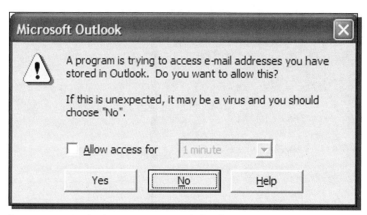

FIGURE 4-15: Outlook security access dialog box.

- If you sync Word documents, you can use the button in the lower-right corner, mysteriously labeled " . . . ", to pick a folder. PocketMac then scans that folder for Word documents and copies those it finds.

- Click "Auto-Sync On Connect" to have PocketMac wake up and do its thing automatically whenever you connect your iPod. If you leave this box unchecked, you have to run PocketMac manually whenever you want to synchronize information from the computer to the iPod.

When you run PocketMac, it latches onto your Outlook information and copies to your iPod. Outlook is smart enough to know that an alien program is trying to get access to its data. In fact, that's been a favorite trick of viruses in recent years: they send e-mail to all your contacts as a way of spreading the virus. To help prevent this problem, Outlook puts up a warning message when PocketMac starts looking at your contacts (see Figure 4-15).

When you see this message, you can decide whether you want to allow the access or not. In this case, you know the access to your data is OK, because you're running PocketMac to sync. A good policy is to use the "Allow access for" pop-up list that grants permission for a fixed amount of time—10 minutes should be enough for PocketMac to do its work.

Once PocketMac starts shipping files off to the iPod, you see one those familiar "flying documents" progress boxes (Figure 4-16). PocketMac helpfully puts the name of the contact, calendar event, document, or other data item in the progress box so you know just what's going on.

Eventually, the sync finishes and the PocketMac window says "Done". When that happens, you can disconnect your iPod and walk away, knowing you're taking the latest info from you computer along with you.

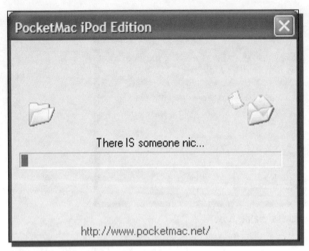

FIGURE 4-16: PocketMac progress.

iPodSync

iPodSync ($14 at `iccnet.50megs.com/iPodSync`; free trial version available) is another tool for off-loading Outlook information to your iPod. iPodSync handles Outlook contacts, calendar items, tasks, and notes. Although iPodSync is a Windows program, its interface is, let's say, strongly inspired by iSync, Apple's Mac-only synchronizing program (see Figure 4-17).

To get going with iPodSync, you click the icons for various kinds of data: contacts, calendar, and so on. You can tell iPodSync what to do with each data type, including not sync it at all. IPodSync provides options for each type that let you specify what you want in detail. For example, when you synchronize calendar events, you can decide whether to include events from the past or recurring appointments, as shown in Figure 4-18.

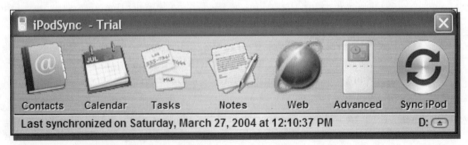

FIGURE 4-17: iPodSync main screen.

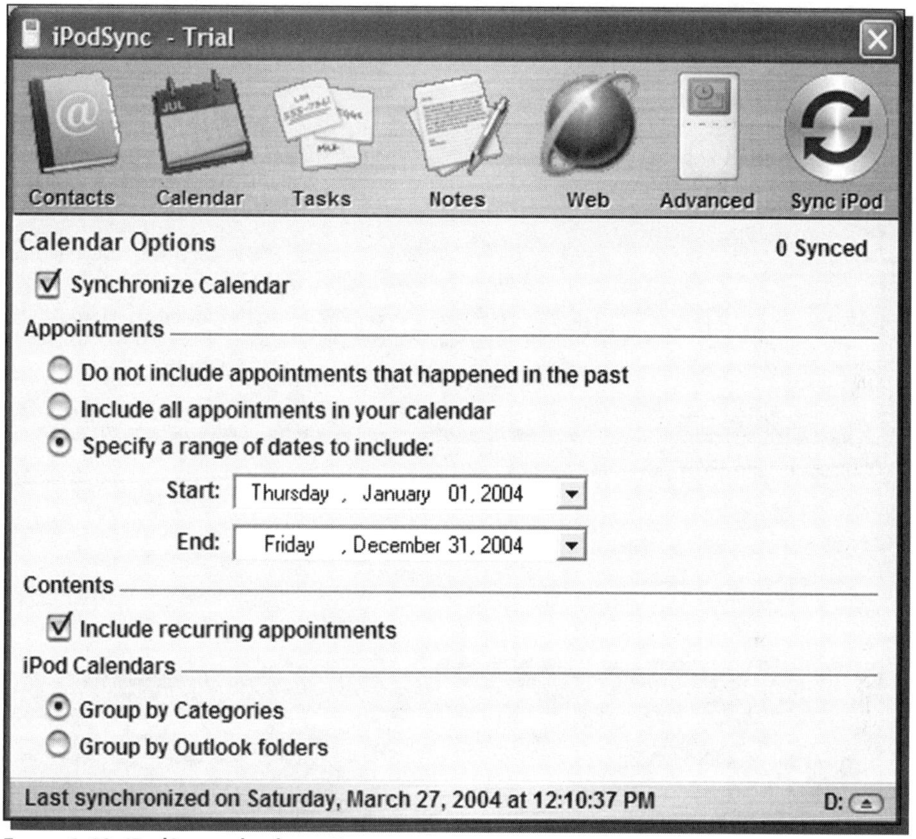

FIGURE 4-18: iPodSync calendar options.

When you click Sync iPod, the program goes to work, grabbing information out of Outlook and copying it to your iPod. The iPodSync screen shows you a progress indicator so you can keep track of the sync in progress (Figure 4-19).

iPodSync includes features that go beyond Outlook synchronization. Click the Web icon to tell iPodSync to get information from the Web and download it to your iPod (see Figure 4-20). You can grab the local weather forecast before you head out, or sync some news headlines so you have something to read while you're waiting for that take-out pizza to be ready.

iPodSync includes a number of settings on its Advanced Options screen. Click the icon that looks like an iPod to see these preferences. Among the advanced options:

- Automatically sync iPod on startup. This option relieves you of having to remember to sync manually.

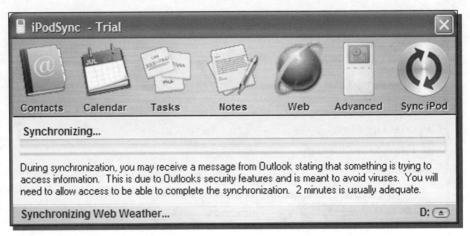

FIGURE 4-19: iPodSync progress screen.

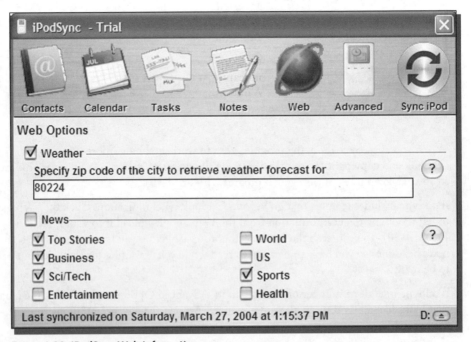

FIGURE 4-20: iPodSync Web information.

- Automatically eject iPod when sync is complete.

- Reset, which removes existing Outlook information from the iPod. Use this if you have inadvertently ended up with multiple copies of the same information on your iPod.

- Choose from specific Outlook folders to synchronize.

- Include or exclude items from specific Outlook categories.

 Cross-Reference Mac users (what are you doing reading this Windows-only section?) can get the news, weather, and lots of other Web-based information onto their iPods with Pod2Go, described in this chapter in the *Get News, Weather, Movie Listings, and More* section.

Export from Windows Address Book

The coolest way to get contacts (not calendar info) from Outlook to your iPod is via the Windows Address Book. If you use Outlook Express, the Windows Address Book is the place where information about your contacts is stored. Windows Address Book has the following awesome feature: if you select multiple contacts and drag them to a destination, the contacts are converted to vCards before they're stored in the new location. What a wonderful coincidence that iPod contacts are stored as vCards! So, if you use Outlook Express, you can easily export all your contacts to your iPod simply by selecting them and dragging them to the Contacts folder on the iPod.

If you want to get contacts from Outlook to the iPod, you can do it, but alas, Outlook lacks the automatic vCard conversion feature of Windows Address Book. However, you can send your Outlook contacts to Windows Address Book first, then to your iPod. Here's how that works:

1. In Outlook, choose File ⇨ Import and Export.

2. Choose "Export to a file" and click Next.

3. Choose "Comma Separated Values (DOS)" and click Next (see Figure 4-21).

4. Type the name of the export file ("my exported contacts" works fine) and click Next, then click Finish. Now your contacts are exported, and it's time to get them into a Windows Address Book.

5. Go to Outlook Express. Choose File ⇨ Import ⇨ Other Address Book.

6. Choose Text File (Comma Separated Values) and click Import.

7. Find the file you saved in step 4 and click Next.

8. In the Mapping dialog box, choose the fields you want to import and click OK.

9. Click Finish to complete the importing process.

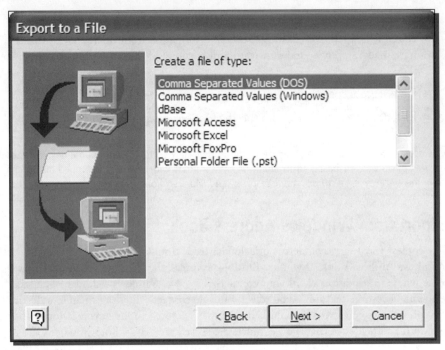

FIGURE 4-21: You can export Outlook contacts to a file.

10. Now that your contacts are imported into the Windows Address Book in Outlook Express, you can select the ones you want to put on your iPod-all of them, if you like—and drag them to the iPod's Contacts folder. They will automatically be converted to vCards and displayed as contacts on your iPod.

Use PocketMac for Macintosh

Note This hack works on Macintosh computers only.

In the preceding section, I mentioned PocketMac iPod Edition for Windows as one of the programs people use for getting information from Microsoft Outlook to an iPod. There's a version of PocketMac for Mac OS X too—not surprising, because it is called Pocket*Mac*, after all (www.pocketmac.net/products/pmipodmac/ipodmac.html, about $23). PocketMac iPod Edition's specialty is syncing with Microsoft Entourage. You can use PocketMac to synchronize your contacts, calendar, to do list, notes, and e-mails to your iPod. PocketMac will even load your iPod with Word documents, just like the Windows version does.

PocketMac iPod Edition on the Mac works by installing itself as an iSync component. PocketMac puts an icon on the iSync toolbar. When you click the icon, its settings appear, and you can set sync preferences, just as with other iSync devices (Figure 4-22).

PocketMac for Macintosh isn't all about Entourage. You can also use it to sync e-mail from Apple's Mail program, PDFs, and Stickies. And because PocketMac works in iSync, you don't have to remember to run yet another application to get everything synchronized.

Read E-Mail on Your iPod

 Note This hack works on Macintosh computers only.

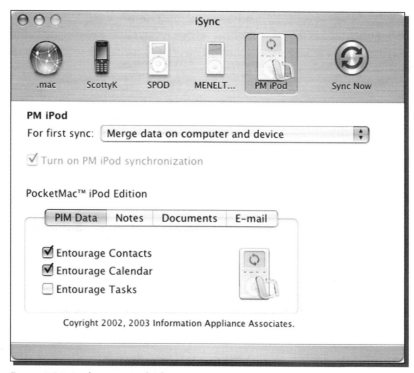

FIGURE 4-22: PocketMac iPod Edition uses iSync to synchronize information between Entourage and your iPod.

iPod lovers, especially those with Macs, have access to plenty of programs that take information from your computer and move it over to your iPod. These "to go" programs take advantage of the precious time when your iPod is hooked up to your computer (and to the Internet). Until Apple makes iPods that can connect to the Internet directly, you can rely on programs like Pod2Go to grab information and ship it to your iPod for later consumption.

PodMail is another "to go" helper. As you might guess by the clever name, PodMail specializes in grabbing e-mail so that you can read it later. PodMail puts your mail in the Notes folder, so you need an iPod that can run version 2.0 or later (that's an iPod with a dock connector, including iPod mini). You can see PodMail's main screen in Figure 4-23.

The most common kind of e-mail account uses a technology called POP, which stands for Post Office Protocol. If you use POP, PodMail requires you to collect your mail with Mac OS X's Mail program before you can move it over. If you subscribe to Apple's .Mac service, or if you have a IMAP account (IMAP is an e-mail technology that leaves mail on the server so you can access it anywhere), PodMail will check your mail for you—you don't have to have it already collected, as with POP mail. When you're ready to move your mail to the iPod, make sure the iPod is selected from the pop-up list of disks, then click the Sync button.

PodMail lets you set up access to as many e-mail accounts as you want. Just click the plus sign at the bottom left to make another one. There's a handy slider you can use to limit the number of messages you get, so your poor little iPod won't be overwhelmed by vast quantities of mail.

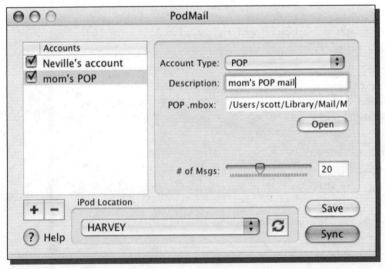

FIGURE 4-23: PodMail grabs your e-mail and moves it to your iPod, where you can read it at your convenience.

Run Linux on Your iPod

Linux is an alternative operating system with a devoted, growing set of fans. The source code for Linux is freely available, and thousands of people around the world contribute to its development. Serious companies like IBM are building and selling products made with Linux. One of the wonderfully hacky traditions of Linux is to *port* it: make it run on new devices, as many different ones as possible. When the iPod appeared, Linux devotees took up the challenge. The result is the Linux on iPod project, created by Bernard Leach and friends.

Apple doesn't provide a lot of technical information about the iPod, so the iPod on Linux project required lots of work to figure out what was happening inside and how to gain control. Leach acted like a detective to learn about the iPod: he looked at Apple's iPod updater to discover how to modify the iPod firmware so that it would boot the Linux kernel he installed on the disk instead of the standard stuff. Figure 4-24 shows you part of what you see when Linux starts up on an iPod.

Why put Linux on the iPod? In his FAQ for the project, Leach gives the classic answer: because it's there. And beyond that standard reason, he hopes that putting Linux on the iPod will result in new applications, such as the ability to play different music formats or add new functions entirely.

 Installing Linux changes your iPod's firmware to allow it to boot the alternative operating system, which voids the warranty. The music and other data on your iPod might get messed up. You could even end up with an iPod that requires you to run Apple's iPod updater to get it working again, and there is a remote chance your iPod will end up unusable. Just so you know—now have fun!

The initial releases of the project require a complex manual process for installing Linux on your iPod, even after all the tough work done by Bernard Leach and crew. This manual process requires you to grab the source code from `ipodlinux.sourceforge.net` and build it yourself using a compiler and other development tools. Then you must navigate through a series of steps that include backing up your iPod's firmware, building the Linux kernel, and finally installing and running Linux on your iPod. You can see the full instructions at `http://ipodlinux.sourceforge.net/build.shtml`.

For Linux fans, this kind of installation process is not unusual. It's part of the pioneering spirit and do-it-yourself joy of Linux. But it's a little daunting for a larger group who are merely curious about playing with Linux on an iPod, One of the coolest aspects of open source projects is that programmers can build on the work of one another. For this project, the community has built an easy-to-use installer that lets you get Linux on your iPod with about 98% less fuss than the original technique. It's not as easy as installing iTunes, but it's a definite improvement.

You can find this version of Linux at ipod.homelinux.com. Here are the instructions for getting Linux onto your iPod:

FIGURE 4-24: Linux booting on an iPod.

1. Go to ipod.homelinux.com/index.php?page=download and download the latest build. If you use Safari, the download will decompress and appear as a disk image.

2. Find the disk image in the Finder. (See Figure 4-25). Copy the contents of the iPodLinux disk image to your hard disk.

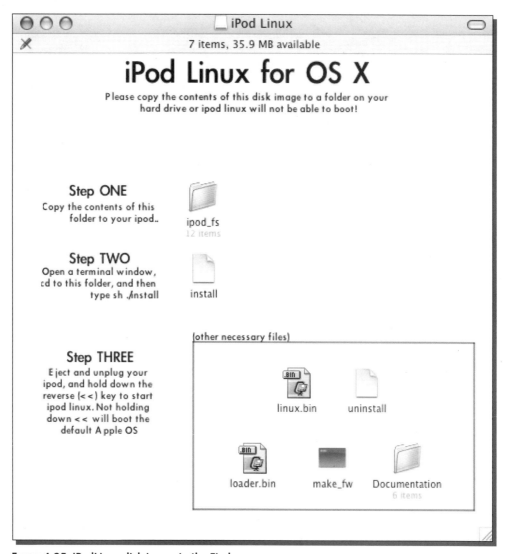

FIGURE 4-25: iPodLinux disk image in the Finder.

3. Run the Terminal application.

4. Next, you'll set the current directory to the iPodLinux folder you just copied to your hard disk. To do that, type **cd**, followed by a space. Then, drag the iPodLinux folder from the Finder into the Terminal window. Press Return. This should result in the Terminal window changing its prompt to show that iPodLinux is now the current directory.

FIGURE 4-26: Tux comes to your iPod.

5. In the Terminal window, type **sh ./install** to start the Linux installer.

6. Before the installer can proceed, it needs to determine the iPod's device name. In Terminal, the installer will display a line like this:

```
/dev/disk2s3 on /Volumes/iGor (local, nodev, nosuid)
```

The device name reported here will always be "diskNs3", where N is usually 2 or 3. To get the installer going, type in **diskNs2**. Note that the name reported to you ends with "s3", but the name you type ends with "s2". And as a reminder, yes, for Linux installs, this counts as easy.

7. Next, the installer will back up the iPod's firmware. Then, you will probably be asked for the password for your Mac's user account. Once you supply this, you should see the following:

```
65536+0 records in
65536+0 records out
33554432 bytes transferred in 20.136763 secs (1666327 bytes/sec)
--> Firmware backup complete.
12742+1 records in
12742+1 records out
6523908 bytes transferred in 8.612815 secs (757465 bytes/sec)

The firmware installer has completed.
```

That's it – Linux is now installed on your iPod. To see it, first reboot by holding down MENU and Play for a few seconds. When the screen goes blank, hold down Previous until you see the Apple logo. You should soon see the pages of scrolling text that indicate Linux is booting. Eventually, you'll be rewarded with a glimpse of Tux, the Linux penguin mascot, on your screen (Figure 4-26).

Linux on your iPod is certainly cool, but you can still use it the regular way, too. To put your iPod into its familiar mode, just reboot normally, without holding down any buttons while it's starting up. To get back to Linux, hold down Previous as the iPod boots.

In Linux, you can make things happen on the iPod by using the command-line tool telnet to talk to your iPod over the FireWire cable. As the Linux on iPod project progresses, we can expect to see games, tools, utilities, and other fun and useful stuff for the iPod. And if you're a Linux hacker, you can join the project as a contributor by signing up on the project Web site at ipodlinux.sourceforge.net.

Summary

Apple built your iPod to be a great music player, and it is—but it's also creeping up on personal digital assistant (PDA) territory with features like news headlines, text documents, e-mail, and lots more. Check out the programs in this chapter and see if they improve life with your iPod. If you like to live on the edge, you can even turn your iPod into the world's coolest little Linux box.

In our next chapter, we'll start getting into nifty things to do in iTunes, your iPod's faithful companion. Chapter 5 covers interesting hacks you can do with the basic feature of iTunes: playing music.

Hacking
iTunes

Play with Your Music

iTunes is all about hearing music, which is why we're starting off the iTunes part of this book with a discussion about hacking your music playing for maximum fun and power. In this chapter, we'll discuss cool tricks you can perform with the basic music playing features in iTunes.

Playlists

Playlists are the ticket to advanced listening in iTunes. Without playlists, you can still use iTunes to listen to your favorite artists and albums, just as you would if you were actually handling physical CDs or LPs. But playlists are the magic digital ingredient that let you take full control of your musical experience by helping you listen to exactly what you want to hear.

Turn Selections into Playlists

Let's say you're listening to music in iTunes when you're struck by an overwhelming urge to hear an unusual set of albums—for example, *Factory Showroom* by They Might Be Giants, Laurie Anderson's *Home of the Brave,* and the latest from Vito Paternoster. What's the quickest and easiest way to collect those diverse tunes so you can hear them together? Try the following steps:

1. Click Library in the sources list to see all your music.

2. Make sure the Browser (artist and album names) is showing above the list of songs. If you don't see the Browser, choose Edit ➪ Show Browser.

3. Look through the list of artists in the Artist column. When you find one whose album you want to include in your eclectic playlist, click to select it.

4. Keep going through the playlist as long as you want to find more artists. For each new artist you want to add, hold down Command (on the Mac) or Control (on Windows),

FIGURE 5-1: Several artists are selected, and all their albums are listed.

then click. This adds the new artist (in technical-ese, it extends the selection) to those you have already chosen.

5. After you have picked the artists you want, you'll see their albums all agglomerated together in the album list on the right (see Figure 5-1).

6. Again using the Command-Click (Mac) or Control-Click (Windows) method, pick the albums you want to hear from the album list at the right.

7. Choose File ➪ New Playlist from Selection. You'll get a new playlist (named "untitled playlist") made out of your wacky album selections.

Now your playlist is memorialized for all time, or at least for as long as your tastes run to that group of artists. And here's a bonus: because it's a full-fledged playlist, you can tell iTunes to sync it to your iPod.

Tip   You can also create a new playlist by dragging the selected items to the source list and dropping them there. For more on how that works, see the section *Drag and Drop to Create a Playlist* later in this chapter.

If you're using Mac OS X, you can use yet another shortcut to create a playlist from the selection: hold down the Shift key and click the "+" button at the bottom of the source list. The new playlist will be created with the selected songs in it. This is one of the unusual cases when a feature is available on the Macintosh version of iTunes but not on Windows. The Windows version uses Shift-click on the "+" button to create a new smart playlist (see *Use Keyboard Shortcuts with Playlists* later in this chapter).

Make a "Freshest Tracks" Playlist

When you get new tunes from your favorite artists, you're probably excited to listen to it as soon as possible. But in the hustle and bustle of our stressful lives, we sometimes forget even pleasurable diversions like listening to new music. iTunes can help you with this problem. Just create a Smart Playlist to keep track of your freshest tracks. Here's how it's done:

1. Choose File ⇨ New Smart Playlist. You'll get the Smart Playlist dialog box.

2. In the boxes that define conditions for the songs you want on the list, choose "Date Added", "is in the last", "30", and "days". You can adjust the "30 days" value depending on how aggressively you acquire new music.

3. Fine-tune your playlist. You can check the "Limit" box to keep the playlist below a chosen number of songs or length of time. If you want to make sure your "freshest tracks" playlist fits on your iPod, use the "Limit" to specify the number of megabytes or gigabytes of music you want.

4. Make sure "Live updating" is checked. This makes sure that tracks are kicked off the playlist when they get too old. Think of this as a "freshness dating" system, like the date stamped on your milk. The dialog box in Figure 5-2 shows what this looks like. Click OK, and you've got your playlist.

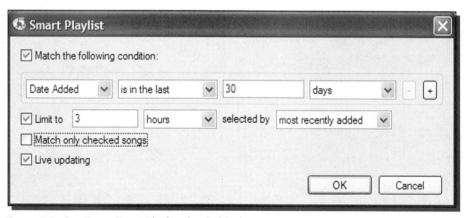

FIGURE 5-2: Creating a Smart Playlist that holds the newest songs.

With a "freshest tracks" playlist, you can make sure you'll never let those new tunes slip through the musical cracks. Any time we can make computers do the remembering for us, it's a plus.

More ideas for Smart Playlists

The Smart Playlist feature in iTunes is one of those technologies that looks very simple while hiding a vast amount of power. You could spend a lot of time coming up with various clever and wonderful schemes for new playlists. Why, you might even devote a whole web site to it! In fact, that's just what's going on at SmartPlaylists.com, a place for iTunes enthusiasts who love to explore what they can make with this great feature. Take a look at the SmartPlaylists.com home page in Figure 5-3.

SmartPlaylists.com is mainly an exchange of ideas on what you can do with Smart Playlists. Here are a few of sample suggestions and ideas for smartening up your music listening:

FIGURE 5-3: SmartPlaylists.com home page.

All "unchecked" songs

iTunes uses the checkbox at the left of every song as a sort of master on/off switch. When iTunes encounters unchecked songs as it's playing music, it skips over them. Many iTunes users uncheck songs that they usually don't want to hear. But sometimes you might find yourself in the mood for those neglected tunes. A Smart Playlist would seem like a handy way to deal with this. But alarmingly, you can't specify "unchecked" as a criterion for Smart Playlists. There's a checkbox for leaving them *out*, but not for allowing them *in*.

What can you do? The answer is to use a two-playlist technique. First, you need to create a playlist that includes all checked songs. You can do that with the following steps:

1. Choose New Smart Playlist from the File menu.

2. Make sure the "Match only checked songs" box is checked.

    This is really the only criterion we want to apply for this smart playlist. But iTunes won't let us create the playlist with only this box checked. We can overcome this problem by specifying a bogus criterion that will not exclude any songs:

3. Make sure the "Match the following condition:" box is unchecked, We won't be using it here.

4. Click the "Limit to" check box to turn it on. Type in **99999 GB** in the boxes on that line. That's the largest number you can enter here, and I'm betting you have less music than that. Your dialog should now look like Figure 5-4.

5. Click OK to create the playlist.

6. In the source list, the new playlist's name is selected. Type a new name: **all checked**.

7. Create another smart playlist by choosing New Smart Playlist from the File menu.

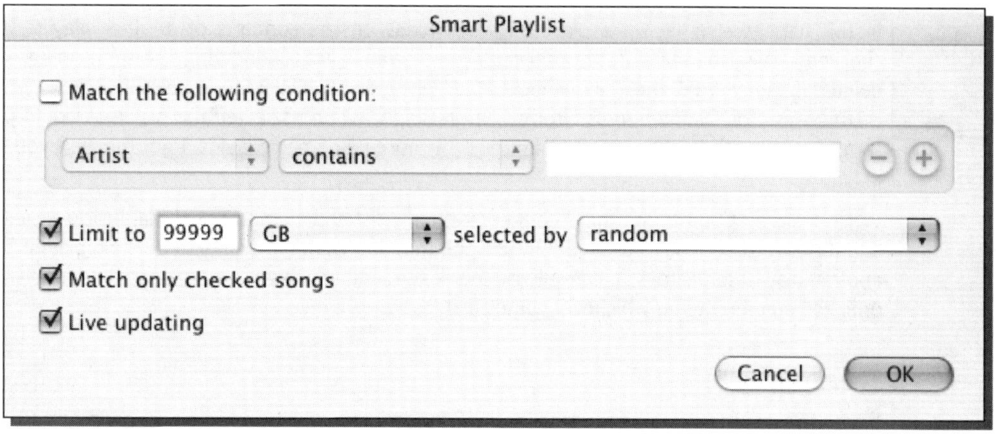

FIGURE 5-4: Smart Playlist dialog box.

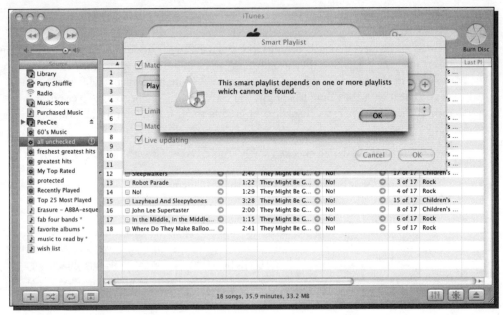

FIGURE 5-5: Broken playlist dependency alert.

8. In the "Match the following condition" section, choose "Playlist is not all checked" and click OK. Rename this new list "all unchecked".

There you go! The new playlist you just created will contain all your unchecked songs and nothing else.

Note

In this hack, we've set up a playlist that depends on the contents of another playlist, "all checked". What happens if "all checked" goes away? I was wondering the same thing, so I deleted it. When I did, the "all unchecked" playlist grew an exclamation point in a circle, which is iTunes-ese for "Something is wrong." Interestingly, when I selected the playlist, I could play songs from it without any problem. But when I chose Edit Smart Playlist, I got the alert you see in Figure 5-5.

When I clicked OK, I found that I could edit the playlist and change its criteria. I clicked cancel, and the playlist continued to work OK, despite that dire warning. So if you delete a playlist that another playlist refers to, you can still use the dependent, which will be frozen in time forever, or until you edit its criteria, whichever comes first.

Themed playlist

Some topics are subjects for thousands of songs: love, hope, and cars are pretty popular. But you might be surprised to find how many songs exist about other subjects that might seem more obscure. You can use the "Song Name contains" criterion of the Smart Playlist feature to see just how many songs you can dig up on a particular topic.

As an example of what you might find, here are the results of a couple of themed playlists I set up:

Song Name contains *jungle***:**

- "Welcome to the Jungle," Guns N Roses.
- "Run Through the Jungle," Creedence Clearwater Revival
- "Bungle in the Jungle," Jethro Tull
- "Jungle Jingle," Love Nation & Ad
- "Jungle Boogie," Kool & The Gang
- "George of the Jungle," Weird Al Yankovic
- "Welcome to the Jungle," They Might Be Giants
- "Jungle Fever," Chakachas
- "Jungle Music," Rico

Song Name contains *summer***:**

- "A Summer Song," Chad & Jeremy
- "Indian Summer," Joe Walsh
- "Let's Loot the Supermarket Again Like We Did Last Summer," Mick Farren and the Deviants
- "Long Summer Days," EMF
- "Summer in the City," Lovin' Spoonful
- "One Summer Dream," Electric Light Orchestra
- "Sausalito Summer Night," Diesel
- "Summer Breeze," Seals & Crofts
- "Summer of Drugs," Soul Asylum
- "Summertime," Billy Stewart

And now you know far more about my musical tastes than you wanted to. You can also use the "Song Name contains" technique to construct your very own romantic playlist. To build this list, try looking for song names containing "love", "girl", "boy", "us", or other telltale terms. iTunes will let you build a single playlist that matches as many different criteria as you want.

Streaming Radio playlist

You might not realize that you can include streaming radio stations in your library and in a playlist. To add a station to the library, just drag the station's icon to the library in the source list. You can then create a smart playlist of radio stations by setting the criteria to "Kind is Playlist URL".

Remember to check out `smartplaylists.com` for many more ideas and to contribute your own.

Drag and Drop to Create a Playlist

You can make wonderful things happen in computer programs by dragging and dropping. Menu items are explicit, because they advertise their functions in words, but drag and drop is more direct, more fun, and feels almost like magic, as if you're reaching into the computer and manipulating real objects. iTunes is loaded with drag and drop features. You've probably taken advantage of being able to add songs to a playlist by dragging from the song list to the playlist. iTunes also includes lesser-known features for creating playlists just by schlepping items around.

The basic rule is this: drag something to an empty space in the source list, below any of the existing playlists, and you'll get a new playlist. Go ahead and give it a try. Look through the browser and pick one of your favorite albums. Then make the album into a playlist by dragging it to the source list, down below the last playlist (see Figure 5-6).

FIGURE 5-6: You can drag an album to the source list to create a playlist.

There are a couple of nuances to notice here. As you're dragging, iTunes provides helpful visual feedback on what would happen if you let go of the mouse button right where you are. If you're over a place that will accept the dropped album, iTunes tells you so by adding a plus sign to the cursor (on the Mac, the plus sign appears in a circle that's a lovely shade of green). This is what you'll see if you drag below the last playlist. The cursor looks different when you're hovering over a place that wouldn't know what to do with the album if you let go. On Windows, you'll see the famous circle with a slash through it, (known to humorous nerds as "the oblique indication of negation"). On the other hand, Mac OS X doesn't give you any cursor feedback when you're hovering over a bad place. With either operating system, if you let go of the dragged item over a target that doesn't want it, nothing happens—iTunes basically just politely ignores you. On the Mac, if you watch closely, you can actually see the dragged item scamper back to where it came from.

Look out below

An interesting thing happens when you drag over the other playlists. As you drag over smart playlists, the cursor lets you know that you can't drop the item there. That's because smart playlists are defined by rules—their contents are picked by algorithms, and they won't let just any old album in there. But when you drag over regular, non-smart playlists, the playlist highlights, and the cursor grows its little plus sign, letting you know that it would be very happy to accept any items you drop inside (see Figure 5-7). If you're trying to create a new playlist by dragging, you have to go right past the existing playlists on your

FIGURE 5-7: Dragging an album over a regular playlist. Note that the playlist is highlighted to show it will add the album if you drop it there.

FIGURE 5-8: You might not be able to see the last playlist when you start dragging.

way to the blank space below. Before you let go of the mouse, be careful you're not accidentally going to drop into a playlist that's already there. You'll be able to tell because iTunes highlights the existing playlist if you're hovering over it.

Another challenge arises if you can't see the space below the last playlist when you start dragging, as shown in Figure 5-8. You're going to have to auto-scroll to get there. Auto-scrolling is the drag and drop feature that lets you make a list or other view start scrolling when you drag into it. In general, you auto-scroll during drag and drop by dragging to the edge of the area you want to scroll. So if you can't see the bottom of the source list, drag to the area just below the last playlist. This will cause the source list to start scrolling down until the last playlist (and the space below it) are visible. Once that happens, you can just drop your item under the playlist.

Sometimes, if you don't drag to exactly the right place, auto-scrolling can be finicky. You might have to scrub around with the mouse a little to make it start. If you just can't seem to get auto-scrolling to work, you have other low-tech options. Before you start dragging, close the album art panel to create more room in the source list, or simply scroll down in the list manually.

Major drag

There are lots of things you can drag in iTunes to create a playlist. For example, drag any album to the source list and you've got a new playlist containing that album's tracks. This

FIGURE 5-9: Make a playlist for the two greatest bands in the world.

is especially useful when you want to burn a CD of an album, because iTunes will only burn a CD from a playlist. You can also select multiple albums, then drag any of them to get them all—it doesn't matter which one you drag, because they'll all come along for the ride.

You can create a new playlist out of songs by selecting all the songs you want, then dragging them to the magic blank spot on the source list. This works fine, although it's probably not the technique you'll normally use for creating new playlists out of songs.

Want to make a playlist containing all the tunes of a particular artist? Just find the artist in the browser, then drag the artist's name to the bottom of the source list, and you've got a highly-focused playlist. Of course, you can do the same thing with multiple artists: make your multiple selection in the usual way with Shift-click and Command-click (Control-click on Windows), then drag 'em over, as shown in Figure 5-9. And if you have the Genre column displayed when you browse songs, you can even drag a genre (or multiple genres) to make a playlist.

The Naming of Playlists Is a Difficult Matter

iTunes is a thoughtfully written program that's been consistently improved since its debut in January 2001. The more you use it, the more nice touches you notice. When you drag songs, albums, artists, or genres to create a playlist, iTunes tries mightily to give the playlist a meaningful name. If the playlist you're cooking up contains just one song, the playlist gets the same name as the song. If the playlist is a single album, the playlist is named after the album, no matter what you dragged to create it. Same thing for a single-artist playlist: it's named for the artist. If the new playlist can't be reduced to a single artist, album, or song, it's just called "untitled playlist", suffixed with a number if necessary to distinguish it from any other anonymous playlists.

One more cool thing about dragging to create playlists: whenever iTunes adds a song to a playlist, it checks to make sure the song is actually stored on the disk where it's supposed to be. If it's not there, iTunes simply doesn't add it to the playlist. In the Library, and in any playlists that already include the song, it's marked with a scary looking exclamation point to let you know that it has a big problem (see Figure 5-10). If all the songs meant for the new playlist are missing, iTunes doesn't even bother creating the playlist (or giving you an error message).

FIGURE 5-10: Tracks are displayed with an exclamation point when iTunes can't find them. These are never added to playlists.

Use Keyboard Shortcuts with Playlists

Point-and-click is great, but to really do cool tricks, you need obscure keyboard combinations. In this section, you'll find out about a potpourri of hacky things you can try at home with playlists and keyboard shortcuts.

Create a new smart playlist

The "+" button at the bottom of the source list is a fast, direct way to make a new playlist. Click it once, twice, 12 times, and get a new playlist every time. What if you want to create a new smart playlist instead of an, uh, un-smart one? You can use File ⇨ New Smart Playlist, or its three-fingered keyboard shortcut, Command-Option-N on Mac or Control-Alt-N on Windows. But here's the niftiest way to create a new smart playlist:

1. Hold down the Option key (Mac) or the Shift key (Windows). You should see the "+" button change into a gear (see Figure 5-11), the icon for smart playlists (Apple uses the gear to indicate features that are a bit nerdier than most.)

2. While you're still holding down the modifier key, click the gear. The Smart Playlist dialog box will appear and you can set the conditions for your new playlist.

Note Because Windows computers don't have an Option key, iTunes uses the Shift key in this case to replace the function that Option performs. On a Mac, if you hold down Shift while clicking the "+" button, you get a new playlist containing the current selection, an entirely different feature.

Tip For much more information on fun things you can do with smart playlists, see the section *More ideas for Smart Playlists* in this chapter, and check out www.smartplaylists.com, where you'll find ideas, discussions, and tips about smart playlists in iTunes.

Figure 5-11: The "+" button that creates a new playlist changes to a gear when you hold down a modifier key.

Reshuffle a playlist

Shuffle play, also called random play, is one of the absolute coolest features of iTunes and the iPod. Without shuffle play, we would be stuck listening to songs in a fixed order, just like it used to be in the old analog days of cassettes and vinyl LP-ROMs. With shuffle play, not only can you change the sequence of songs you hear, you don't even have to think up the new order yourself: just ask the computer to do it for you.

You can shuffle any playlist. To turn on shuffle play, click the crossed-arrows button at the lower-left edge of the iTunes window. This works for the Library as well as playlists. Each playlist remembers its own shuffle setting, which is handy when you want to randomize the tunes in your personal "greatest hits" list while playing favorite albums from the Library in their correct song order.

When you create a new playlist, smart or otherwise, the songs are listed in the order they're going to be played. The first column, the one with numbers, shows this play order. If you click another column, you'll sort the playlist and change the play order. Turning on shuffle is like throwing the play order out the window. If you have Shuffle turned on and you want to see the order in which the songs will play, you have to click the Play Order column, as shown in Figure 5-12.

FIGURE 5-12: When you're listening to a shuffled playlist, you can see the play order by clicking the first column.

Let's say you've turned shuffle on and clicked the Play Order column. Maybe you're not happy with the order, even though you've trusted iTunes to mix things up, because you really wanted to hear several tunes that are tragically stuck near the bottom. How can you change the play order of a shuffled playlist? When you have Shuffle turned off, and the Play Order column is selected, you can rearrange songs in the playlist just by dragging them around (try it). But when Shuffle is turned on, iTunes is in control of the play order. If you try to usurp its power by dragging a song to a new position, it simply ignores you.

Although you can't explicitly move songs around in a shuffled playlist, you can force iTunes to pick a new random order. Turn Shuffle off, then on again, either by clicking the Shuffle button twice or by choosing Controls ⇨ Shuffle twice. Every time you do this, iTunes reshuffles, so you can see if you like the new order better.

Turning Shuffle off and on again is not a very elegant solution to this problem, so the iTunes folks invented a shortcut for reshuffling a playlist. Hold down the Option key on Macintosh or Shift key on Windows, then click the Shuffle button. Your playlist will get rerandomized. Note that if you're looking at the playlist with another column selected, such as Song Name or Artist, you won't see the song order change, because you're not looking at the songs in play order. To see the listing change when you reshuffle, be sure the Play Order column (the first one) is selected.

Tip

If you're about to start listening to a shuffled playlist and there's a song in the list that you really want to hear right away, you don't have to suffer the tyranny of iTunes by waiting until its turn comes. For instant gratification, just double-click that song to start your listening. When your song is done playing, iTunes will continue through the rest of the playlist in random order.

Shuffling Madness

You might think that shuffle play would be simple and straightforward. Like many features in Apple products, there's an easy way to use shuffle, which is good enough for most users, most of the time. But then Apple added tweaks that enable greater control for those who are interested.

Here's an example: every playlist has its own shuffle setting, as we noted earlier. This feature lets you turn on shuffle play in your "Hip-hop goodness" list, while keeping shuffle play turned off for "Les Filles de Sainte-Colombe's greatest hits".

Per-playlist shuffle setting doesn't work on the iPod, however. When you listen to tunes on your iPod, there is a global shuffle setting that's used no matter what music you're playing. The iPod shuffle feature has some nuances of its own. Rather than a simple on and off setting, the iPod lets you choose from two different kinds of shuffle: songs and albums. The "albums" setting is useful if you have a playlist of favorite albums—your iPod will play whole random albums from the list, one after another. The "songs" mode simply jumps from tune to tune regardless of album. iTunes has a similar setting on the Advanced tab in the Preferences dialog box.

Delete a song via a playlist

A playlist in iTunes is a list of songs that that get played together. The Library is like a special playlist, a master list of all the music on your computer that iTunes knows about. Playlists and the Library are simply *lists* of songs, not the songs themselves, which are stored in files on your hard disk. When you delete a tune from a playlist, it's removed from that list—nothing happens to the song in the Library or the actual song file on the disk. When you delete a song from the Library, iTunes forgets all about it, which means it vanishes from any playlists it belongs to.

Even when you delete a song from the Library, the actual file on disk that holds the song isn't affected. However, when you delete a song from the Library, iTunes figures there's a good chance you want to nuke the song file too. So, if you delete a tune from the Library, iTunes asks you if you want to trash the song file too. If you say yes, iTunes will put the file in the appropriate receptacle: the Trash (Mac) or the Recycle Bin (Windows).

Here's a shortcut you can use if you're looking at songs in a playlist, not the Library, and you decide there's a song you want to banish from iTunes entirely by removing it from the Library and all playlists. If you hold down Option (Mac) or Shift (Windows) and press Delete, iTunes deletes the song from the Library and all playlists automagically. iTunes then asks if you also want to delete the song file from your hard disk. Neat!

When iTunes Doesn't Delete

When you remove a tune from the Library, iTunes doesn't always offer to delete the song's file from the hard disk. Here's why: iTunes has a default folder for the music it knows about. On the Mac, this folder is in your User directory at Music/iTunes/iTunes Music/, and on Windows, it's located inside My Documents at My Music\iTunes\iTunes Music\. Not every song file in iTunes needs to be in this default folder. Any song file can be added to the iTunes Library, no matter what folder it's in. If it's in the default folder, iTunes assumes it owns the file, so it offers to delete the file when you remove it from the Library. If the file is not in the folder, iTunes figures it belongs to somebody else, so it shows good manners by not deleting it.

iTunes has a setting that ensures it will put all the song files it knows about into its default folder. You can turn this feature on by going to Preferences, Advanced tab, and checking "Copy files to iTunes music folder when adding to library". After turning on this setting, new music will be copied to the default folder when it's added to the Library. If you have tunes scattered around your hard disk and you want to unite them all in the default folder, choose Advanced ➪ Consolidate Library to bring them all home.

If you like, you can move the default folder to another location. Just click Change on the Advanced tab and pick out your new location.

Change the Play Order

In iTunes, every song knows its place—in the play order of playlists, that is. Every playlist maintains a play order for its songs. This is the default sequence in which the playlist's tunes will be heard. Every playlist displays its play order in the first column of the song list. There's no way to move or turn off the play order column—it's guaranteed to be there. In this section, we'll discuss how play order works and provide some ways to monkey around with it.

Play songs in a different order

You can get around a playlist's play order if you want to—Apple believes in freedom! The most obvious way is by turning on shuffle mode—when you do, play order isn't used. Another way to play songs in a different order is to click one of the columns in the song list. For example, if you click the Song Name column and make sure shuffle mode is off, iTunes will play the tunes in alphabetical order. Click it again to sort the list from Z to A and get reverse alpha order (Figure 5-13). Click the Last Played column to hear songs that haven't been played in awhile.

FIGURE 5-13: Click the selected column again to reverse the sort order.

Tip   iTunes provides lots of cool columns you can display in your playlists. To see them all, choose Edit ⇨ View Options, or *right-click* (on the Mac, Control-click) the song list headers. Every playlist remembers which columns it shows. For an especially cool hack in this area, check out *Use a List Column for Equalizer Settings* in this chapter. And for more on song list columns, see *Fine-tune the Music Library's Appearance* in Chapter 10.

Permanently change play order

If you're not happy with the play order of your playlist, there are a couple of ways to change it permanently. The direct way is by dragging and dropping songs around in the playlist: just grab the one you want to move, and put it where you want it to be. This works great, as long as you meet two conditions: the play order column must be selected, and shuffle play must be turned off. If either of these isn't true, you can drag songs until your wrists ache, and you still won't be able to change the play order. If you're successfully dragging songs to change the play order, iTunes will show you feedback as you move up and down the playlist, as shown in Figure 5-14.

Another even slicker trick lets you change the default play order to match the current order. You can use this to adopt a shuffled order, time-length sequence, or any other order as the

FIGURE 5-14: You can drag a song in a playlist to change the play order.

permanent setting for the playlist. To adopt the current order as the default, right-click (or on the Mac, Control-click) on a song in the list, then choose "Copy to Play Order" from the menu. iTunes changes the playlist's default play order to match the current order.

Hacking the Culture: Silence Is Golden

Here's a story about a different kind of song for your playlist: nothing. Macintosh is still Apple's flagship product, despite the tremendous success of the iPod since it was introduced in 2001. As you probably know, Macs comprise a small minority of the computers used in homes, offices, and schools. iPod, however, is a different story: according to Steve Jobs' keynote speech at Macworld Expo in January 2004, iPod is the most popular digital music player in the world, representing 31 percent of all sales. The iTunes Music Store is even more successful: in late 2003, Nielsen SoundScan reported that an amazing 80 percent of all online music is sold by Apple.

Apple is the big cheese of digital music. So it shouldn't be surprising that the company has to field the occasional wacky news story about its role in this emerging technology. In February 2004, the media picked up on the fact that among the tracks available for 99 cents at the iTunes Music Store are several that are nothing but silence. These include the aptly named "10 Seconds of Silence" by R-Three and "(Silence)" by Ciccone Youth. There's even Slum Village's "Silent", a completely silent track that's on iTunes in both "clean" and "explicit" versions. Although all the online music services have some silent tracks, apparently because the artists and labels simply delivered albums that include them, Apple got all the attention because it's the leader. And it looks like all the attention embarrassed somebody: after the story was reported, most of the silent tracks were available only as part of an album—you couldn't buy them individually for 99 cents anymore.

See Precise Playlist Statistics

When you select the library or a playlist in the iTunes source list, iTunes displays vital statistics about that source at the bottom of the window: number of songs, elapsed time, and disk space consumed by the songs in the playlist. You can see an example in Figure 5-15.

If you click the text in the statistics, the total time display changes from a decimal value to an exact count of days, hours, minutes, and seconds (Figure 5-16). This is a perfect feature for those of you who need to know exactly how long you can listen to your music before it starts to repeat.

Click the text again to change the display back to the decimal value.

719 songs, 1.6 days, 1.85 GB

FIGURE 5-15: iTunes displays
statistics for every playlist.

719 songs, 1:15:54:54 total time, 1.85 GB

FIGURE 5-16: After you click the display,
iTunes shows the precise total time of all the
songs in the playlist combined.

Reset Play Counts

iTunes keeps track of a play count for each song in its library, a running total of the number of times a song has been played. Whenever you play a song all the way through, its play count goes up by one. Playing it on your iPod counts, too: when you sync the iPod with your computer, the iPod tells the computer how many times the song was played, and the play count is adjusted accordingly.

Play count is one of the most powerful variables you can use when building Smart Playlists. When you create a Smart Playlist that selects songs by most or least often played, iTunes uses play counts to determine which songs to pick.

Sometimes it's handy to be able to manipulate the play count directly. The easiest way to do this is to right-click (or control-click on a Mac) on a song and choose "Reset Play Count". After a confirmation dialog box, iTunes returns the track's play count to zero.

This trick works just as well with multiple tracks. Select as many tunes as you want, then right-click any of them and choose "Reset Play Count". They'll all be reset to zero.

Cross-Reference   A less convenient, but more powerful way to mess with play counts is via AppleScript. Every song has an AppleScript property named "played count" which is settable from a script. For an example of how this works, see the section *Change the Play Count* in Chapter 6.

Move Your Playlists to Another Computer

On that happy day when you get a shiny new computer, you'll probably want to take your tunes with you. It's easy enough to move your music to the new computer: just copy the song files and use the "Add File to Library" command in iTunes to build up your new library. You can even use drag and drop folders and files of songs into the iTunes window, and they'll be added automatically.

But what about getting your playlists to make the move to the new computer with you? Moving playlists is slightly trickier, but still easy. You do it with a couple of steps and a few simple ground rules. First, here are the steps to take:

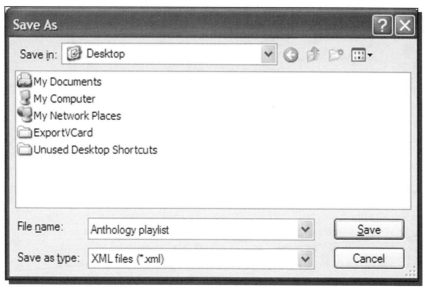

FIGURE 5-17: Use iTunes to export your playlists.

1. In the source list, click the playlist you want to move to another computer.

2. Choose File ⇨ Export Song List.

3. In the Save As dialog box, give the exported playlist a name, and choose "XML files" in the Save as Type box (see Figure 5-17).

4. On the new computer, choose File ⇨ Import. A new playlist is created with the same contents as on the old computer.

When you move a playlist from one computer to another, you're only moving the list of songs, not the songs themselves. If the songs exist in the iTunes library on the new computer, the playlist will find them and hook them into the playlist.

How does the playlist connect with the songs on the new computer? It looks in the library for a song with the same title, artist, and album. If it finds a match in all three of those categories, it puts the song in the playlist. If any of those tags is different, the song isn't added to the playlist. Note that other information, such as the song's file name and what folder it's in, aren't considered here.

Exporting and importing playlists even works across platforms, between Macs and Windows computers. It's so nice when everbody gets along.

If you import a playlist with songs that aren't in the new computer's library, iTunes will give you an error message (Figure 5-18). In this case, the playlist is created anyway, without the missing songs.

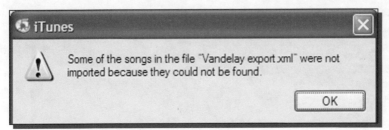

FIGURE 5-18: iTunes warns you when it can't find a song in an imported playlist.

Listen to Streaming Radio

Apple has focused its digital music efforts on selling songs and albums through the iTunes Music Store, and iTunes and the iPod are optimized for playing those songs and albums. So it might surprise you to learn that iTunes includes a powerful radio tuner for listening to thousands of music broadcasters who stream their signal on the Internet.

You might have noticed the Radio icon in the source list, up there in a prominent position right under Library—yep, there it is. This icon is your ticket to the wide world of listening to Internet radio in iTunes. With few exceptions, streaming radio stations are not the same as the commercial stations you can hear over the air, although non-commercial broadcasts such as NPR are widely available. This means you won't hear a lot of the same stuff you get on broadcast radio, which opens up a huge variety of musical tastes and genres.

To check out the stations available in iTunes, follow these steps:

1. Click the Radio icon in the source list. You'll get a list of categories, each with a triangle next to it.

2. Click a triangle next to the category of music (or other programming, such as Talk/Spoken Word) that you're interested in hearing. iTunes will take a moment and download a list of available stations, with descriptions, as shown in Figure 5-19.

3. Double-click a station you want to hear. After a few seconds, you should hear its stream in iTunes. The iTunes status display gives the name of the stream, the current track, and the length of time you've been listening.

In general, you'll get better quality streaming from sources with higher bit rates (see the Bit Rate column). But don't shy away from the streams with lower rates, such as 56K or even 32K bits per second. Depending on your surroundings and the kind of music the station is playing, those bit rates can be very listenable, especially if you're stuck somewhere with a feeble Internet connection.

You'll find hundreds of stations listed in iTunes—you're bound to like at least some of them. And if not, many other stations are available on the Web at sites like Live365.com and

FIGURE 5-19: The iTunes radio tuner shows its categories.

ShoutCast.com. You can also listen to lots of public radio stations in iTunes. For exam-ple, you can hear NPR on KCRW radio, available at http://www.kcrw.com/grid/.

Another cool way to listen to radio from Live365 is Radio365, a custom tuner application created by Live365.com (see Figure 5-20). With Radio365, you can create you own pre-sets, see the current station's playlist, and search for stations by artist or musical style, There's even a side panel for displaying album art and buttons you can click to buy the current track on the iTunes Music Store or at Amazon. You can get a free copy of Radio365 at www.live365.com/downloads.

Cross-Reference Want to find out how to record songs from Internet radio and add them to your music library? See *Convert streams to songs* in Chapter 8.

Turn off streaming radio

Streaming radio provides a fabulous source of free music you would probably never get to hear otherwise. I love listening to streaming radio, and I hope you will too. But if you have

FIGURE 5-20: Radio365 is a custom tuner for `Live365.com` stations.

managed to read all the way through this section and are unmoved by the promise of all this streaming radio, I suppose it's only fair that I tell you how to get rid of it.

1. First, you have to make sure you're running iTunes version 4.5 or later, using the About iTunes menu item. On Macintosh, look in the iTunes menu; on Windows, it's in the Help menu.

2. Open Preferences (in the iTunes menu on Mac, the Edit menu on Windows).

3. Click the General tab in Preferences. You should see a dialog that looks like Figure 5-21.

4. To turn off streaming radio, uncheck the box next to Radio, then click OK.

When the Preferences dialog closes, the Radio icon in the source list will go away. If you change your mind and realize you really do want to fool around with this great feature, all you have to do is go back to Preferences and check the box again to restore your radio.

FIGURE 5-21: iTunes Preferences, General tab.

Use a List Column for Equalizer Settings

As we discussed elsewhere in this chapter, you can display various columns to reveal information in a playlist's song list. You can directly edit some of the settings right in the song list. For example, click a song to select it, then click the song's title, and you can type to change the name of the song. This works with artist, album, genre, and comments, too. Other settings are calculated for you and can't be changed, such as the track time and size, date added, and play count.

One column is not like the others: equalizer. When you display the equalizer column, you can actively choose the equalizer setting for any track. This is also the only column that doesn't display text. Instead, it shows a little double-arrow control. When you click the control, you see a pop-up list of all available equalizer settings, shown in Figure 5-22. Pick the setting you want for that track. When you let go of the mouse button, your chosen setting appears next to the double-arrow for that song.

Tip iTunes has a global equalizer setting. If you don't have a custom equalizer setting for a track, iTunes uses the global setting. To see the global equalizer setting, click the equalizer button in the lower right corner, third button from the right.

Open Multiple Windows in iTunes

Many applications are organized around documents, with each document represented by a window. For example, in a word processor or text editor, you might have three documents open at the same time, each in its own window. But iTunes doesn't work that way. When you use iTunes, you're probably used to doing all your "work" in one window, which is fine most of the time.

FIGURE 5-22: Equalizer column lets you choose a setting.

But iTunes actually supports multiple windows, which you can use to your advantage if you're doing some serious fooling around. iTunes lets you open any playlist, or the radio list, in a separate window. To open a new window, double-click a playlist in the source column. The playlist will open in its own window. This is useful if you want to work on one playlist, maybe cleaning up song titles or rearranging things, while listening to a different playlist. Pretty soon, you can have your nice, neat iTunes screen just as cluttered as you like with a bunch of different windows.

Note that you have to double-click to open the new windows—this feature isn't in any menu.

Use iTunes Window Modes

iTunes lets you resize its main window in various ways so that you can have it just as you like it. The easiest, and least scientific, way to resize the iTunes window is to grab the size control in the lower right corner and drag it around to make the window bigger or smaller. There are other, cooler ways to boss the iTunes window around.

FIGURE 5-23: The smallest iTunes windows: just the controls (left), and with status display (right).

If you want to keep your tunes playing, but you don't want the big iTunes window to get in your way, click the zoom box in the title bar of the window. On the Mac, that's the green circle; on Windows, it's the "maximize" control next to the "X". When you click this control, the iTunes window shrinks down to itty-bitty size, with only the most basic controls visible (see Figure 5-23, on the left). If you want more information and you don't mind using up a little more space, you can drag the size control to the right and add the status display to the mini-window, as shown on the right side of Figure 5-23.

No matter how you have resized the iTunes window, you can instantly return it to pleasing dimensions by holding down Option (on Mac) or Shift (on Windows) and clicking the zoom/maximize box. This results in iTunes centering the window on the screen and resizing it to leave a reasonable margin around each edge.

If you're using another application while listening to music and you can't see the iTunes window at all, you can still exert your control. On Mac OS X, you can Control-click (or right-click) the iTunes dock icon; if you're running Windows, right-click the iTunes icon in the system tray. This pops up a menu with commands that let you play, pause, change songs, and perform other functions.

The ultimate way to get rid of the iTunes window is to make it vanish completely, by hiding the application. On the Mac, you can accomplish this by choosing Hide iTunes from the iTunes menu. On Windows, click the minimize icon in the title bar, or click "iTunes" in the taskbar.

If you're using a Mac, there is an extra-geeky way to hide the iTunes window: just click its red close control. Yes, close it! The window closes, but the music keeps playing, as if from a phantom jukebox somewhere. When you want to regain control, click the iTunes icon in the dock and the window reappears. If you're already in iTunes, you can also choose Window ⇨ iTunes, or just press Command-1.

Use SnapBack Arrows

When Apple shipped its Safari web browser in 2003, it included a built-in box on the toolbar for searching Google (Figure 5-24). That's not a new idea: Google itself ships a toolbar for Windows browsers that provides the same feature. But true to its innovative nature, Apple added something more: SnapBack.

FIGURE 5-24: SnapBack arrows in Apple's Safari browser.

See the little arrows on the right side of the address box and the Google box? Those are SnapBack arrows, sort of an enhanced version of the browser's Back button. When you click a SnapBack arrow in the address box, Safari goes back—not to the previous page, as with the back button, but to the first page you opened in that window, the last address you typed into the address box, or last bookmark you opened in that window.

The SnapBack arrow in the Google box on the right works in a similar way. Clicking that arrow takes you back to the last Google search you performed. Having SnapBack arrows in two different places shows that Apple was thinking about using SnapBack as a general concept.

Apple proved the general usefulness of SnapBack by adding it in an entirely different program: iTunes 4.5, released in April 2004. SnapBack, shown in Figure 5-25, comes in handy when you're listening to music and browsing around iTunes at the same time.

For example, let's say you're listening to your All-Time Favorites playlist, and you go exploring your Library to look for forgotten gems in your collection. Or, you might want to visit the iTunes Music Store to see what's new this week. When you want to see the current song again, you can simply click the SnapBack arrow that appears at the right side of the iTunes display. Instantly, you'll be cyber-whisked back to your playlist, with the current song selected in the list and scrolled into view.

SnapBack also works when you're playing previews in the Music Store. If you go wandering off while listening to a preview, just click the SnapBack arrow to go back to the Music Store page you were looking at.

You don't even have to be off in a distant playlist to use SnapBack. If the current song is in the playlist you're looking at, clicking the SnapBack arrow will make it appear on the screen. Cool! Note that although SnapBack is new, iTunes has had the ability to locate the current song for a long time, by choosing Show Current Song from the File menu. But many users were not aware of the feature buried deep in that menu, so SnapBack provides a more discoverable way to find out what you're listening to.

FIGURE 5-25: SnapBack arrow in iTunes.

Get Album Art

Fun with music is mainly about what you hear, but it's also what you see: the physical package. Album art might not be the crucial reason you buy a CD, but it's cool anyway. Unfortunately, album art has been diminishing over the past 20 years or so, as music technology has progressed from LP to CD to digital. The smaller the box, the less room there is for cool album art. Digital music does away with the package entirely.

When Apple opened the iTunes Music Store, it provided a small victory for lovers of album art: when you buy a song, you get an image of the album cover. You can display this picture in the lower left corner of the iTunes screen while the song is playing.

That's a great solution for music you buy at the iTunes store, but what about your zillions of CDs that you spent weeks ripping? You don't get album art for those when you import them into iTunes.

Although album art doesn't appear automatically when you rip a CD, iTunes lets you copy an image from somewhere else and paste it into the album art space. The album art is out there on the Web, on sites like `Amazon.com` that sell music. Using this feature, clever folks have figured out a solution: programs that grab the art on the Web and put it into iTunes for you. There are at least a couple of programs that do this for Mac users. Although I couldn't find one that runs on Windows, there is a Web-based tool that makes the process easier, if not fully automatic.

iTunes Catalog

iTunes Catalog is a nifty program that makes getting album art effortless. When you run iTunes Catalog, it shows you all your playlists. You can then pick a playlist, or the whole music library, and ask iTunes Catalog to grab the art for the albums from Amazon, then copy the covers back to iTunes. The grabbing is quite fast—the copying to iTunes takes a little while.

Getting album art is not even the prime function of iTunes Catalog. As the name suggests, its main feature is creating a catalog that lists all your albums and tunes. iTunes Catalog will make a PDF, text, or HTML file, and it will even publish directly to your .Mac site.

iTunes Catalog costs $10, and you can download a free demo to see if you like it before buying. Find out more at `http://www.kavasoft.com/iTunesCatalog`.

Clutter

Clutter is another cool iTunes pal for Mac OS X users. Clutter grabs album art for the song that iTunes is playing and displays it in its own "Now Playing" window. You can then do cool things with the art, such as dragging it out into its own window, or copying it to iTunes. The clutter in Clutter happens after you play a bunch of albums and drag their covers into separate little windows. You can then double-click one of the windows to play the album, turning Clutter into a kind of visual interface to your music collection.

Clutter will let you assign art to your playlists as well as to songs, and you can set Clutter to change its dock icon to show the art for the song that iTunes is currently playing, which is pretty cool. Clutter is free at `http://www.sprote.com/clutter`.

art4iTunes

Windows users: although there's no automated tool for grabbing art for all your songs at once, you can get some help from art4iTunes, a Web-based tool. To use art4iTunes, you start with the File ⇨ Export Song List command in iTunes to make your playlist into an XML file. Then, you go to the art4iTunes Web site and point it at the XML file you just made. The site chews on your list for awhile, then constructs a Web page right there in the browser that includes album covers for all your songs. Of course, that leaves you with the tedious task of dragging the covers to iTunes, one at a time. But once you do, you'll revel in seeing all those beautiful album covers once again.

Cross-Reference   For more on displaying album art in iTunes, check out Chapter 10, "See Album Art".

Summary

Playing music is the most fundamental feature of iTunes, so it's probably also the most well-developed. Take advantage of the nuances in the music playing features of iTunes, especially for playlists and streaming radio, to enhance your listening pleasure.

Coming up next in Chapter 6, we'll move beyond the melodious basics we covered here and into more advanced musical hackiness, including fun with the iTunes visualizer (it's like iTunes for your eyes), cool scripts, and interesting helper applications.

Extreme Music Playing

In this chapter we'll keep pushing iTunes in our quest to take control of all its features and to find more cool stuff for it to do. The stars of this chapter are AppleScript, Apple's amazing user scripting system, and the Visualizer, the trippy visual effects system built into iTunes.

AppleScript is a Macintosh-only technology, so there's no way to take advantage of this feature in the Windows version of iTunes. In fact, the lack of AppleScript support is probably the most significant difference between the Mac and Windows versions. It's unfortunate for Windows users, but there's not really anything to be done about it.

AppleScript

Note AppleScript only works on the Macintosh version of iTunes.

One the most powerful features of Mac OS X (and previous versions of Mac OS before it) is a wonderful technology called AppleScript. According to Apple's Web site, "AppleScript is an English-like language used to write script files that automate the actions of the computer and the applications that run on it." Luckily for us music lovers, iTunes provides excellent support for AppleScript. Using cleverly written scripts, you can gain great mastery over iTunes and its functions. And the best part is that you don't even have to write the clever scripts: they're available in abundance, for free. Scripts can help you with hundreds of tasks, including finding song and artist information for your tracks, adding comments to many tracks at once, or cleaning out missing items from your library and playlists.

AppleScript is practically a cult feature in Mac OS X, and it's a rich source for hacking. AppleScript users can be fanatical in their support for the technology, while Apple itself often manages to send mixed messages by seeming to neglect the development and promotion of AppleScript at times. But a dedicated core of developers, evangelists, and fans, led by AppleScript Product Manager Sal Soghoian, keeps the community strong.

Turn on AppleScript in iTunes

To take advantage of scripts in iTunes, the first thing you have to do is enable AppleScript. This is a very easy task, as iTunes is all ready to support scripts. All you have to do is create a folder, then put the scripts in the folder and iTunes will find them. You'll then find yourself knee-deep in AppleScript. Here are the precise steps:

1. If iTunes is running, stop it: choose iTunes ➪ Quit iTunes.

2. In the Finder, open your Home directory. If you're not sure how to do that, a fool-proof technique is to choose Go ➪ Home.

3. In your Home directory, find the Library folder, and inside Library, find iTunes.

4. In the iTunes folder, choose File ➪ New Folder. Rename the new folder "Scripts". You can also call it "scripts", or even "sCrIPts" if you want to make a fashion state-ment. Spelling is important here, but case is not.

5. Now you're ready to install some scripts in the folder. For starters, you can go to `http://www.apple.com/applescript/itunes` and download Apple's own script collection. Once you have downloaded the scripts, put them in your new Scripts folder.

6. Run iTunes. You should see something new in the menu bar: a little scroll of paper icon representing the script menu that holds the scripts you just put in the folder (see Figure 6-1).

Note You must put scripts in the folder in order to enable AppleScript. If you run iTunes with an empty script folder, you won't see the Scripts menu. Although you can move scripts into and out of the Scripts folder while iTunes is running, the contents of the Scripts menu won't change until you quit and restart iTunes.

Let's take a quick tour of Apple's scripts for iTunes. Some of the scripts are interesting, but they're really more of a proof-of-concept exercise than a killer collection of the finest pos-sible scripts you could ever want. Also, it's instructive to note that these scripts haven't been updated since the days of iTunes 2, more than 2 years ago, which reminds us that Apple sometimes forgets it has this great technology. Despite their age, the scripts work fine with iTunes 4.2, the current version as of this writing.

Note iTunes looks inside all subfolders within the Scripts folder and adds any scripts it finds to the Scripts menu. Because of this, you can't organize your scripts inside subfolders—the scripts are displayed in alphabetical order regardless of which subfolders they're stored in.

FIGURE 6-1: If you see a Scripts menu like this, you've correctly enabled AppleScript in iTunes.

Get Information from the Web

Because computers see CDs as just big hunks of data, it would be really cool if CDs were encoded with information about their songs, such as title, artist, composer, and so on. Unfortunately, nobody asked us geeks about this when audio CDs were invented. Instead, CDs you import with iTunes have to look up their information from a net-accessible database called GraceNote CDDB.

CDDB's main function is to automatically get song and album information when you import music. By default, iTunes is set up to grab information from CDDB whenever you rip a CD.

Tip   If you don't have an Internet connection available when you rip a CD, iTunes won't be able to look up track and artist information. However, you don't have to type this data in manually. Just wait until you are connected to the Internet, select the tracks that need names, then choose Advanced ⇨ Get CD Track Names. iTunes will get the info from CDDB and fill it in.

But CDDB can do more; there's also a CDDB Web site where you can look up album and artist information. This is useful if you want to see all the albums released by an artist, or look at the track list from an album you don't own. Some CDDB pages also include links to fan sites and news stories.

You can use Apple's scripts to get quick access to the CDDB Web site. Just select a song and choose one of the CDDB Search scripts, such as CDDB Search by Artist. Or, you can look up information directly on the site by artist, album, or song title. Ever wonder how many songs there are with a particular word in the title, such as "old" or "myxomatosis"? Now you can find out! Here's how:

1. Go to the Gracenote site at www.gracenote.com/music (Figure 6-2).

2. Enter the information you want to search for. You can look specifically in the artist, album, or song fields, or choose to search in all fields.

3. To avoid bogus results that include your search term as part of a word (for example, searching for "old" and getting results that include "hold", "cold", and so on), click the "Exact Phrase" box.

4. Choose to see 10 or 25 results at a time.

5. Click Search to get your first set of results.

Each item in the search results is a link to that song's entry. You can click a song to get more information about that song.

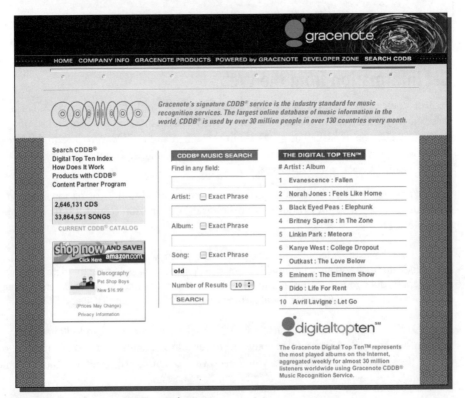

FIGURE 6-2: Gracenote CBBD search page.

Cross-Reference For more cool scripts from Apple, see *Use Apple's iPod Scripts* in Chapter 2.

Check or uncheck multiple tracks

The "Enable | Disable Selected Tracks" script lets you turn the checkbox on or off for all the songs you have selected. iTunes uses the checkbox as a sort of master on/off switch for playing songs. If an unchecked song is due to be played in a playlist, iTunes simply skips over it. When you set the rules for a new smart playlist, you can specify whether you want to allow unchecked songs. To use this script, select the songs whose status you want to change, then run the script. You'll get a dialog box asking you to give thumbs up (enable) or thumbs down (disable) on the songs (Figure 6-3).

Tip Here's a way to enable or disable a bunch of songs en masse without a script. Command-click (Control-click on Windows) any song's checkbox. All the songs in that playlist will have their checkboxes turned on or off.

Export library listings

iTunes includes a built-in command (File ⇨ Export Library) for exporting your music library to an XML file. XML is a great format for exchanging data, but it's not very easy on human eyes. To demonstrate this point, Figure 6-4 has an example of part of an exported library XML file.

If you want to produce a text file of your library that's intended for people rather than computers, use Apple's "Library Summary" script. This script gives you a choice of several formats for your summary. To see the available formats, click the "Set Prefs" button when you run the script. You'll get the list shown in Figure 6-5.

After you pick a format, the script then ponders your library contents and produces a simple text file showing all your music. A companion script, "iPod Library Summary", performs the same function for your iPod.

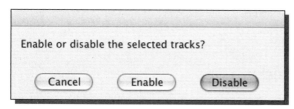

FIGURE 6-3: Enable | Disable Selected Tracks script shows you this dialog box.

```
Library.xml
They%20Might%20Be%20Giants/Robot%20Parade/Robot%20Parade%20(Demo)</string>
                        <key>File Folder Count</key><integer>6</integer>
                        <key>Library Folder Count</key><integer>1</integer>
            </dict>
            <key>36</key>
            <dict>
                        <key>Track ID</key><integer>36</integer>
                        <key>Name</key><string>Deep Blue Something - Breakfas</string>
                        <key>Kind</key><string>MPEG audio file</string>
                        <key>Size</key><integer>4114480</integer>
                        <key>Total Time</key><integer>257097</integer>
                        <key>Date Modified</key><date>2004-02-21T22:01:52Z</date>
                        <key>Date Added</key><date>2004-02-20T01:03:02Z</date>
                        <key>Bit Rate</key><integer>128</integer>
                        <key>Sample Rate</key><integer>44100</integer>
                        <key>Normalization</key><integer>3350</integer>
                        <key>File Type</key><integer>1347174745</integer>
                        <key>File Creator</key><integer>1397375309</integer>
                        <key>Location</key><string>file://localhost/Users/scott/Music/
iTunes/iTunes%20Music/!!!already%20on%20Musica/!!!fixup%205-17-03/Unknown%20Artist/
Unknown%20Album/Deep%20Blue%20Something%20-%20Breakfas</string>
                        <key>File Folder Count</key><integer>6</integer>
                        <key>Library Folder Count</key><integer>1</integer>
            </dict>
            <key>38</key>
            <dict>
                        <key>Track ID</key><integer>38</integer>
                        <key>Name</key><string>Robot Parade (Demo)</string>
                        <key>Artist</key><string>They Might Be Giants</string>
                        <key>Album</key><string>Robot Parade</string>
                        <key>Kind</key><string>MPEG audio file</string>
                        <key>Size</key><integer>452936</integer>
                        <key>Total Time</key><integer>28290</integer>
                        <key>Track Number</key><integer>1</integer>
                        <key>Date Modified</key><date>2000-03-14T23:55:11Z</date>
                        <key>Date Added</key><date>2004-02-20T01:03:03Z</date>
                        <key>Bit Rate</key><integer>128</integer>
                        <key>Sample Rate</key><integer>44100</integer>
                        <key>Normalization</key><integer>2475</integer>
```

FIGURE 6-4: iTunes exports library files as XML.

Cross-Reference   You can use XML exporting to transfer playlists to a new computer. For details, see *Move Your Playlists to Another Computer* in Chapter 5.

Miscellaneous quick tricks

A few scripts in Apple's collection simply provide shortcuts for features you could achieve in other, less hacky but more tedious ways. These include "Open Scripts folder", "Play Random Track", and "Set Genre to Specific EQ". I'll describe each of them in this section.

FIGURE 6-5: Choose from various formats for your library summary.

If you want to look at the iTunes script folder, you can navigate to the Finder, find your Home directory, then drill down to the iTunes Scripts folder. But it's much quicker to use the "Open Scripts folder" AppleScript in iTunes. This script will switch to the Finder and open the folder in a new window.

You can use the "Play Random Track" script to quickly find and play any track from your library. Of course, you could achieve the same result by going to the library, closing your eyes, and double clicking somewhere in the song list, but the script is better, because when you click with your eyes closed, you might miss and accidentally launch missiles or something bad like that. Another advantage to using this script is that it doesn't take you away from your current playlist.

The "Set Genre to Specific EQ" script is handy for making sure, for example, that all your jazz tracks have a Jazz equalizer setting. To use the script, you just pick a playlist, a genre, and an equalizer setting. Here's how it works:

1. Choose "Set Genre to Specific EQ" from the Scripts menu.

2. You can decide whether to apply a specific EQ setting to all tracks of a particular genre in the entire library or only in a chosen playlist (Figure 6-6). Click the option you want.

FIGURE 6-6: Select whether to change EQ settings for all songs of a genre or only those in a specific playlist.

3. If you chose "playlist" in step 2, the script will ask you to pick the playlist you want.

4. Next, you'll get a list of all possible genres. Pick the one you want to look for.

5. In the next step, you choose the EQ preset you want to apply.

6. After picking the EQ preset, the script displays a progress dialog box as it goes through your tunes and applies the setting you selected.

Tip You can set any bunch of tracks to the same equalizer setting with a few additional steps. Start by selecting all the tracks you want to set. Then choose File ⇨ Get Info and go to the Options tab. Pick the setting you want from the Equalizer Preset pop-up, click OK, and you're done.

Doug's AppleScripts for iTunes

The undisputed king of iTunes scripting sites is Doug's AppleScripts for iTunes at `http://www.malcolmadams.com/itunes`. This popular site's proprietor is Doug Adams, who has been writing, collecting, and publishing iTunes scripts since early 2001. The site now contains more than 260 scripts. Many of the scripts are clever and extremely useful, and a few reach the "what would I ever do without this?" level. The scripts are available for free, and if you use them and like them, you can make a donation on the site to help keep it running, a practice I highly recommend.

In this section, I'll discuss some of the niftiest scripts available from Doug's AppleScripts. The site is very dynamic, with new scripts always arriving, so you should be sure to return often to check out the latest.

Handle duplicate tracks

As your digital music collection grows, you'll inevitably have to deal with the problem of duplicate tracks. Sometimes you'll forget which CDs you've ripped, or you'll move music from one disk to another, or you might even buy a track you've already ripped. You can use a set of handy scripts described in this section to help clean up duplicates.

Remove duplicates

This script simply looks through the selected playlist for multiple copies of the same track. If it finds any, it removes the superfluous copies from the playlist. To be considered duplicates, two (or more) playlist entries must refer to the exact same track: that is, the same file on disk. So, different tracks that have the same song name, or even tracks with the same name and artist that are on different albums (such as a "greatest hits" collection), are not considered duplicates. Remove Duplicates provides a report when it's finished, as shown in Figure 6-7, but it doesn't give you a chance to preapprove its work before it deletes duplicates—you just have to trust it.

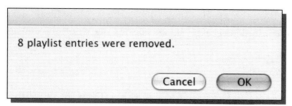

FIGURE 6-7: Remove Duplicates tells you what it's done.

Sometimes you end up with multiple copies of the same song on your hard disk, with playlist entries pointing at each one. Remove Duplicates can't help with that, because it has no way of knowing that the songs on disk are actually identical copies. For that, you need human intervention, as described in *Trash Duplicates*.

Trash duplicates

Use this script when you suspect that two disk files are really copies of the same song. You start by selecting the two tracks in iTunes, and then you run the script. Trash Duplicates posts a neat summary of details about the two tracks to help you decide if you want to throw away one or the other (see Figure 6-8).

If this information is enough to convince you that the tracks are duplicates and one of them must die, you can click either of the Trash buttons to throw the track away and remove it from all playlists. Neat! But maybe you're not sure. In that case, click the Sample button. You will then be treated to 10-second clips from the beginning, middle, and end of each track, then asked again to decide whether to trash one or the other. Each sample is preceded by a nifty voice-synthesized announcement: "beginning of 1", "middle of 2", and so on. It's very space-age.

When you get to the dialog box asking you whether to trash a track or hear a sample, you might be alarmed to note that there's no Cancel button. The author says this is due to the

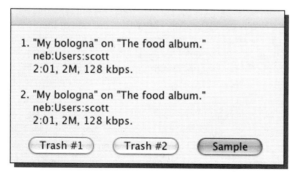

FIGURE 6-8: Trash Duplicates gives information about the tracks you're comparing.

AppleScript limitation of three buttons in a dialog box. To end the script without trashing anything, just click one of the Trash buttons, then cancel the trashing when the confirmation dialog box appears.

Wrangle same-named tracks

The Wrangle Same-Named Tracks script is another tool in the war against unwanted duplicates. Wrangle Same-Named Tracks finds all tracks that have a given word or words in their title, then moves them all to a new playlist. Here's how it works:

1. Click a track in the library or any playlist. (Note: if you don't select a track before you run the script, it will ask you to type in a track name when you run it.)

2. Choose "Wrangle Same-Named Tracks" from the Scripts menu. The script then searches the library for other tracks with the same name, creates a new playlist, and puts all the same-named tracks into that playlist.

At this point, you're on your own. The idea is to look at the contents of the new playlist, listen to the songs, check their tags, and decide which ones to keep and which to trash.

Note that using this script to search for tracks is not the same as typing text in the Search box at the top right corner of the iTunes window. When you type in there, iTunes looks for the text you typed in *any* field of the song. Wrangle Same-Named Tracks searches track names only.

Corral all dupes

Check out these cool script names: Corral, Wrangle—it's like a musical rodeo!

But seriously, Corral All Dupes goes through your library looking for tracks that have the same song name, artist, and album. When it finds such tracks, it puts them in a newly created playlist called Dupes that it constructs for just this purpose. After Corral All Dupes has finished its work, you can go through the new playlistand get rid of unwanted tracks.

Note

AppleScript is an easy language to use because of its English-like syntax. But one of the tradeoffs for this ease of use is leisurely speed. Some scripts, such as Corral All Dupes, can take a long time (like hours) to work. The best thing to do is run the script as the last thing you do before going to bed, and let it run overnight. That should be enough time to get the job done, assuming you get enough sleep.

Get rid of dead tracks

Tracks in playlists that become dislodged from their song files present another problem for ever-growing music libraries. As you rip new tunes, buy new computers and hard disks, and move music around, you're bound to end up with playlist entries referring to songs that iTunes can't find. These are called dead tracks, items that show up with an exclamation point to the left of their name. This is what happens if you delete a song file in the Finder: iTunes keeps the entry in the library and any playlists, but it no longer knows where the song is, so it puts up the exclamation point. In this section, I'll discuss a few scripts that help you bury your dead tracks.

List MIAs

Use the List MIAs script to scour your library to look for dead tracks. List MIAs creates a report of the missing tunes it finds, as shown in Figure 6-9. The report includes a list of the playlists that contain the wayward track. Once you have the report, you can decide whether to proceed with deleting the tracks (see *Remove Dead Tracks*) or trying to resuscitate them (see *iTunes Track CPR*).

Remove dead tracks

If you want to take direct action to get rid of dead tracks, you can use this script. Start by selecting the playlist that you want to cleanse of deceased tracks, then run Remove Dead Tracks. You'll soon get a dialog box reporting how many dead tracks there are in the playlist, and offering to remove them for you. There's no way to confirm or check each deletion individually, so use this script with care. Because this script can take a while to run, it tells you its progress after it checks every 100 songs.

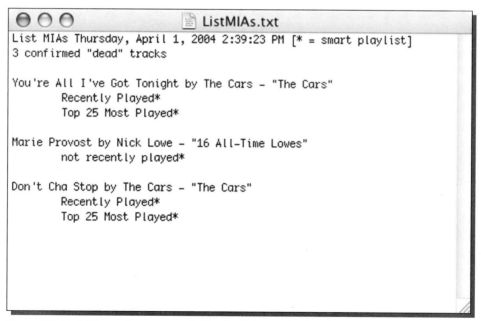

FIGURE 6-9: ListMIAs produces a report of tracks that can't be found.

Note Many scripts change playlists by adding or removing songs from them. When a script deletes a song from a playlist, you might not see the change reflected on the screen right away. If you're seeing the ghost of a song that you're sure was just deleted from the playlist, you can nudge iTunes into updating the display by clicking a column to resort the playlist or by clicking another playlist, then back to the original one.

Super remove dead tracks

This script is like Remove Dead Tracks, except that it works on the library instead of an individual playlist, which is what makes it "Super". When you run this script, it checks your library for dead track listings, and if it finds any, it wipes them out. If any playlists end up completely empty after this process, Super Remove Dead Tracks deletes the playlists. As with Remove Dead Tracks, you don't get a chance to confirm each deletion, so use this with caution. If you're going to try resurrecting any dead tracks with iTunes Track CPR, do that before running Super Remove Dead Tracks.

iTunes Track CPR

Sometimes you don't want to remove the dead tracks—you want to make them work again. You can accomplish this if the track listing has been cut off from the song file's location but the file still exists. This is a fairly unusual situation, but it can happen, for example, if you move song files around on the hard disk. In this case, the songs still exist, but iTunes might lose track of them. iTunes actually provides a built-in manual way to do this: if you try to play a dead track, iTunes will ask if you can locate the song file and connect it to the track listing (see Figure 6-10). If you can and you do, the dead track will be fixed.

Wouldn't it be great if iTunes could automatically reconnect dead track listings with their song files in cases like this? That's exactly what a lot of folks told Doug Adams. So Doug set out to write a script to do the job, and iTunes Track CPR is the result. Unfortunately, this turns out to be a tricky job for a number of reasons, and the resulting script helps with the task but is also kind of a work in progress. If you use iTunes Track CPR, Doug implores you to study the Read Me file so you understand what's going on. See www.malcolmadams .com/itunes/scripts/ss.php?sp=itunestrackcpr for more information.

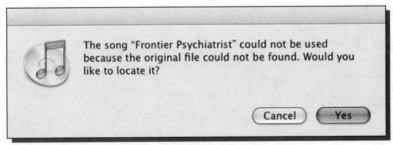

FIGURE 6-10: iTunes asks you to find the song file for a dead track.

Tip

With Mac OS X 10.3 or later, it's easy to set up keyboard shortcuts for menu commands, including AppleScripts in iTunes. Here's how to do it:

1. Open System Preferences from the Apple menu or from the dock.

2. In System Preferences, click Keyboard & Mouse.

3. In the Keyboard and Mouse panel, click the Keyboard Shortcuts tab.

4. Click the + button on the left, under the list box. You'll see a dialog box for defining a new keyboard shortcut.

5. In the "Application" pop-up menu, choose iTunes.

6. In the "Menu Title" box, type the exact name of the menu item-in this case, an AppleScript, from the Scripts menu—that you want to make a shortcut for. If you misspell the name of the script, the shortcut won't work, and you might become sullen.

7. In the "Keyboard Shortcut" box, type the combination of keys you want to use as a shortcut. Figure 6-11 shows an example.

8. Once you have defined the keyboard shortcut, quiet iTunes if it's running, then start it again. Take a look under the Scripts menu. You should see your newly defined shortcut. Go ahead and try it out!

For many scripts, assigning a keyboard command makes them far more useful. For example, the script that plays a random track is very handy when you can trigger it just by pressing a couple of keys.

Fix bad tag info

When you rip a CD, iTunes gets the name of the song, artist, and album (collectively called the tag info) from the CDDB online database. But this and other music databases have plenty of errors. You can correct typos in your tags by clicking the mistaken text in the library or playlist column, then typing the correction. But some errors can be fixed with more elegant, scripted solutions. In this section, we'll talk about a couple of scripts that help you automate the process of correcting tag errors.

Swap track name and artist

Sometimes the folks who type in the CBBD information for a CD accidentally reverse the artist and track name fields. When this happens, you can end up with a ripped CD filled with a whole bunch of songs named "The Beatles" by artists called "Eleanor Rigby", "Yesterday", and so on. That's just not right.

Instead of making you manually retype every name and artist, you can use Swap Track Name & Artist to automate your task. Just select one or more tracks, or even a whole

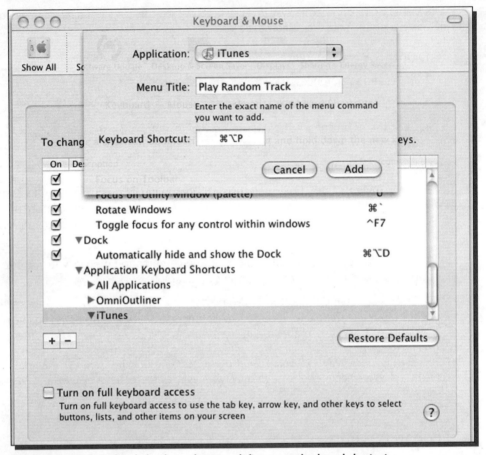

FIGURE 6-11: You see this dialog box when you define a new keyboard shortcut.

playlist, and run the script. And if you happen to run it on the wrong songs accidentally, just run it again to put things back the way they were: the script is its own "undo" command.

This tag, that tag

This Tag, That Tag is a package of four scripts that provide a more general version of Swap Track Name & Artist. The four scripts are as follows:

■ Swap This With That lets you trade information between any two tags. For example, if your tags for a CD mistakenly have the album name where the song name should be and vice versa, use Swap This With That to put things right.

- Put This Into That copies one tag to another, which wipes out whatever was previously in the destination tag.

- Put This Before That and Put This After That copy information from one tag to another without deleting what was already in the destination tag.

This group of scripts is a more general version of Swap Track Name & Artist. Swap This With That lets you trade information between any two tags. For example, if your tags for a CD mistakenly have the album name where the song name should be and vice versa, use Swap This With That to put things right.

Other scripts in this set give you more control over moving tag info. Put This In That copies one tag to another, which wipes out whatever was in the destination tag. To preserve what's already in the tag instead of replacing it, use Put This Before That or Put This After That.

Make iTunes an alarm clock

iTunes plays music, which makes it sort of like a radio . . . so why not turn it into an alarm clock radio? The scripts in this section will let you do just that.

Start iTunes . . . when?

"Start iTunes . . . When?" lets you specify a time for iTunes to start playing. It's a simple script that lurks in the background waiting for its time to come. When you run the script, you get to specify the time you want it to start rocking out, as shown in Figure 6-12.

Alarm clock applications

For the most features in an alarm clock, check out MP3 Alarm Clock (Figure 6-13) from Sugar Cube Software at www.sugarcubesoftware.com/sw/index.php?alarm. This

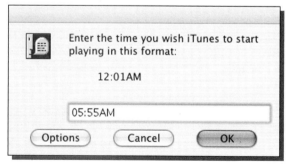

FIGURE 6-12: Use iTunes as an alarm clock if you have to get up pretty early in the morning.

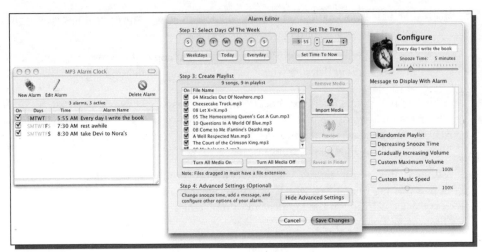

FIGURE 6-13: MP3 Alarm Clock lets you set multiple alarms.

free program offers great flexibility in choosing alarm patterns—you can have one alarm for weekdays and another for weekends, for example. And you can't lose—it's cool, and it's free!

MP3 Alarm Clock wins the "coolest hack in an alarm clock" award. By using the "Custom music speed" setting, you can make your MP3s play faster than normal, creating a powerful Chipmunks effect.

Another advanced alarm clock is iRooster (Figure 6-14) at www.sixdollarchimp.com/irooster.aspx. iRooster lets you choose an iTunes playlist for your wakeup music, has automatic wake-from-sleep for Mac OS X 10.3 users, and supports the iTunes Visualizer, although it's not as flexible in setting repeating alarms. iRooster is free for 14 days and $10 if you want to keep using it after that. Try them both!

Street spirit fade out

This script is the opposite of an alarm: it's a sleep timer. This is a great tool for ensuring that iTunes goes to bed shortly after you do. If you like, you can have the Mac go to sleep when it's time, too. And, in a nice touch, this script even fades the music out before it stops.

Tip For a non-AppleScript, full-featured alarm clock that works with iTunes and other applications, check out Alarm Clock Pro, a shareware application available at http://www.versiontracker.com/dyn/moreinfo/macosx/13639. And if you have an iPod, don't forget that it has both a sleep timer and alarm clock settings, which you can read about in Chapter 2.

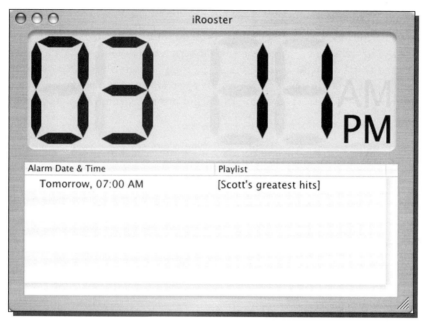

FIGURE **6-14**: iRooster lets you make the window more or less transparent.

Change the play count

Most properties of songs, such as the name, artist, and album, are set and rarely change. Others, like play count and last played date, are more dynamic. Play count increases by one every time a song is played, either in iTunes or on an iPod.

In iTunes 4.1, Apple added a feature that was happily welcomed by scripters: you could now change the play count property (officially known as "played count") from a script. So, if you want to fake the number of times a song has been played, you can do it with AppleScript. This can be useful for artificially increasing or decreasing the apparent popularity of a song in your library, which can affect how it appears in smart playlists.

Two scripts on Doug's AppleScripts for iTunes site are useful for fooling around with play count. New Play Count lets you enter a new value for the play count. Add or Subtract Play Count changes a track's play count by a specified value.

More fun with scripts

In this section we present a few miscellaneous scripts from Doug's site that are suitable for long hours of fun and goofing around with your music.

Find album artwork with Google

If you love having album art for your music, you might be interested in this clever script. To use it, you select a song, then run the script, which tells your Web browser to go out and search Google for a picture of the song's album cover. After you run the script, you'll see a Google image search results page. If you see an image you like, you can drag it into the album art space in iTunes and just stare, admiring it and your cleverness.

 Caution Album covers are protected by copyright law. Getting album covers for your personal use is probably OK, but distributing them to other folks is not legal.

 Cross-Reference See the section Get *Album Art* in Chapter 5 for other ways to acquire album covers for your collection.

Google lyric search

The Google lyric search script is cool if you want to figure out just what they're singing while you're listening. When you run Google Lyric Search, the script calls upon your Web browser to search the Web for lyrics to the current song. Rather than displaying the lyrics, your browser will show a list of search results. You can then click the one that looks most promising to you. Don't be shy about singing along!

Now Playing in iChat AV

The Now Playing in iChat AV script shows your iChat buddies what song you're listening to in iTunes right now, thus advertising just how cool (or lame) you really are. When you run Now Playing in iChat, the script stays active in the background, posting the current song and artist as your status message in iTunes, as shown in Figure 6-15. To make it stop, find the Now Playing in iChat AV application and quit it.

FIGURE 6-15: This script shows your iChat buddies what you're listening to.

Tip

Another way to tell the world what you're listening to is Kung-Tunes, an application you can download at `http://www.kung-foo.tv/itti.php`. Unlike Now Playing in iChat AV, Kung-Tunes lets you publish your current iTunes song to a Web page, so you can let the whole world know your taste in music.

Find More Scripts for iTunes

Although Doug's AppleScripts for iTunes is the best site of its kind, there are a few other sources for scripts. Be sure to check out `MacScripter.net` at `scriptbuilders.net/category.php?search=iTunes` to see what's going on there. You might also be able to find scripts by searching VersionTracker (`www.versiontracker.com`) and MacUpdate (`www.macupdate.com`).

Create Your Own Scripts

It's easier to write programs in AppleScript than in conventional programming languages. This fact has lured many folks to AppleScript who were never programmers before. If you're intrigued by AppleScript, this section is for you.

Looking at scripts

One of the cool things about AppleScript is that most scripts are distributed as editable source files. You can open them in the Script Editor, an application that comes with Mac OS 9 and X. In the Script Editor, you can study how they work and even modify them to suit your whims. As an example, take a look at Figure 6-16, which shows a listing of the Play Random Track script.

Note

Although AppleScript uses a friendly English-like syntax, it's a real, honest-to-goodness programming language, with power and complexity. Don't be too concerned if the script shown in Figure 6-16 is baffling to you—I included it here just to show you what an AppleScript looks like, not as an introduction to programming. And if you are interested in learning more about AppleScript, even if you've never programmed before, see *How to find out more* at the end of this section.

Almost half the script listing is devoted to making sure the user has a version of iTunes that supports the script. (That's the section of the script that starts "if this_version is not greater than or equal to the required_version".) If the current iTunes version isn't at least 2.0.3, the script asks the user to upgrade, and even offers to go to the iTunes download page. If iTunes passes the version check, the script picks a track at random in this line:

```
set this track to some track
```

```
property required_version : "2.0.3"

tell application "iTunes"
        activate
        -- VERSION CHECK
        set this_version to the version as string
        if this_version is not greater than or equal to the required_version then
                beep
                display dialog "This script requires iTunes version: " & required_version & ¬
                        return & return & ¬
                        "Current version of iTunes: " & this_version buttons {"Update", "Cancel"} default button 2 with
                                icon 2
                if the button returned of the result is "Update" then
                        my access_website("http://www.apple.com/itunes/download/")
                        return "incorrect version"
                end if
        end if
        tell source "Library"
                tell playlist "Library"
                        set this_track to some track
                        set this_name to the name of this_track
                        set this_artist to the artist of this_track
                        set this_album to the album of this_track
                        play this_track
                end tell
        end tell
        display dialog "Now playing..." & return & return & ¬
                "Name: " & this_name & return & ¬
                "Artist: " & this_artist & return & ¬
                "Album: " & this_album buttons {"•"} default button 1 giving up after 10
end tell

on access_website(this_URL)
        ignoring application responses
                tell application "Internet Explorer"
                        GetURL this_URL
                end tell
        end ignoring
end access_website
```

FIGURE 6-16: Play Random Track script shown in Script Editor.

The "some track" syntax is AppleScript's cool way of selecting a random track. Once the random track is chosen, the script fills up some variables that will display the track info for the user. Finally, it plays the track and displays the dialog box with song information.

How to find out more

Plenty of information is available on the Web and in books to help aspiring scripters. Start with Apple's site at www.apple.com/applescript for basic information. If you want to get to the juicy technical info, check out developer.apple.com/documentation/ AppleScript. You should also take advantage of the very active AppleScript forum at iPodLounge, where Doug Adams and many of the contributors to his site hang out and swap tips. To get there, go to Doug's AppleScripts for iTunes and click the Forum link. Good luck becoming a super scripter!

Master the Visualizer

Playing beautiful music is not enough: iTunes turns your tunes into art. The Visualizer feature replaces most of the iTunes window with groovy animation that soothes and hypnotizes. Starting the Visualizer is easy: just choose Visualizer ➡ Turn Visualizer On. When you do that, you'll no doubt be distracted by the pretty colors for awhile. Go ahead and stare. I'll be here waiting when you get back.

Set visualizer options

Although the Visualizer displays nifty images by default, you can play around with a bunch of settings to control it more precisely. To see the settings, click the Options button at the top right corner of the iTunes window while you have the Visualizer turned on (not in Full Screen mode). You'll see a dialog with four check boxes (five on the Mac version). The options are as follows:

- *Display frame rate*: When you turn this one on, the Visualizer display will show you how many times per second the screen effect is being redrawn.

- *Cap frame rate at 30 fps*: This option limits the amount of processing power devoted to the visual effect being drawn so it doesn't cause everything else on your computer to slow down.

- *Always display song info*: Turn this checkbox on to keep the name of the song, artist, and album showing in the lower left corner of the visual effects. See Figure 6-17 for an example.

- *Faster but rougher display*: If your visual effects seem to be redrawing too slowly, try turning this checkbox on.

- *Use OpenGL*: (Mac only) This option determines whether the Visualizer uses Apple's OpenGL graphics technology to draw the effects. Depending on which Mac you have and what modes you're using, turning this setting on might make your display smoother —try it and see.

The preceding options are a little tricky to find, but there are others that are even more well-hidden. To see them, type ? while the Visualizer is running. When you do, you'll get a list of additional settings right there in the Visualizer screen. They only stay onscreen for a few seconds before vanishing into the ether, but I have thoughtfully preserved them for you here:

- *? Display more help*: If you press the ? key again, you'll get a second list of options that are even more gnarly than these (see the following).

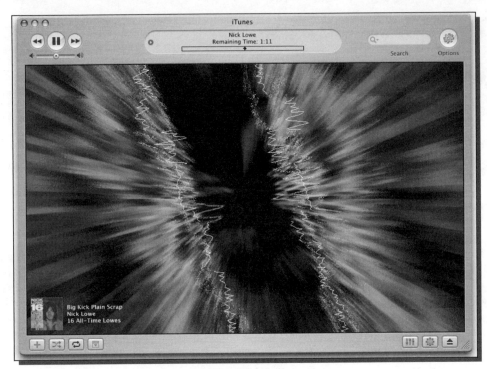

FIGURE 6-17: Visualizer with "Always display song info" turned on.

- **F** *Toggle frame rate display*: You can use this option to show or hide the number of frames per second of animation. Yes, this is the same option you can set with a checkbox in the main options dialog we discussed earlier.

- **T** *Toggle frame rate capping*: Use this option to let your visual effects run free and draw just as often as it wants to. Again, this setting is also available in the main options dialog box.

- **I** *Display song information*: If you have "Always display song info" turned off in the main options dialog box, press I to temporarily see which song is playing. The info display fades into the psychedelic mist after a few seconds.

- **D** *Reset settings to default*: Start the current effect over again.

If you follow the advice suggested by the first item and press ? again, you'll see even more commands:

- **M** *Select config mode*: This option cycles between three different display modes. The default is "Random slideshow mode", in which the Visualizer keeps changing the effect parameters. The other modes are "User config slideshow mode", which cycles through effects chosen by the user, and "Freezing current config", which prevents the display mode from changing.

- **0-9** *Select user configs (shift to set)*: When you see a visual effect that you really like, you can save it by pressing Shift and a number key. Then, when you want to relive the past and call the effect back, just press the number.

- **R** *New random config*: If you're tired of the current effect and you want to see something different, press R to change it up. By pressing R repeatedly, you can take control of the visual effects without having to think too much.

- **C** *Display current config*: Use this option to show the current Visualizer settings. You'll see three parts to this information, as shown in Figure 6-18. The first line is the pattern, the foreground object that's most visible. The second line gives the shape, the background objects that swoop out of the main object. The third bit of information is the effect's color scheme.

As if these hidden options aren't hidden enough, there are a few more that aren't documented at all. Here they are:

- **Q and W** *Cycle through patterns*: Press *W* to see the next, and *Q* for the previous pattern.

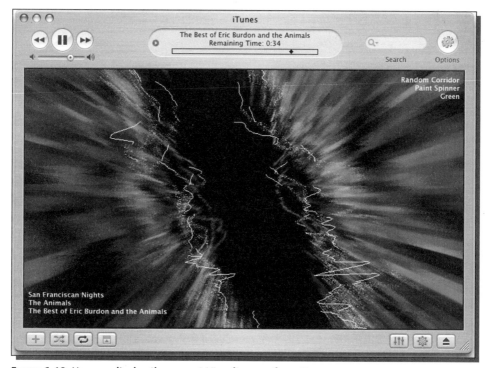

FIGURE **6-18: You can display the current Visualizer configuration.**

- **A and S** *Cycle through shapes*: Use *A* for the next and *S* for the previous.

- **Z and X** Cycle through color schemes: *Z* for the next and *X* for the previous scheme.

- **Caps Lock** *Display configuration when it changes*: If Caps Lock is on, you'll always see new configurations displayed.

- **N** *Toggle between high contrast and normal contrast colors*.

- **B** *Show the Apple logo*: "B" is for "bite".

Set the size of the visual effect

You can make the Visualizer's effect appear in any of four different size formats, all available as menu items in the Visualizer menu. All the formats are relative to the size of the iTunes window. The Large format fills the window, while the Medium and Small settings occupy smaller fractions. To get the most out of your Visualizer, choose Full Screen to have the visual effect take over your entire monitor. When you want your computer back, just press Esc to end the light show.

Note

iTunes respects the size setting (Large, Medium, or Small) even when you're watching in full screen mode. If you want your full screen effects to take over the entire full screen instead of just part of the full screen, make sure you choose Visualizer ⇨ Large before going to full screen.

Use the Visualizer as a screen saver

You might not have realized that you don't actually have to be playing music for the Visualizer to be working. Try it: turn on the Visualizer, but make sure iTunes is silent. You'll still see a lovely slide show.

Get Visualizer plug-ins

Although Apple provides awesome visual effects with the Visualizer, you don't have to settle for the built-in features. The Visualizer in iTunes is actually a platform that allows programmers to create their own visual effects modules. If you scour the Internet, you'll find a few very cool Visualizer plug-ins that offer alternatives for visual effects. To install a new plug-in, you just download the file, then put it into the Plug-ins folder inside the iTunes folder (see iTunes Help for full details). When you install Visualizer plug-ins, they show up in the Visualizer menu. To use one, you select it in that menu.

Most Visualizer plug-ins are only available for the Mac version of iTunes, because it's been around for much longer than the Windows version, but there are some for both operating systems. Here are a few for you to check out:

- Fractogroovalicious draws lots of big, colorful fractals. You can get it at `www.2tothex.com/fractogroovalicious.html`.

- WhiteCap, available in both Mac and Windows versions, is a visual plug-in with over 180 effects, the ability to export video, and a lot of flexibility. It's available at `http://soundspectrum.com/whitecap/download.html`.

- ArKaos Visualizer is a plug-in that matches beats with the music and displays fast-moving, dynamic images. See Figure 6-19 for a sample. Download ArKaos Visualizer at `http://versiontracker.com/dyn/moreinfo/macosx/8315`.

Create your own Visualizer plug-ins

If you're a programmer, and you're looking for a fun musical project, consider building your own Visualizer plug-in for the Mac or Windows versions of iTunes. You'll need the

FIGURE 6-19: ArKaos Visualizer sample image.

iTunes Visualizer Plug-in Software Development Kit (SDK), which you can get from Apple at `http://developer.apple.com/sdk/#iTunes`. There are two versions of the kit, one for Macintosh and one for Windows. To develop a Mac plug-in, you can use Apple's free Xcode tools or Metrowerks CodeWarrior. The Windows SDK works with Microsoft Visual Studio.

Summary

Adding AppleScripts to iTunes can make your music listening and management a lot smoother, especially for tasks like cleaning out duplicates and dead tracks. If you want something to look at while you're listening to great music, the Visualizer has an almost infinite variety of nifty graphics to see. And if you're a programmer type, or you want to be, you can learn how to create your own scripts and visual plug-ins for iTunes.

In the next chapter, you'll move beyond mere software and into the realm of hardware add-ons to extend the reach of iTunes and your computer.

iTunes and Hardware

If you're a typical iTunes user, your goal is to move as much of your music collection as possible onto your computer. Once it's there, you can put iTunes in control of playing all your tunes. But you probably don't do all your music listening while you're sitting (or standing, or kneeling) in front of your computer. So it's important to find ways for your music to escape from the prison of your computer. Well, maybe prison is too harsh an analogy, so let's just say that your music shouldn't stay cooped up in your computer all the time —just like you, it needs to get out once in awhile.

Of course, the best way to get your music out into the world is on an iPod, a topic that's discussed in great detail in Part I of this book. But as marvelous as our iPods are, they're lacking some features that computers have:

➤ They have a lot less capacity for music. As of this writing, iPods are limited to a mere (!) 40 gigabytes, while computers can store hundreds of gigabytes. And you can always add more storage just by buying additional external hard disks.

➤ They lack a method for easy networking. A bunch of computers in your home or office can share music directly, but a gang of iPods can't.

➤ By virtue of their more powerful CPUs, bigger screens, and external connections, computers can do a lot more stuff and can provide a more thorough user interface. This one cuts both ways: the small screen and limited space for controls force a wonderful simplicity that is one of the reasons why iPods are so well-liked. But iTunes and other music players on computers give you the power to rip CDs, create and rearrange playlists, rename and delete songs, edit tag information, and do much more.

For these and other reasons, playing your music collection directly from iTunes will likely be an important part of your personal musical strategy. In this chapter, we're going to see how to use additional hardware to get the most out of iTunes music playing.

Broadcast Your iTunes

This section discusses a couple of different ways you can listen to iTunes music wirelessly: cordless headphones and WiFi. Take a look at these solutions and see if one of them works for you. The world doesn't need any more wires.

Listen with cordless headphones

Here's a neat trick: you can play music in iTunes and listen through cordless headphones. This is useful in your home late at night so you can listen without disturbing others, in classrooms where more than one person might need to hear the same music while others are working on something else, and at parties attended by the very geeky.

Cordless headphones have been around for a long time, a lot longer than digital music. They're handy because they eliminate wires and because they allow more than one listener to share music. Cordless headphone systems include a transmitter along with the headphones. You plug the transmitter into your computer's audio out connection, and away you go. Anyone wearing headphones tuned to the same frequency can listen to the tunes.

You can get cordless headphones that use a couple of different technologies:

- Infrared systems require you to be in line of sight with the transmitter plugged into your computer. These models are great if you're going to be sitting on the couch across the room from your computer, up to 20 feet away, grooving to the beat while you catch up on some reading. Infrared systems include the SC2600 from Arkon Resources (www.arkon.com/ir.html). The SC2600 costs about $40, and extra headsets go for about $30. Other well-reviewed infrared cordless headphones include the Sony MDR-IF140 (crutchfield.com or amazon.com), Emerson EHP1000 (www.ravefactory.com or amazon.com), and RCA WHR50 (www.shoptronics.com). All sell for $50 or less, some as low as $28. The Sony MDR-IF140 is pictured in Figure 7-1.

- 900 MHz systems operate by radio waves and give you the freedom to wander away from the transmitter's all-seeing eye and into other rooms. These headphones also work over a much greater range than infrared, with some systems claiming up to 300 feet. Folks who use 900 MHz headphones sometimes report problems with sound quality, such as hiss and breakup, so try before you buy, if you can. Popular sets include the Jensen JW160 for about $48, Magnavox PM-61571 ($55), JVC HAW250 ($60), and the ever-present Sony with the MDR-RF915RK and other models. Prices range from $60 to $120. Audiophile cordless headphones run $200 – $400 and more. The most popular models in this range are from Sennheiser (www.sennheiser.com). Check amazon.com, crutchfield.com, and sepharus.com when you're ready to go shopping.

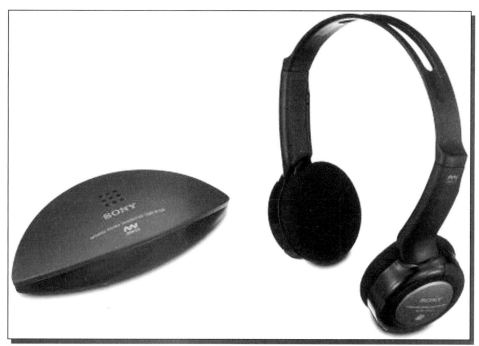

FIGURE 7-1: Sony MDR-IF140 cordless headphones.
Courtesy of Sony Electronics Inc.

Blue, Blue, My World Is Blue

If you have a Macintosh made since 2003, there's a good chance it includes the ability to communicate using a wireless technology called Bluetooth. If your computer is a Mac older than that or is a Windows PC, you can add Bluetooth to your computer via a USB adapter. Because Bluetooth transmits data wirelessly, it would be very cool if you could get Bluetooth headphones and hear music from your computer without having to plug in a separate transmitter. As of this writing, Bluetooth headphones that can receive stereo music were not available, but several companies seem to be on the verge of shipping such products, including TEN Technology (www.tentechnology.com).

For more information on cordless headphones, see www.headsets.com, or go to froogle.com or shopping.yahoo.com and search for "cordless headphones".

Play music over WiFi

Another way you can get your music into the air is through a wireless music adapter that uses WiFi technology, also known as 802.11 or AirPort, Apple's brand name. These devices have two parts: software that broadcasts music from your computer, and hardware that connects to your stereo, receives the broadcasts, and plays the music. You can have as many receivers as you want, and different receivers can receive different music at the same time. Each receiver acts as a window on all the music stored on computers in network range. From the receiver, you can browse among computers, playlists, albums, artists, and songs. It's like having your computer and its music in the room without actually having to carry it around.

Apple makes a simpler, slightly different solution for playing music over WiFi. AirPort Express is a WiFi access point (also known as a base station) that provides a full range of wireless services, like its big brother, AirPort Extreme. In addition to doing standard wireless stuff, AirPort Express hooks up to your stereo or speakers and streams audio to them from iTunes, as discussed below.

Tip   Instead of having a wireless receiver to play your iTunes music, you can connect another computer to your stereo, run iTunes, and play music via iTunes music sharing. The advantage is that you get a full-powered computer running a full version of iTunes; the disadvantage is that a computer will likely cost more and take up more space than one of the wireless receivers described in this section. If you do hook up a computer to your stereo in order to run iTunes, take a look at this chapter's *Run iTunes by Remote Control* section.

You can choose from among several WiFi music receivers:

- Squeezebox, from Slim Devices (www.slimdevices.com), looks right at home as a stereo component (see Figure 7-2). This small black box includes a bright multi-

Now Playing (1 of 40)
1. Symphony No. 9 in D Minor

00:48

FIGURE 7-2: Slim Devices Squeezebox.

line fluorescent display that walks you through setup, helps you choose music, and provides "Now Playing" information. There's a mode that switches the display to one big line, which makes it easier to read from across the room. The accompanying open-source software runs on Mac OS X, Windows, Linux, and Unix. Squeezebox works great anywhere your wireless network reaches. It also comes in a wired version, but that's not nearly as much fun. Squeezebox sells for about $250. One more cool thing about the Squeezebox: it has Easter eggs. There's a screen saver that simulates falling snow and spells out a holiday greeting: from the Home screen, choose Settings ➪ Screensaver ➪ Snow Screensaver. And Squeezebox plays Tetris: go to Home ➪ Plugins ➪ SlimTris. Press right-arrow to drop a piece, up-arrow and down-arrow to move the piece, Add and Play to rotate. Excellent!

■ AirPort Express, from Apple (Figure 7-3), is the newest way to play your music from afar. This device is a full 802.11g WiFi access point. It includes audio connectors to hook it up to your stereo or other powered speaker system. AirPort Express is also nicely compact and lightweight, so you can take it with you.

AirPort Express works together with AirTunes, a feature that was added to iTunes in version 4.6. To get AirTunes going, you just make sure it's enabled in iTunes preferences (see Figure 7-4) at the bottom of the Audio tab.

FIGURE 7-3: AirPort Express.
Courtesy of Apple.

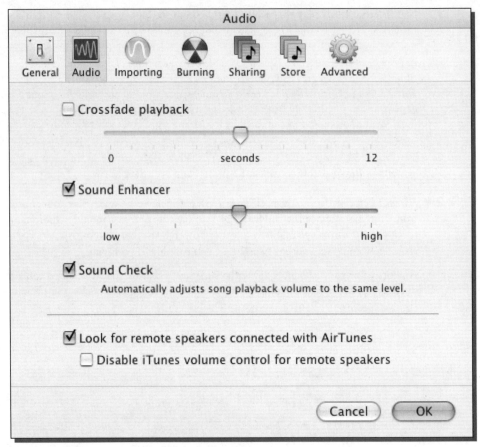

FIGURE 7-4: AirTunes setting in iTunes preferences.

When AirTunes finds an AirPort Express, it adds a pop-up menu to the bottom of the iTunes window that lets you pick where your music will go: the computer's speakers, or a distant AirPort Express somewhere.

Because AirPort Express carries Apple's brand and legendary ease of use, it's destined to become the most popular way to broadcast your tunes to another place in the house. But there are definite drawbacks when comparing Apple's little base station to products like Squeezebox. The most notable limitation is that AirPort Express has no user interface. While that certainly makes it easy to use, it also means that if you're listening to remote music with AirTunes and AirPort Express, you can't change playlists, skip songs, or even pause the music without going to the computer that's running iTunes. That can be annoying if the computer is in a distant room or on another floor.

When this obvious flaw was pointed out to Steve Jobs at the AirPort Express product introduction, he responded by saying that walking is good for you, according to a report on AppleInsider.com. Most likely, Apple is working on a new product or feature that will remedy this problem. Maybe a remote control, or even an iPod that also functions as a remote?

- Macsense's HomePod (`www.macsense.com/product/homepod/`) is an iPod-white box that plugs into your stereo and plays music it receives from your Macs and Windows PCs via the WiFi network. HomePod includes built-in speakers and plenty of connections for your stereo, and costs about $250.

- Roku (`www.rokulabs.com`) makes the Roku SoundBridge Network Music Player, which gives you WiFi access to your tunes in a really cool aluminum package. Roku makes two models, starting at $225.

- cd3o (`www.cd3o.com`) makes various models of their stylish Network MP3 Player, two of which have WiFi connections. The cd3o products only work on Windows computers. Prices for wireless models start at about $180.

- Sound Blaster Wireless Music (`www.soundblaster.com`) from Creative Labs is another Windows-only WiFi solution. This model is notable because it plays all WMA files in addition to MP3s. Another nifty feature is the remote control: it includes a multi-line display for choosing music, and it uses RF instead of infrared for a much greater range. Sound Blaster Wireless Music goes for about $200.

- Linksys Wireless-B Media Adapter (`www.linksys.com`) plays MP3 and WMA songs from your Windows computers (no Macs) and displays pictures (JPEG, GIF, and so on) on your TV. The Wireless-B Media Adapter uses your TV as a display for its user interface. This product sells for about $150.

Inside AirPort Express

How does AirPort Express work its magic? AirPort Express teams up with the AirTunes feature of iTunes to stream music wirelessly across your network. You start by plugging in an AirPort Express and enabling it in iTunes preferences, When you play a tune, iTunes first converts the song from its source format (MP3, AAC, and so on) to an audio stream. Then, iTunes re-encodes the music using Apple Lossless compression, which is a way to reduce the size of the music without losing any fidelity. After compressing the music, iTunes encrypts the data so it can't be "stolen" while it's going over the air, then streams it off to the AirPort Express.

When the AirPort Extreme receives the data, it decrypts it, decompresses it to restore its original fidelity, then pumps it through its audio out jack and into a waiting stereo or set of speakers. The cool thing about this setup is that you still play music pretty much as you did before: through iTunes. Of course, that's also the main drawback to AirPort Express: if you want to make any changes in what you're listening to, you have to go to your computer, which is likely to be in another room.

Run iTunes by Remote Control

If you've decided to connect a computer to your stereo, and not just a wireless receiver, you're faced with the prospect of running software that might be on the other side of the room from where you are. Software designers call this "the ten-foot interface", describing how far away you are from the computer you need to run.

The best solution is to get a remote control for your computer. Sure, that's kind of comical: yet another remote. But give it a try and you might see that it's the best way to deal with that distant computer. In this section, we'll take a look at two of the best remote controls for computers: the Remote Wonder II from ATI, and the Keyspan Digital Remote.

Control your computer with ATI Remote Wonder

The ATI Remote Wonder II is the Swiss army knife of computer remotes: it does just about everything. In fact, it does so much that simply controlling iTunes is a little job for it. The 50-key Remote Wonder looks a lot like a remote for a device in your entertainment center, as you can see in Figure 7-5. It includes keys for running your computer's DVD player as well as iTunes (or any other music player). The remote has a thumb pad that you use to move the cursor across the screen, and keys that cause the computer to think you have clicked mouse buttons. The Remote Wonder operates via RF, not infrared, which gives it a range of 20 feet or more, and it can even work through walls.

The Remote Wonder works with both Macs and Windows PCs. Installing the software is simple. To set up the hardware, you just plug the receiver into a USB port, and you're set. You can configure global settings for the remote, or set up custom profiles for each application, reprogramming every last button if you want. You can even program the keys to perform a different function after you hold them down for a couple of seconds.

ATI sells the Remote Wonder II for about $60. The original Remote Wonder, with fewer features, is about $50. You can find out more at www.ati.com.

Get Keyspan Digital Media Remote

For about the same price ($50) as the Remote Wonder, Keyspan's Digital Media Remote takes an entirely different approach (see Figure 7-6). Instead of providing full control of the computer, the Digital Media Remote is minimalist: it has only 17 keys and is much smaller and easier to handle than the Remote Wonder. This tiny device provides everything you need for controlling iTunes on a computer across the room, but no super-duper features such as cursor control. You can set up application-specific functions for the Digital Media Remote's buttons.

This remote communicates with its receiver via infrared, which means you have to be able to see the receiver in order for commands to work. The Keyspan Digital Media Remote run on Macs and Windows PCs. You can learn more about it at www.keyspan.com.

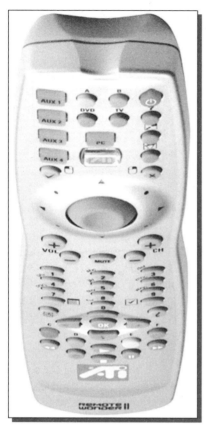

FIGURE 7-5: ATI Remote Wonder II.
There is also a receiver that plugs
into your computer via USB.

FIGURE 7-6: Keyspan Digital Media Remote.

Playing a Borrowed Tune

Usually, there's no reason to play music directly from your iPod while you're using your computer, because the music on the iPod normally *comes from* the computer when you sync. Let's say, however, that you're borrowing someone else's iPod, and you want to play the iPod's music through iTunes to take advantage of cordless headphones or a WiFi receiver you have connected to that computer, or just to use the computer's speakers. You can play iPod music through iTunes, but only if you have the iPod set to "Manually manage songs and playlists", which is usually not the best way to wrangle your music. When the iPod is set to this mode, all its songs magically become available in iTunes, and its playlists are visible. You can play any song or playlist, or even turn on the music browser and pick out albums or artists to hear.

Even if the borrowed iPod is set to automatic update mode, you can play songs from the iPod by switching to manual mode temporarily. Here's how:

1. Connect the alien iPod to your computer. You'll see a scary looking warning message asking if you want to wipe out the iPod and replace it with your music (Figure 7-7). For the sake of your friendship, just say no. (If you don't see the warning, the iPod is already set for manual updating, and you can skip the rest of the steps. The iPod's songs and playlists will appear in iTunes without any further coercion.)

2. Make sure the iPod is selected in the iTunes sources list.

3. Click the iPod button at the lower right to get the iPod Preferences dialog box.

4. Note whether it's set to "Automatically update all songs and playlists" or "Automatically update selected playlists only", and write the setting down somewhere. If "Manually manage songs and playlists" is selected, skip the rest of the steps—you can already play this iPod's music through iTunes without any further monkeying around.

5. Click "Manually manage songs and playlists". Acknowledge the not-so-important warning you get (Figure 7-8) by clicking OK, then click OK again in the Preferences dialog box.

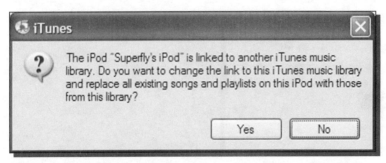

FIGURE 7-7: iTunes warns you if you attach an automatically updating iPod from another computer.

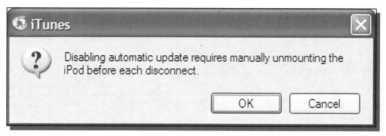

FIGURE 7-8: You'll see this dialog box when you switch to manual management.

Caution

When the iPod is set to manual mode, you can change its contents directly in iTunes, which is not possible in automatic mode. You can mess around with playlists, change tags, delete songs, and just generally hose everything. Assuming you want to preserve the contents of your borrowed iPod just as you got it, be sure not to change anything while you're listening to the music.

6. The iPod's music comes to life! You can pick playlists, choose songs to play, and turn on the browser (Edit ⇨ Show Browser) to look through artists and albums.

7. Enjoy the music. When you're done with the iPod and ready to return it, go on to the next step.

8. Select the iPod in the iTunes sources list and click the Eject iPod button at the lower right.

9. Recall the setting you wrote down from step 4. (You did write it down, didn't you?) Return the iPod to your good, good friend. Tell your friend to connect the iPod, click the iPod button at the lower right, and choose the appropriate "Automatically update" setting that you wrote down in step 4. After your friend clicks OK, all will be back to normal, and your friend will still be your friend. (Note that you can't set the iPod back to automatic update mode on your computer, because then it will try to update the iPod with *your* music. That's why you need to ask your patient, saintly friend to perform this step.)

Play Tunes on Your TiVo

If you have a TiVo Series2 digital video recorder, you might not realize that in addition to taking over your TV life, your TiVo can play your computer's music, as long as you have the TiVo connected to your home network. There are two parts to the process:

- Download and install TiVo Desktop software on your computer (www.tivo.com/4.9.4.1.asp). There are versions for Mac OS X and for Windows.

- Buy the Home Media Option from TiVo. You can get this $100 option at www.tivo.com/4.9.asp.

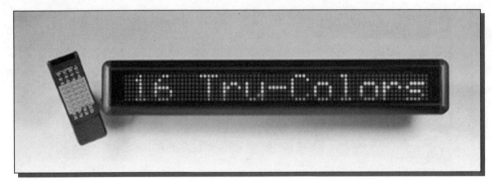

FIGURE 7-9: TruColor programmable message sign.

Once you've installed TiVo Desktop and turned on Home Media Option, you'll be able to use your computer to "publish" music to the TiVo. If you have a Macintosh, you can specify which iTunes playlists to publish. On Windows, you get to pick folders or individual songs. When you're on the couch and enjoying your TiVo, you can pick Music & Photos to get to your computer's tunes. Now you can spend even more time in front of your TV!

Set Up a "Now Playing" Sign

Want to advertise your obsession with iTunes and music? There are few better ways to show off than by getting a programmable LED sign, like the one in Figure 7-9 ($250 at http://www.neon-das.com/TruColor112.html) connecting it to your computer, and having iTunes display the current song, maybe mixed in with a trivia quiz or the latest stock prices. You can program this sign and others like it via Ethernet or e-mail. If you hook it up to a Mac, a simple AppleScript will post the current iTunes song on the sign for you. And then you can have a blast as you attract every fellow tunehacker within shouting distance.

Summary

For several years Apple has been pushing the idea of a "digital hub" in which all your music, pictures, and movies pass through a computer (preferably one of theirs). iTunes is the most successful software piece of that strategy, but to really take advantage of iTunes, you have to get the music into your stereo. In this chapter, we looked at various solutions, including broadcasting your music over the airwaves of your home, and running your computer by remote control.

Coming up in Chapter 8: we'll focus on how to get all kinds of music into your computer so you'll have even more to enjoy in iTunes.

Music In

Before we can listen to all our favorite songs in iTunes, before we can make tunes flow into our iPods, we must go through the essential step of getting music into iTunes. There are two basic methods for doing this: copying from CD, and buying from the iTunes Music Store. But those aren't the only ways you can collect music to listen to—far from it. In this chapter, you'll discover some of the coolest techniques, nuances, variations, and obscure features for getting music into iTunes.

To copy songs from your CDs, you insert a CD, at which time iTunes translates the music from the CD into a compressed form, usually MP3 or AAC. These compressed versions retain most of the qualities of the original CD, but have the virtue of taking up far less space on your hard disk than the uncompressed versions would— usually, about 90 percent less.

The other major technique for getting music into iTunes libraries and iPods is to buy songs from the iTunes Music Store. Apple is especially fond of this method. You visit the iTunes Music Store by clicking the Music Store icon in the sources column in iTunes, where you can buy lots of songs for 99 cents each, or albums for $9.99.

Although most music in iTunes comes from these two sources, there are other ways of getting music in. For example, most artists, especially those who are little known and would like to be more popular, provide free songs and samples on their Web sites. Some online merchants do the same thing.

There is also the world of peer-to-peer file sharing programs that provide access to free music. Courts have ruled that these programs have legitimate uses, but they are also widely used for illegally sharing copyrighted material. If you use file sharing programs, don't share copyrighted songs. Not only is it a bad idea, it's against the law.

In other parts of this chapter, I'll talk about tips for efficiently getting music from your CDs into iTunes, how to add music by recording the tunes your computer plays, and much more. By the time you finish this chapter, you should be able to fill every spare byte of your hard disk with beautiful music.

in this chapter

☑ **Keep Your Music CD-Quality**

☑ **Automate Your CD Ripping**

☑ **Get All Your Music Together in One Place**

☑ **Record Whatever Your Computer Plays**

☑ **Convert Streams to Songs**

☑ **Get Legal Free Tracks**

Rip but Don't Tear

You probably know that the process of copying music from a CD is called *ripping*. Well, this bit of knowledge apparently came late to some music industry execs. This descriptive term, which predates iTunes, was coined to describe the way you're (figuratively) ripping the music from the confines of the disc and putting it into your computer. When Apple shipped iTunes and its first CD burners, and made music a key part of the "digital hub" strategy, the company adopted the slogan "Rip. Mix. Burn." to describe the process of copying music from your CDs, arranging it the way you like, and then creating your own custom CDs.

"Rip" reminds people of "rip off", as in "steal", which is much on the minds of sensitive folks trying to sell music during these turbulent days, and some people in the music biz were not happy with Apple's choice of words. The similarity between "rip" and "rip off" has caused more than a little confusion in the music business and in the press over the past few years. But when you take CDs you've bought, copy their music into your computer for your own use, there's no rip-off involved.

Keep Your Music CD-Quality

The music on a typical CD takes up 500 to 600MB of storage, or about 10MB per minute of music. If you stored music at that rate, it would consume a typical hard disk in a hurry. The development of the MP3 format was a milestone in the brief and recent history of digital audio. MP3 provided a way to take a hunk of music, sift through it, remove most of the data, and yet end up with something that sounds quite faithful to the original version. This process, called *encoding*, is what happens when you rip a CD with iTunes or any other program that creates MP3s. When an MP3 encoder gets through with a CD, it manages to produce music that takes up only about 10 percent of its original size, or 50 to 60MB per disc. A companion program called (surprise) a decoder is required to play back the music. Programs like iTunes usually have both encoders and decoders (players) built in.

In 2003, when Apple opened the iTunes Music Store, iTunes added support for a new format called AAC (Advanced Audio Coding), which Apple says produces files that sound better than MP3s. When you buy songs from the iTunes Music Store, they come in AAC format. And by the way, AAC allows Apple to add some restrictions to music files, which you can't easily do with MP3 files. These restrictions are the rules imposed by the iTunes Music Store: for example, tracks you buy can only be played on three different computers, and you can only burn the same playlist to CD ten times.

The hard part of encoding music is knowing which data can be thrown away without wrecking the sound. Over the years since the invention of MP3, encoders have gotten much more clever at this key task. One way to make your files sound better is by keeping more data and throwing away less. Both MP3 and AAC let you choose to make better sounding files by increasing the data rate, or the amount of information that's stored for every second of music. The typical rate is 128K bits per second of music. You improve the sound quality by using the iTunes preferences settings to increase the rate, all the way to a maximum of 320K bits per second. The higher the setting, the more disk space you use up. But if you have sensitive ears, you'll probably be glad to make this tradeoff.

Even if you use the highest compression rate, some people can clearly hear the difference between music played from CD and encoded (compressed) on a computer. If you're one of those cursed with marvelous hearing, rather than compressing your tracks, you can suck in the original full-length music from a CD to iTunes. All it will cost you is disk space.

You can easily tell iTunes to import your CDs without compression, using the WAV or AIFF format. To do so, perform the following steps:

1. Choose Preferences from the iTunes menu (Mac) or Edit menu (Windows).

2. Click the Importing tab.

3. Click the Import Using menu and choose WAV Encoder or AIFF Encoder.

4. Click OK.

From then on, whenever you insert a CD to be ripped, iTunes will simply copy the tracks from the CD without encoding them. The music will sound just like it does on CD, but it'll take up about 10 times the disk space that MP3 or AAC files do. Once you have imported WAV or AIFF files, iTunes and iPod play them happily.

How much will it cost you to keep all your music uncompressed? Not as much as it would have last year, and more than it will next year. In recent times, hard disks have gotten much bigger and much cheaper. You can now buy big disks for less than $1 per gigabyte (GB), which means you could store the uncompressed music from about 500 CDs for about $300 on a 300GB hard disk.

Do You Hear What I Hear?

Most music lovers (like me) are perfectly content with the quality of standard MP3 or AAC files. Other folks prefer to use one of the solutions for getting better quality, such as increasing the bit rate for MP3 or AAC encoding, or even using WAV or AIFF to copy the CD audio. For some audiophiles, though, CD quality and digital recording in general are a sonic disaster. Rock legend Neil Young might be the most famous critic of digital recording. He has said that digital recording lacks the warmth of analog, and that music has produced a generation of recordings that have lost quality forever because they're digital. So you can imagine what he thinks of MP3. In an interview a few years ago, Neil said that "CDs don't sound good no matter what you do," and "The MP3 is less than CD. I mean, MP3 is dog. The quality sucks. It's all compressed and the data compression—it's terrible."

You can read the text of the whole interview on the Web at `www.angelfire.com/rock2/traces/pages/kgsr.html`.

Add Files to Your Library by Dragging

The first time you start iTunes, it thoughtfully asks if you want it to scour the farthest reaches of your hard disk and look for music to add to your music library. You might decide to skip that step and gain greater control over which audio files go into your library. Whether you accept iTunes' offer to look for music or not, you can always add tunes at any time. When you rip a CD or buy songs from the iTunes Music Store, the new tunes are automatically added to your library.

What about getting other music into the library? You might have songs on your hard disk from some other source, or that somehow has been removed from the library. iTunes provides a couple of easy ways to get those songs into your library: with menu commands, or by using drag and drop. Here's how to use the menu commands:

1. On Macintosh, choose File ➪ Add to Library. On Windows, it's File ➪ Add File to Library.

2. In the dialog box that appears, choose a file on the disk that iTunes understands (MP3, AAC, WAV, or AIFF).

3. Click Choose (on Mac) or Open (on Windows) and iTunes will add it to the library.

You can add a bunch of tracks to the library at once if they're in the same folder:

1. On Macintosh, choose File ➪ Add to Library. On Windows, choose File ➪ Add Folder to Library.

2. In the dialog box, pick the folder that holds the music you want to add.

3. Click Choose (on Mac) or OK (on Windows) to select the folder. iTunes will search inside for music files and add them to the library.

When you're adding a whole folder at once, you don't even have to make sure all the files in the folder are valid music files—iTunes will happily ignore tone-deaf files.

By taking this folder-full feature to its logical extreme, you can get iTunes to add all the files on your hard disk by choosing the hard disk itself in the Add to Library or Add Folder to Library dialog box (see Figure 8-1).

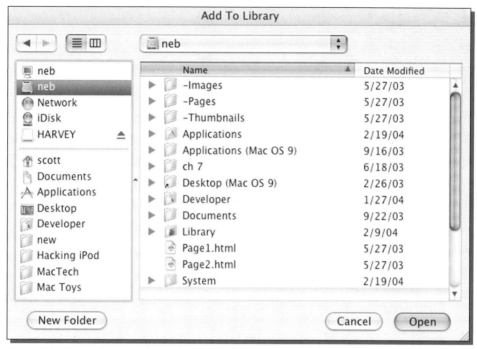

FIGURE 8-1: If you choose the hard disk itself, all files on the disk that iTunes can play are added to your music library.

As I mentioned, you can also use drag and drop to add files to your library. This works the same whether you're using Windows or a Mac: just drag a folder from a Finder or Explorer window to the iTunes window, and iTunes will find all the music files in the folder and put them in your collection.

Note that although you can drag your hard disk folder and add all the audio files on your computer to your iTunes library, you probably won't like the results. Your disk is filled with zillions of little sound effects, bits of narration from movies and lessons, and other bizarre chunks of sound. Unless you really want all of those in your library, avoid adding the entire hard disk.

Automate Your CD Ripping

Ripping CDs is a mindless process that ought to be as automatic as possible. All you want to do is just get the CD into the drive, copy the music and encode it in your choice of formats, then get the CD out and go on to the next. Wouldn't it be cool if you could hook up some kind of laser scanner to your computer, put your CDs nearby, and just tell the computer to rip everything? Well, as far as I know, that device is still a dream. But there are still a few steps you can take to make it easier on yourself before you dive into the job of ripping that massive stack of CDs.

Setting up iTunes

There are several settings you can take advantage of for massive bouts of ripping in iTunes. Here's what you do:

1. Open Preferences (that's in the iTunes menu on the Mac, and in the Edit menu on Windows).

2. Choose the General tab.

3. Click the "On CD Insert" menu and choose Import Songs and Eject (Figure 8-2).

   This setting ensures that when you put a CD in your computer, iTunes will do what you want: rip the songs, put them in your library, then eject the CD and make a little boodle-boot noise so you know it's time for the next one.

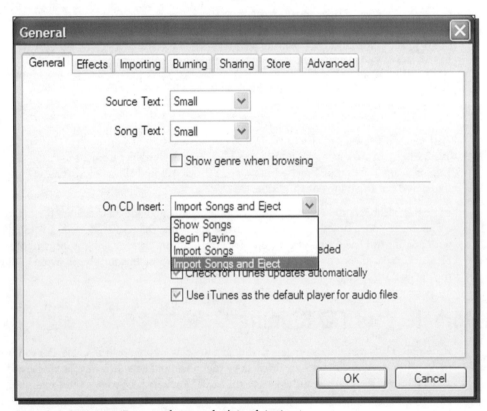

FIGURE 8-2: Setting up iTunes preferences for lots of ripping.

4. Also on the General tab, make sure "Connect to Internet when needed" is checked. This gives iTunes permission to look up the CD and track names when you insert a disc.

5. Click the Importing tab.

6. Make sure "Play songs while importing" is turned off.

If you're doing bulk ripping, you probably don't want to listen to the songs as you're adding them.

Best hardware

If you have a choice of computers you're going to use for ripping, there are several points to consider that will smooth the process. These include computer speed, loading mechanism on the CD drive, and whether you have more than one computer handy.

First, and most obviously, use the fastest machine you can spare. The encoding process requires the computer to do a lot of thinking, so the faster the computer, the quicker the ripping. Don't worry about whether that's the computer that you'll be using to actually play the music. You can copy ripped files from one computer to another.

A computer with a slot-loading CD drive, like the CD player in a car, will save you lots of time and hand fatigue. Most recent Apple laptops come with this handy device, as do some desktop models.

Finally, try to do your CD ripping on a machine that's not the one you're doing other work on at the same time. Even though iTunes is very good at ripping CDs in the background while you work, you'll find it more convenient if the ripping is happening on a secondary computer. You really did want a new computer anyway, didn't you?

Doing the ripping

Once you've set the iTunes preferences on your best (spare) computer, the one with the slot-loading CD drive, you're ready to go. Insert the first CD and let 'er rip. You can watch as iTunes tracks the progress of the CD being ripped, but unless you have huge amounts of free time on your hands, you'll want to be doing something else while waiting for the encoding to finish. When it's done, the computer will make a happy sound and eject the CD.

Once in a while, when you insert a CD, iTunes will report that it can't get the CD's track name information from the Gracenote CDDB service. If this happens, it's usually a momentary glitch with the service. You can have iTunes try again by going to the Advanced menu and choosing Get CD Track Names. That will usually fix the problem. But if not, you'll have to stop and manually enter the CD and track names by selecting tracks and choosing File ➪ Get Info, This is an annoying process, but if you don't do it, you'll be left with a bunch of unnamed tracks.

FIGURE 8-3: If you insert a CD that has already been imported into the iTunes library, you'll get this helpful message.

If you have to enter track names manually, or there are any other problems that cause you to stop and start the ripping process, such as a CD that isn't seated properly, you might have to click the Import button in the upper right to get things going again, and you might have to eject the CD manually when it's done. It's OK, the exercise will be good for you.

Despite your studious attention to the task, you might find yourself mixed up about whether you have already ripped a particular CD or not. There's a quick and easy way to find out. Just go ahead and insert the CD. When iTunes sees the CD, before starting to rip, it checks to see if the CD is already in its library. If so, you'll get a message like the one in Figure 8-3, pointing out that it's already in there and asking whether you really want to rip it again. Pretty cool!

Rip City

Maybe you would rather not bother with the task of ripping all your CDs. If so, you'll be happy to know that you can throw money at the problem. A service called RipDigital will take your CDs and perform the manual labor of ripping them, to your specifications, and then ship the CDs back to you along with external hard disks or DVDs containing your ripped tunes. RipDigital charges about a buck per CD in quantity. For more information, check out the company's Web site at www.ripdigital.com.

Get All Your Music Together in One Place

If you love music and you have more than one computer, or even one computer with more than one hard disk, you might find yourself with music scattered across various places as you scramble for nooks in which to store your digitized tunes. This can also happen if you use one computer for ripping and a different one for playing music. With some file copying and the help of a little-used iTunes command, you can easily collect all your music together on one hard disk, as long as you have enough space on that one disk.

The first step in getting your music together is to make sure that it's all on disks that are connected to the computer you use for playing. It doesn't matter whether the songs are scattered across multiple hard disks or not. For best results, you should use drives that are either internal or externally connected, rather than any network volumes.

Once you have all your musical disk drives connected to one computer, verify that all your music is in the iTunes library. If it's not, your very next act should be to get the music into your library. Use the File ⇨ Add to Library menu item, or just drag and drop it in, if you prefer the direct method.

iTunes keeps track of the location of every music file that's represented in its library. To unite all your tunes on one drive, you could move files manually, remove them from the library (because the library items are now pointing at the old locations), and then add them back in. Gee, that sound tedious and error-prone! Luckily for us, iTunes has yet another really cool feature that helps us out: Consolidate Library. If you choose Consolidate Library in the Advanced menu, iTunes will brilliantly copy all your music to one place, the iTunes Music folder. Your music, previously scattered to the four winds, will come together in one place, creating peace and harmony.

To see how this works, take a look at Figure 8-4, which depicts a bunch of music scattered around a disk in various folders.

In iTunes, we choose Advanced ⇨ Consolidate Library, and iTunes copies all your music into the iTunes Music folder and organizes it by artist and album. Figure 8-5 shows the same music library after it's been consolidated.

Your Main Library

When you add music to iTunes CDs by ripping or buying songs from the music store, the files are stored in a particular folder on your hard disk. By default, iTunes uses /Music/iTunes/iTunes Music/ on Mac OS X and \My Documents\My Music\iTunes\iTunes Music on Windows. If you prefer to specify your own choice of folders before consolidating your library, just open Preferences in iTunes, click the Advanced tab, and click Change... to select the folder you want.

Merge Tracks from Live CDs

Having all your music in iTunes is like owning a magical jukebox. One of the best features of this jukebox is the ability to achieve almost instant gratification by listening to any song you want to hear, just by searching or browsing for the name of the song or artist.

Some CDs aren't particularly well suited to song-at-a-time listening. For example, it's more fun to listen to CDs made of live concerts from beginning to end rather than by plucking

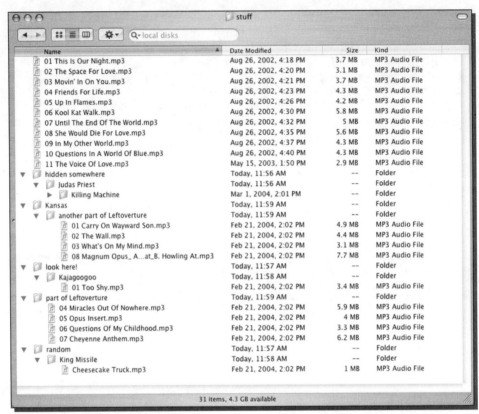

FIGURE 8-4: Before using Consolidate Library, music is in various folders with no particular pattern.

out individual songs. Side 2 of The Beatles' "*Abbey Road*" is basically one long composition. But when you rip a CD into iTunes, song-at-a-time is what you get. And, when you play songs back in iTunes, there's a gap between songs that you can't get rid of, unlike a CD, which flows smoothly even when switching from one track to the next. This gap, which is a consequence of the encoding process and has been around to annoy iTunes users since the beginning, messes up the flow of live CDs or multi-track compositions, as you have to pause for a beat in between tracks.

There is a way to remove the gap and play adjacent tracks, or even an entire CD, without pause. You have to take action at the time your rip the CD. Here's how it goes:

1. If you have iTunes set to automatically rip CDs when they're inserted, turn that off. Go to Preferences, click the General tab, and choose Show Songs from the "On CD Insert:" menu. Click OK.

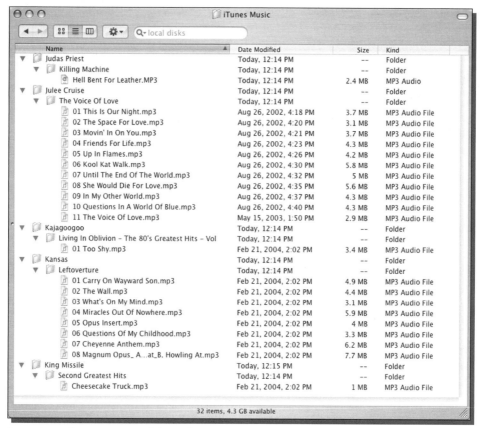

FIGURE 8-5: After using Consolidate Library, music is copied to the iTunes Music folder and organized according to artist and album.

2. Insert the CD you want to rip. The CD should appear in the iTunes source list, with its tracks listed to the right.

3. Figure out which tracks you want to hear without a gap. To select them, click the first, then shift-click the last.

4. Pull down the Advanced menu and choose Join CD Tracks. Your song list should look like the one in Figure 8-6.

5. Click Import to rip the tracks on the CD. The joined tracks will be ripped, glued together, and placed in your iTunes library as one track. The new track's name will be the names of all the joined songs, with hyphens between them. If you join all the tracks on the CD, the name will be the CD's name. Of course, you can rename the track once it's been ripped.

FIGURE 8-6: When you insert a CD and join tracks together, you can see the individual track names with a line connecting the joined tracks.

Note

iTunes has a feature called *Crossfade playback* which plays the last part of the current song at a decreasing volume level while playing the first part of the next song at an increasing volume. This effect is similar to joined tracks, but not the same. The Crossfade playback setting is on the Effects tab of iTunes preferences.

When you play the joined tracks from your library, you'll hear them one after the other without any gap, just as if you were playing them from CD. Of course, you won't be able to access them individually in your library. If you want to have it both ways, you can gain the ultimate flexibility by ripping the CD twice: once without any joining, and once with some tracks joined. That will give you entries in your library for all the songs individually, as well as the version that plays through the songs without any gaps.

If you've already ripped the tracks without joining them, and you're using a Mac, you can stitch the tunes together again using the audio features of Apple's iMovie, as follows:

1. In iMovie, click the Audio button.

2. Drag the first tune you want to use from the song list on the right to the timeline at the bottom of the screen.

3. Drag the playhead (that's the cursor with the inverted pointer at the top) all the way to the right.

4. Select the next song and click Place at Playhead (Figure 8-7).

5. If you want to add more songs, repeat steps 3 and 4 for each one.

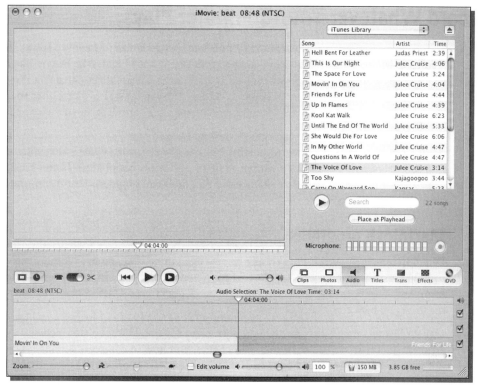

FIGURE 8-7: Songs imported into iMovie, one after the other.

6. Choose File ➪ Share.

7. Click the QuickTime tab.

8. Choose "Expert Settings" from the "Compress movie for" pop-up menu and click Share.

9. In the "Save exported file as" dialog box, choose "Sound to AIFF" from the "Export" pop-up and click Save.

When the file is done being exported, you can add it to your iTunes library and you'll be able to enjoy the tracks one after the other, although you might hear minor "seams" where the songs were glued together.

Note The steps here are for iMovie 4. You can do the same thing in iMovie 3, although some of the menus and dialogs have different names. In particular, the Share command has the less utopian name Export.

Record Whatever Your Computer Plays

This section is about one of the most flexible ways to get music into your iTunes library: recording whatever audio you can convince your computer to play. Maybe you like to listen to streaming audio. Lots of cool radio stations broadcast their signals on the Internet. Many popular commercial radio stations are available this way. Other sources of streaming audio are Web sites for musical artists, song samplers on sites that sell music, and online music stores.

All these streaming services are wonderful, but one problem with them is that you can't save the recordings—you can only listen to them, and then they're gone. In this hack, we'll discuss some very cool tools that neatly solve that problem: programs that record the audio your computer is playing.

Macintosh programs

WireTap is a cool program that simply records everything that you hear coming out of your Mac's speaker. This wonderful application is available for an incredible price—free—from Ambrosia Software. WireTap provides an eloquent user interface, most of which you see in Figure 8-8. Yep, that's all there is!

If that's just too simple for you and you want more control, WireTap also includes a preferences panel that lets you set values like whether and how to compress sounds, where to put recorded files, what to name them, and which application should be used to play them back. Because WireTap saves standard audio files, iTunes is happy to play them for you. You can even add them to playlists and ship them off to your iPod.

WireTap is wonderful and free, but you should also check out Audio Hijack and Audio Hijack Pro, published by Rogue Amoeba Software. These nifty programs have a bunch more features you can use when recording audio on your Mac. You can record from specific applications only, start and stop recording at predetermined times, and add DSP effects to your recorded files. You can also record directly to MP3 files. Audio Hijack Pro

FIGURE 8-8: WireTap's user interface is about as simple as you can get. There are buttons to start recording, pause, and stop. The window tells you if WireTap is recording, paused, or idle, and displays the length and file size of the current recording.

is $30, and Audio Hijack, which doesn't have quite as many cool tweaks, costs $16. Both have free demo versions. Like the other programs described here, they're all available at download.com.

Windows programs

If you're running Windows, you have it both better and worse than your Mac pals: better because you have more choices for recording programs, most of which have plenty of features; worse, because the programs all cost money, and none is as elegant and easy to use as WireTap. C'est la vie.

SoundCapture from MagicSofts has a wacky user interface and documentation written in a language that's not quite English, but it's easy to use and creates MP3 files directly, at various configurable quality settings. SoundCapture is free to try, and costs $10 to register.

All Recorder is another utility for recording sounds your PC is playing, but does a lot of other stuff too. For example, All Recorder opens MP3 files directly and lets you edit sound files by selecting a hunk of sound and saving it to its own separate file. You can add effects like tremolo and reverb to files, or even play songs in reverse to check for satanic messages. (For a big fun example, play the introduction to "Fire On High" by Electric Light Orchestra in reverse.) There's a free trial version of All Recorder that only records 30 seconds at a time. The full version is $30.

Advanced MP3/WMA Recorder by Xaudio Tools, as its name implies, will create Windows Media Audio files as well as MP3s. It doesn't have all the editing features of All Recorder, but its interface is clean and simple, and it seemed to produce fewer clicks and pops in its output. And hey, it's skinnable! (That means you can change the way it looks, for those who missed the height of this nutty trend a few years ago.) The free trial version is limited to recording 60 seconds at a time, and the full version costs $30, which seems to be the going rate for tools like this on Windows. You can see Advanced MP3/WMA Recorder in Figure 8-9.

FIGURE 8-9: Advanced MP3/WMA Recorder, which has a long, prosaic name, provides a clean interface that makes it look a lot like a mere music player.

If you're using Windows, be sure to quit the recorder application before you play back files with iTunes. Having a recorder running seems to add crackly sound to anything that's playing. As with WireTap and Audio Hijack, all the Windows recording programs we've discussed in this section can create MP3 or WAV files, which you can then feed into iTunes. And once again, all these programs are available at download.com.

If you're interested in recording streaming audio and you want to find out more cool stuff you can do, see the section *Convert Streams to Songs*, which discusses how you can create individual songs while recording Internet radio stations.

Hacking the Culture: Music store construction kit

The iTunes Music Store wasn't the first attempt to sell digital music online. Before Apple opened its virtual storefront in April 2003, there were several attempts to entice music lovers into legitimacy and reliability, and away from free file-sharing programs. But services such as Rhapsody and Pressplay treated the paying customers warily, with severe restrictions on downloading and burning songs, and odious requirements such as membership fees just to buy and keep stuff. Apple got past all that and simplified things with its policies of 99 cents per song, three computers per account, and virtually unlimited CD burning and iPod use, along with making the store extremely easy to use. Apple's store was considered revolutionary at the time because it cut through the daunting red tape of music industry contracts and egos, which were tougher problems to solve than any technical issues.

Once Apple established a successful formula, others started to copy it, repeating the history of a lot of other innovations in the personal computer industry over the past 25 years or so. Existing music stores were redesigned, and new ones started to appear, almost all with only slight variations on the standards Apple set.

Late in 2003, Microsoft announced that it would be working with another company, Loudeye, to sell prebuilt online music stores to anybody who wants to open one. They set up the software, they provide prenegotiated contracts with music publishers, and you get to put your name on the service. In less than 8 months, Apple's revolutionary store had become virtually a commodity. Can Apple continue to be the leader? Only by continuing to do what it has always done when it's been successful: innovating to stay ahead.

Convert Streams to Songs

Streaming radio is a great way to discover eclectic, non-commercial, obscure music. Using the built-in radio tuner in iTunes, you can explore dozens of Internet-only radio stations in categories ranging from pop to classical to religious. In the section *Record Whatever Your Computer Plays*, we talked about saving streamed music to your hard disk so you can enjoy it any time in iTunes or on your iPod. In this hack, we'll go one step beyond: we'll discuss tools that not only record streaming music, but also slice it up into its component songs for you, almost like magic.

How does it work? When Internet radio stations broadcast their music, most of them also send along information about the songs they're playing, such as the name of the song and artist. When you're tuned to an Internet station, iTunes uses this information to show you what's playing. Clever programmers have written applications that tap into this data to find out when one song ends and the next one begins so that they can save the streamed music as separate songs. They use the artist and track information to label the saved songs.

On Windows, you'll use StreamRipper32 or RipCast. If you have a Mac, you should get RadioLover. Whether you have a PC or a Mac, you can find radio stations by using the Radio icon in the iTunes source list. But that's not all—there are hundreds more radio stations on the Internet. See *Listen to Streaming Radio* in Chapter 5 to find out all about this subject.

Windows programs

StreamRipper32 is a free program for recording streaming radio stations and saving the results as individual song files. StreamRipper provides a rather geeky interface (remember, it's a free program!) that lets you connect to streaming radio stations and record their streams. It includes a directory of `Shoutcast.com` stations so you can pick the one you want.

For more features and a better user interface, check out RipCast from Xoteck Software. Figure 8-10 shows RipCast as it records music and displays a list of what it's already procured for you.

RipCast has Internet Explorer built in, which makes it easy to connect to `Shoutcast.com` streams. Once you've connected to your favorite station, RipCast starts recording tunes to disk as MP3 files, tagging each file with the name of the song and the artist. Cool! You can set up timed recordings so you don't have to wake up at 3:00 a.m. to record your favorite shows. And RipCast really takes advantage of your Internet connection: it can record multiple streams at the same time. There's a free demo version of RipCast, which limits you to 30MB of downloading before it hits you up for money. The full version removes the download limitation and costs $18.

Macintosh programs

The most popular Mac OS X application for recording streaming radio and splitting it into songs is RadioLover (`www.bitcartel.com/radiolover`). This program is a descendent of the Mac version of StreamRipper. RadioLover works in conjunction with iTunes. You start by selecting the radio tuner in iTunes and clicking one or more genre items to display the names of stations. Then, you switch over to RadioLover and pick a station to tune. You can listen while you're recording, or just record the songs silently. This is handy if

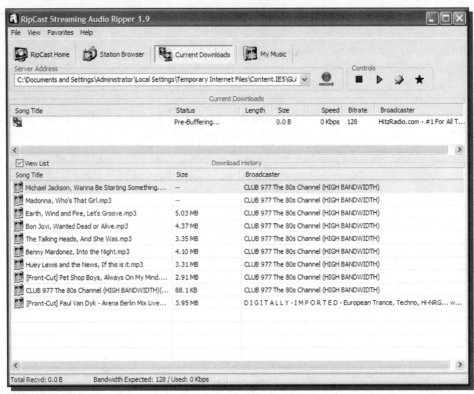

FIGURE 8-10: RipCast can record more than one stream at a time, and it can show you the list of what it has recorded.

you're ripping streams while talking to your agent on the phone negotiating your new multi-million dollar recording contract.

You can use RadioLover to record multiple stations at the same time, although you need a beefy network connection to make sure you have enough bandwidth for that. Like RipCast on Windows, RadioLover has a timer feature so you can schedule recordings in advance. RadioLover costs a modest $15. You can use it without paying, but it stops recording every 30 minutes.

Making adjustments

As Internet radio stations broadcast their music, they send information about the next song just as it's about to start playing. That's how the programs in this section know when to start a file for a new song. Sometimes the timing is a little off, which results in a little bit of the start of song B getting tacked onto the end of song A. To correct this annoying problem, the recording programs include settings that let you specify how long to wait after the new song info is detected before splitting off a new file. With a little tweaking, you should be able to get songs split just right when recording from your favorite stations.

Get LPs into iTunes

Once upon a time, music came on big black vinyl platters. They were called LP records, and they weren't that good, but we didn't know any better. If you're a person of a certain age, you probably have a few crates of LPs somewhere, and you haven't listened to them in years. You could pay 99 cents a track to buy them all over again at the iTunes Music Store, but that's not very economical, and many old tracks aren't available in digital form.

Instead, why not look into digitizing your LPs and getting them into iTunes? The process is relatively inexpensive and straightforward, although it is time-consuming. The basic steps:

- Connect the output from a turntable (that's sort of an LP-ROM drive, kids) to the input of your sound card or sound capture hardware, such as the iMic (www.griffintechnology.com).

- Record the LP with sound capture software, such as Peak for Macintosh (www.bias-inc.com) or Adobe Audition for Windows (www.adobe.com/products/audition/main.html).

- Use your sound capture software to split the files into songs.

- Enjoy your new old music!

For more on to ripping LPs into digital files, see www.techtv.com/callforhelp/howto/ story/0,24330,3333231,00.html . If you're going to use a Macintosh for the process, I highly recommend Chapter 9, "Convert Your Old Vinyl LPs to CDs" in the book *Mac Toys*, published by Wiley, ISBN 0-764-54351-2. (Full disclosure: I wrote *Mac Toys* with John Rizzo. But that chapter really is the best, most detailed treatment of this subject I've ever seen, and I didn't even write it—John Rizzo, my co-author on *Mac Toys*, did.)

Rip Stubborn CDs

One of the great things about getting your music into iTunes is that digital songs never wear out, unlike CDs (and, of course, vinyl records). Once you've got your music ripped, you have it forever, assuming you're diligent about backing up your hard disk, just in case.

Once in a while, when you dig out an ancient CD and serve it up to iTunes for importing, the process doesn't go smoothly. The ripping slows down, or even stops entirely, and the

CD starts making scary clicking or wobbling noises as it spins around in the CD drive. Yikes! What can you do?

The first trick to try is simply cleaning the CD, just as you would if it failed to play in a regular CD player. Take the CD out and examine it under a light. Be sure you look at the silver side—the bottom—because that's the business end, where the music is stored. You'll often see a fingerprint or other hunk of goo, which you can clean off with a tissue or similar delicate article. When you put the CD back in the drive, make sure it's firmly seated on the spindle (if your computer doesn't have one of those slick slot-loading drives).

If you've made sure your CD is sparkling clean, you've snapped it firmly into place, and it still balks at being imported, there's one more trick to try. Go to iTunes preferences, click the Importing tab, and turn on "Use error correction when reading Audio CDs". This feature will get iTunes to try its best to figure out what's on the CD so you don't have to live without an old favorite.

Get Legal Free Tracks

There has been a lot of press the past couple of years, and plenty of lawsuits, about shady ways to get free music by using file sharing networks. But while courts, record companies, and governments battle that out, you might be surprised to learn that there are plenty of fully legitimate sources of excellent free tracks on the Web, mostly available as MP3s. You'll find obscure and rare tracks by big commercial artists, first efforts from bands you've never heard of, and very old but good tracks. This hack tells you about how to get your hands on some of that music.

Most of the sources in this section understand that MP3 is the standard for exchanging free music tracks, so they provide their wares in that format for you to download. Other sites, most often the more commercial ones, put their stuff in proprietary formats, such as RealAudio or Windows Media Audio. These often have restrictions: either they're only streamed and not downloadable, or they have digital rights restrictions, such as a 30-day expiration date. Some only work on Windows. As long as you can get them to play at all, you can always use one of the audio recording programs discussed in "*Record Whatever Your Computer Plays*", elsewhere in this chapter.

The Web sources in this section are divided into the following broad categories:

- Many artists provide free MP3s for downloading on their Web sites. You can often grab whole songs from albums or unreleased live tracks.

- Lots of record companies—especially the more enlightened ones—take advantage of the Web by offering MP3 tunes by their artists. Labels that are far from the mainstream and don't get their records played on the radio are fond of this practice.

- Other commercial sites, such as `Amazon.com` and MTV, provide a selection of free music for you. Some non-commercial sites have free music, too.

We'll take a look at each of these groups. There's no way this can be a comprehensive list, of course, with tens of thousands of artists and record companies posting music for you to enjoy. You can easily kill a few hours or an entire day discovering new music this way, and it's free!

Artists

The best way to find out if a particular band provides free music downloads is to check it out yourself. Use a search engine, such as Google, to find an artist's site, then see what you can find. Even if you thought you had everything ever recorded by your favorite band The Obscuros, you might be surprised to see some rare or live tracks available on their Web site. And as you go surfing through your favorite artists' sites, be sure not to go blind watching all that groovy Flash animation they insist on foisting upon you to show you how cool they are.

We'll list a few artist sites here just to get your started.

- Janis Ian, who has spoken out about how much downloadable music has helped her career, provides music for you at
  `http://www.janisian.com/mp3_downloads.html`.

- They Might Be Giants have done a lot of pioneering work in distributing digital music. They serve up a good collection of nifty free tunes at `www.theymight-begiants.com/ mp3.shtml`. And don't miss They Might Be Giants Clock

FIGURE 8-11: They Might Be Giants Clock Radio has three stations: one that plays rare tracks, another for live music, and an Emergency Broadcast System that streams the latest cool news and stuff. Plus, because it's a clock radio, it tells the time!

Radio, an incredibly cool free toy that sits on your desktop and streams music to you from several channels. Figure 8-11 has a picture of the TMBG Clock Radio, which you can download by going to www.tmbg.com and clicking the clock radio in the upper right.

- The princess of pop—or is she the queen by now?—Britney Spears offers music on her site, www.britneyspears.com. There's a jukebox that has mostly 30-second clips, but some full songs as well. Keen.

- Some artists, such as Guster, Sonic Youth, and Madonna, stream their music to you while you're on their sites. You can use recording software such as WireTap or All Recorder to save the music so you can listen later.

- R.E.M. gives away exclusive remixed tracks at www.remhq.com/shared_assets/ extras/remix/remixFLASH/remix.html.

- There's free music from Journey and its members at www.journeymusic.com/ themusic/multimedia.html.

- Find John Mellencamp tracks, especially from recent albums, at www.mellencamp.com/albums.htm.

- The Grateful Dead has never stopped its fans from trading live recordings. Find more live Grateful Dead music than you can possibly imagine at www.gdlive.com/ deadmp3.asp. Also, see the following sidebar "*Live music is better*".

- If you like Crosby, Stills, Nash, and Young, don't miss the download page at www.4waysite.com/download/mp3.html. And you'll probably enjoy the rest of the site, too.

- Rage Against the Machine's former front man Zack de la Rocha has a site at www.marchofdeath.com where you can check out his recent music.

- Sampling pioneers Negativland have lots of cool freebies at www.negativland.com/audiogadgets.html.

- Discover some excellent music you might not know about at John McCutcheon's site, www.folkmusic.com/f_mp3.htm.

- For something that's probably *very* different from what you usually listen to, check out Hamsa Lila at www.hamsalila.com/audio.html.

- Finally, be sure to get some funny stuff. Try MC Frontalot and MC Hawking, two of the nerdiest rappers you'll ever hear, at http://www.frontalot.com/ music.html and www.mchawking.com/multimedia.php?page_function=mp3z. And don't miss the wacky tunes of Strong Bad and the gang at www.homestarrunner.com/homester.html.

Record companies

Lots of smart record companies have figured out that offering free MP3s on the Web is a great way to promote their bands. Here are some record label sites for you to check out:

- Rhino Records has lots of cool releases, and you can get some free tracks from them at `www.rhino.com/fun/downloads.lasso`. Unfortunately, the free songs stop working after 30 days (they're Windows Media Audio).

- Find various free MP3s from Matador Records at `www.matadorrecords.com`.

- You can get tunes from well-known artists like Steve Earle, Warren Zevon, and the Reverend Horton Heat at `www.artemisrecords.com/downloads.aspx`.

- Lookout Records has more free MP3s than most record companies. They're available at `www.lookoutrecords.com/sounds`.

- Check out tracks from Tom Waits, Joe Strummer, and others at `www.anti.com`.

- Visit Blind Pig Records at `www.blindpigrecords.com/contact.html` to download songs from that company's artists, including Reneé Austin.

- The eclectic label Telarc has a bunch of free tunes for you. Go to `www.telarc.com` and click the link to Free Digital Downloads.

- Clear Blue Records is one of many small labels that lets you download MP3s so you can hear how its artists sound. For example, try the Style Kings: `www.clear-bluerecords.com/stylekings/songs.html`.

You can use a search engine to find hundreds more record companies on the Web, most of which offer some free music to download. You can also peruse the list of record labels at `singer-songwriter.com/resource/resource.php3?offset=0&r=record`.

Web sites

If you do any shopping on the Web, you've probably bought stuff from `Amazon.com`. Even if you're a regular Amazon visitor, you might not know that Amazon serves up thousands of free tunes for your enjoyment, a practice the *San Francisco Chronicle* compared to having "a dish of penny candy at the sales counter". The free songs at Amazon are in a section called Music Downloads. Most are MP3s. To get there, go to `Amazon.com`, click See More Stores on the navigation bar, click Music (it's under Books, Music, DVD), then click Free Downloads in the second navigation bar that appears at the top of the page. Once you're there, you'll get a page that looks something like what you see in Figure 8-12.

The ArtistDirect site at `www.artistdirect.com` has a massive collection of information about thousands of bands, and downloadable songs for many of them. Just search by band or click the Downloads link at the top. AristDirect has a few quirks; some of the

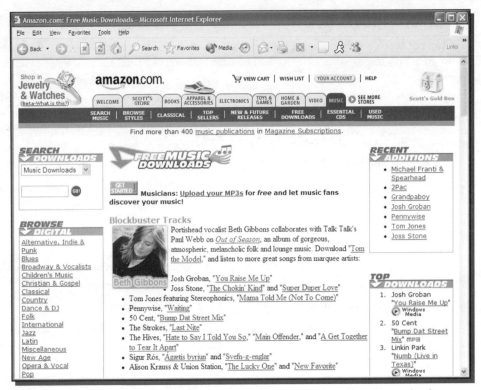

FIGURE 8-12: `Amazon.com` is best known for selling stuff, but it also offers thousands of songs for free in its Music Downloads section.

songs labeled as "downloads" are actually streamed, not downloadable, and some of MP3s have their links hidden so you can't easily download them.

Emusic has tons—or even megatons—of MP3s. The only catch is that you have to sign up for a free trial, and then you start paying once the free trial is up. Go to www.emusic.com to find out more.

Apple sells music creation software called GarageBand, but `GarageBand.com` had the name first. This site, which has the tagline "Discovering the best independent music", has tens of thousands of free tunes for you to download.

Microsoft is keenly interested in the music business, and the company uses its Windows Media site to offer free downloads. Naturally, the songs come in Windows Media Audio format, which you can't play in iTunes or on an iPod, but you can convert them to MP3 or capture them with a recorder program like All Recorder. Go to `windowsmedia.com/mediaguide/ThisWeekInMusic/Downloads` for more information.

As you might expect, MTV provides free song downloads. The MTV site is at www.mtv.com/music/downloads.

Finally, when you're in the mood to discover eclectic music that you haven't heard before, try www.epitonic.com and www.peoplesounds.com. These sites collect music from hundreds of independent bands and provide songs for you to download. Check 'em out!

Live Music Is Better

Many music fans take part in recording and trading live concerts. Without the band's permission, this is illegal, and you shouldn't do it. Some acts, such as Pearl Jam, try to head off this practice by producing huge numbers of live recordings. On the other hand, the Grateful Dead famously encourages taping and trading, as long as there's no financial gain, and even sets aside seating areas for those recording their shows.

Summary

The obvious ways to get songs into iTunes, ripping CDs and buying tunes from the iTunes Music Store, aren't the only ways. In this chapter, we discussed lots of other sources for music. Take advantage of free songs on the Web, manipulate the tracks on CDs to get just the right format, and discover whole new kinds of music with streaming radio. The more time you spend looking for all the music that's available to you, the more you'll be rewarded by finding great tunes that you didn't even know existed.

Coming up next in Chapter 9, we'll talk about cool things you can do to get music away from your computer and into the world at large. We'll discuss burning CDs and DVDs full of music, dragging songs out of iTunes, and backing up your music.

Music Out: Burning and Beyond

iTunes is a haven for your music, not a prison. Whenever you want, you can borrow your songs from iTunes so they can go with you out into the world, not just in an iPod, but also on CDs and DVDs. In this chapter, we'll talk about hacks and tricks you can use to make your music better and more accessible as you get it out of iTunes.

When consumer CDs first appeared in the early 1980s, they were meant as a replacement for vinyl records and prerecorded cassettes. The industry had to apologize for the fact that people couldn't record their own CDs—that simply wasn't what the technology was invented for, and it would probably never be possible, they said. But demand proved to be a powerful motivator, and CD recording—or *burning*, a much more colorful term—became a national pastime.

Apple missed out on the start of the CD burning obsession. Apple was one of the last major computer companies to include CD burners in its machines. This is especially ironic for several reasons: Apple was a big booster of CD-ROMs when they first appeared; while he was at NeXT Computer, Apple CEO Steve Jobs introduced the first computer that had *only* an optical drive; and given Apple's strong position in digital music now, you would have guessed the company got an early start on trends like CD burning. They didn't, but they seem to be all caught up now.

iTunes is best known for a few key features: playing music, importing tunes from CD, buying songs from the iTunes Music Store, and burning CDs. Although you probably know all about burning your own CDs to play in the car or the living room stereo, there's a lot more you can do with your music. In this chapter, we'll discuss cool and sometimes useful features for getting the music from iTunes onto optical discs and beyond.

in this chapter

- ☑ Use MP3 to Make a 12-Hour CD

- ☑ Make a Mix DVD

- ☑ Create Gapless Music CDs

- ☑ Burn as Many Songs as You Want

- ☑ Change the "Volume Up" and "Volume Down" Sounds

- ☑ Back Up Your Music

Use MP3 to Make a 12-Hour CD

Hey, kids! Not to sound like an old guy here, but back in the day, records were records, and record players played them. The only format differences you had to worry about were turntable revolution speed (33 1/3, 45, or 78 revolutions per minute [RPM]) and the physical size of records. You might have thought that digital music would make format differences easier to deal with. If so, you would have been wrong. Format wars and convenience factors have made dealing with digital music trickier than it ought to be.

Standard CDs, like the ones you buy from record stores, cause few problems. They'll play in almost any consumer CD players, like the ones in your car, bedroom, or bathroom, and they work in your computers, usually, although unpleasant copy protection schemes sometimes interfere with that. The latest technology allows standard audio CDs to hold up to 80 minutes of music. The CDs you burn on CD-R discs with iTunes are like this: they can hold up to 80 minutes of music and will play in most CD players.

Meanwhile, while we've been learning to play and burn audio CDs, Apple and the rest of the digital music industry have been training us to love MP3s. As you probably know, the main innovation provided by the MP3 format is that it manages to squish music down to about a tenth of its size while still sounding a lot like the original: CD music takes up about 10 megabytes per minute, while MP3s only use about 1 megabyte per minute. That's one of the reasons we can fit so many songs onto our hard disks and iPods.

When you burn a CD, the music is inflated back to the larger size. That's because most CD players only understand CDs with music in that format. But what if you could put MP3-sized files onto a CD, then listen to them in your CD player? Because MP3s are about a tenth the size of their full-audio counterparts, you would be able to get 12 hours of music or more onto a single CD. Using a feature of iTunes and the right CD player, you can actually make this happen. (The precise length of time you can fit onto a CD depends on the particular songs you choose.)

To make this work, you need two things: a CD player that can read and play the disc, and a way to burn a CD full of MP3 music. The first part, finding a compatible CD player, requires a little investment, but the second part, burning the CD, is cheap. Many CD players for homes and cars, especially newer models, are smart enough to understand a disc filled with MP3s. You can play MP3s on CD players from Alpine, Sony, Aiwa, Kenwood, Panasonic, JVC, and many others. You might have to shop a bit for a new player, but you can find MP3-capable CD players in all price ranges, starting at less than $100.

iTunes makes it simple to burn a CD full of MP3s. Here's how you do it. First, you need to make a playlist containing the songs you want to put on the CD. Then, pull down the iTunes menu (Mac) or Edit menu (Windows) and choose Preferences. Click the Burning tab. In the Disc Format section, choose MP3 CD and click OK. The next time you proceed to burn a CD, iTunes will create a CD filled with MP3s instead of full-audio music. You can play that CD on a computer or on an MP3-savvy CD player.

Before you rush out and buy a new CD player to listen to your 12-hour discs, hang on for a second. You might already own one. If your CD player is new-ish, it might be MP3-capable. You can find out for sure by burning an MP3 CD, as described earlier, and then putting it into your CD player. If it starts playing, you're a winner. If your player just sort of sits there and looks at you as if to say "What did you just feed me?", it's a strong clue that you'll need to look into getting a new CD player if you want to use this hack.

Safe at Any Speed

Dealing with various music formats is nothing new. If you're too young to remember vinyl records, you probably didn't know that they were made to spin around turntables at either 33 1/3, 45, or 78 RPM. And if you, like Eddie Vedder of Pearl Jam, do have some classic vinyl stashed around, you might wonder why those values were chosen.

Early records (before vinyl) were designed for playback at speeds between 64 and 100 RPM—there was no universal value. You had to set your gramophone differently for each recording. There are various stories about how 78 RPM came to be a standard. One theory says that the British Gramophone Company decided on 78 RPM based on listening tests performed with their record catalog, while another account claims that inventor Eldridge Johnson had created a sewing machine mechanism that rotated at 78 RPM, and this technology was adapted for gramophone use.

The first 33⅓ RPM records were developed in conjunction with sound films. The film reels ran for about 10 minutes, so engineers needed to double the five minutes available on a 78 RPM record. Projectionists played the sound records along with the film, and you could hear what the actors were saying.

RCA Victor developed the 45 RPM standard for popular vinyl records in the 1940s. Supposedly, this speed creates an acceptable balance between recording quality and music capacity.

Now, of course, we don't have to worry about any of this stuff—unless you count MP3, AAC, Windows Media Audio, Ogg Vorbis, AIFF, WAV, and many others. When it comes to having lots of music formats, the more things change, the more they stay the same.

For more on this subject, see the article at `members.tripod.com/~Vinylville/spindoc.html`.

Make a Mix DVD

 Note This hack is Mac-only

iTunes is part of Apple's iLife set of programs—as Apple says, iLife is "like Microsoft Office for the rest of your life." The other programs in iLife let you manage your photos (iPhoto), make and edit your own videos and DVDs (iMovie and iDVD), and create your own music (GarageBand). One of the coolest features of iLife is the integration between the applications. Because all the programs know about each other, and their information is stored in well-known places, they can do some neat tricks together. For example, you can make a slide show in iPhoto, using a playlist from iTunes as the soundtrack, or you can compose music in GarageBand starting with an iTunes track.

There are plenty of ways for the iLife applications to work together, and amazingly, Apple hasn't yet thought of them all. They're trying, though. Just about the same time as Apple shipped iLife 04 in January 2004, it also released a free application called Playlist to DVD (clearly, the Clever Names section of the marketing department is not responsible for that one). This program is a cool tool if you have a Mac with a DVD-burning SuperDrive.

Playlist to DVD takes a playlist of your favorite tunes and burns a DVD that plays those songs, complete with real DVD menus, a "now playing" display, and a list of upcoming songs. Your disc can contain up to 90 minutes of music. The DVD you make doesn't need a computer—it will play in virtually any DVD player. This is great for making a disc of party music, favorite tunes for a special occasion, or just for geeking out. If nothing else, you'll get to use that blank DVD that came with your new Mac.

Here's what you need to do to try out Playlist to DVD:

1. First, make sure you have the required hardware and system software. You need a Mac with a SuperDrive—that's a DVD burner—and you must be running Mac OS X 10.3 or later.

2. The next requirement is QuickTime Pro. You need this because Playlist to DVD actually works by creating a QuickTime movie with the music, track list, and album art you select. Every Mac already has the free version of QuickTime, but QuickTime Pro provides extra features, mainly for creating movies, and costs money, about $30. If you don't have QuickTime Pro, you can download and pay for it at www.apple.com/quicktime/download/.

3. Finally, you need a copy of iLife 04. Specifically, you'll need iTunes and iDVD. iLife has a retail price of $49, and you can buy it at the Apple store online or in the physical world, or at many computer stores.

4. Once you're done collecting all that for-pay software, you can get the free Playlist to DVD application. Download it at www.apple.com/applescript/playlisttodvd/. Run the application after you have downloaded it.

5. In the Playlist to DVD window, you'll see your iTunes playlists listed at the left. Pick the one you want to make into a lovely DVD. On the right, choose a template style. Click Create DVD, and watch the magic. Figure 9-1 shows you what the Playlist to DVD window looks like.

FIGURE 9-1: The Playlist to DVD application lets you choose from all your iTunes playlists (on the left) and one of four template styles for your DVD presentation (on the right).

Playlist to DVD provides a valuable feature by making slick DVDs out of your favorite music. Playlist to DVD was created using Apple's powerful AppleScript Studio software, which makes programming far more accessible than it is with traditional technologies. If you're interested in finding out how it's done, and possibly learning more about becoming an AppleScript programmer, Apple provides all the source code and other pieces of the project at www.apple.com/applescript/playlisttodvd/downloads/ Playlist2DVDProject.dmg.

Create Gapless Music CDs

When iTunes imports music from a CD, it rips each track separately and leaves a gap between them. As we learned in the section *Merge Tracks from Live CDs* in Chapter 8, you can eliminate the gap between songs by using the "join tracks" feature before ripping a CD.

What happens to the gaps between tracks when you want to burn a CD? Take a look in iTunes preferences, on the Burning tab. (Every time I think about something named the Burning tab, I feel like I need to call the fire department.) You'll see a promising setting labeled "Gap Between Songs" (see Figure 9-2).

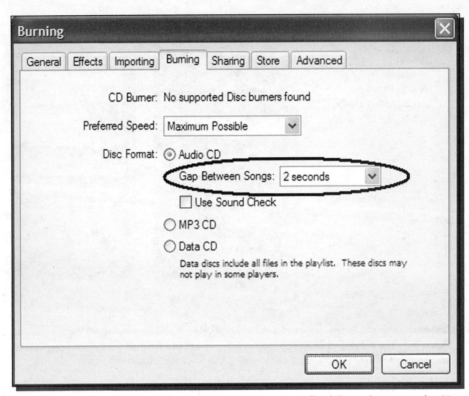

FIGURE 9-2: The "Gap Between Songs" setting gives you some flexibility in burning audio CDs.

You can use this setting to create CDs with no gaps between the tracks, but only in certain cases:

- You joined the tracks on the CD before importing them.

- You're burning a CD from an uncompressed format (AIFF or WAV) rather than a compressed format (such as MP3 or AAC).

Unfortunately, if you create a CD from MP3, you will always get a gap between the songs. The gap is still there even if you use the "none" setting in Burning preferences, although it's tiny and almost imperceptible in many cases. The only way to ensure a gapless CD is to rip the CD with joined tracks, or in an uncompressed format (either AIFF or WAV).

Burn a CD from an Album

One of the iron rules of iTunes is that you can only burn a CD from a playlist, not from an artist or an album. But there is a shortcut if you want to create a CD consisting of a single album. While looking at the library or any other song list, make sure the Browser is visible (choose Edit ➪ Show Browser if not). Pick an album, any album, and drag it to the source list, in the white space under your last playlist. If your source list is full, this is a little tricky—you have to tuck it in there in a tight space just below the last playlist.

When you drag an album this way, you instantly create a new playlist of the album you dragged. You can then click Burn Disc and you're ready to make a CD. This trick works for any items you drag from the Browser to the source list. You can select an artist, or even multiple artists or albums. Go wild!

Burn as Many Songs as You Want

If you like to put together CDs of your favorite songs, iTunes helps you figure out when you've filled up your CD. If you're putting together your playlist by hand, you can keep an eye on the time indicator that iTunes displays at the bottom of the song list. As long as you make sure you keep the total playlist time under the capacity of your blank CD (usually 74 or 80 minutes), you'll be fine.

If you're not very picky about what's going on the CD, you can get even more help from iTunes by employing a smart playlist. Let's say you want to burn a CD filled with the music you listen to the most, so you can play it in your car's CD player. Pull down the File menu and choose New Smart Playlist. Uncheck the box at the top next to "Match the following condition". Check the box for "Limit to", fill in "80" in the first text box, "minutes" in the second, and "most often played" in the third. Then click OK. The Smart Playlist dialog box should look like the one in Figure 9-3.

When you choose these settings for a Smart Playlist, you're asking iTunes to find the songs you've played the most and grab them for a playlist, collecting songs until it has

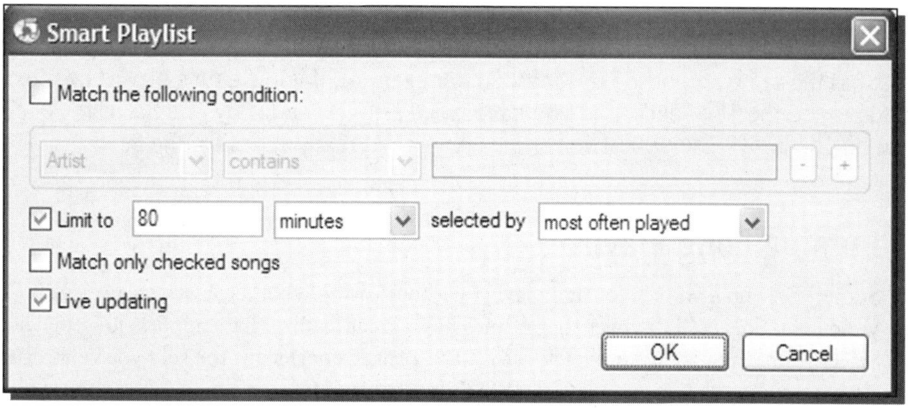

Figure 9-3: You can ask iTunes to create a smart playlist with exactly (almost) as much music as you want, to fit it on a single CD.

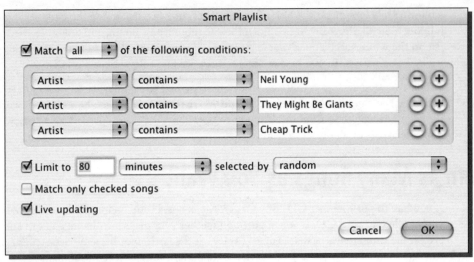

Figure 9-4: This playlist is more complex. iTunes will randomly choose 80 minutes of music. Each song must be by one of the three artists.

80 minutes of music. You can use other smart playlist settings to find songs with different criteria. For example, the settings in Figure 9-4 will build another smart playlist that fits on a CD, and containing randomly chosen songs by any of three different artists.

Equal Opportunity

When you create a smart playlist with more than one condition, and you use the "Match any of the following conditions" setting, as we've done here by making a playlist with three artists, iTunes does some clever figuring to make sure the playlist has a fair distribution of music. iTunes determines how much of your library is represented by each condition, then makes sure the playlist has the same proportion of songs. So, for example, if you create a playlist of songs from The Buoys and the The Seeds, and you have twice as many songs by The Seeds in your library as you do The Buoys, the playlist will also have twice as many songs by The Seeds.

Burning Long Playlists

Sometimes you'll want to burn a playlist without caring whether it fits on a single CD. When you do, you'll discover that iTunes has a great feature that supports long playlists. Select your long playlist and click Burn Disc. iTunes checks out the CD you've inserted and compares it to the selected playlist. If the playlist won't fit on a single CD, iTunes will tell you so. But it's not an error message! No, instead it's a *helpful* message that offers to burn the playlist on multiple CDs automatically. (See Figure 9-5 to examine this nice message.)

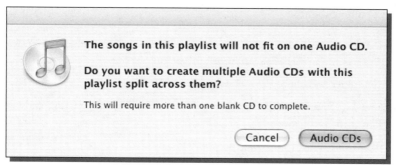

Figure 9-5: When you ask to burn a playlist that won't fit on a single CD, iTunes provides this helpful message.

If you get this message and click Audio CDs, iTunes will methodically burn multiple CDs, one at a time, until it's all the way through the playlist. As iTunes burns each CD, the song list helpfully shows the songs that are going onto that CD in black, with songs meant for other CDs in gray. When all the burning is done, you have your playlist of songs, spread neatly across as many CDs as necessary.

Change the "Volume Up And Down" Sounds

Note This hack is Mac-only.

Mac OS X is loaded with pretty visual features. You see one of these whenever you use the Mac keyboard to change the volume. When you press the keys that turn the volume up or down, or turn volume muting on or off, Mac OS X puts a big transparent image on the screen that shows you what's happening, and then the image fades away like mist. In addition, whenever you change the volume or turn off muting, the Mac plays a little "squirt" sound so you can hear the current volume setting.

The Sound panel in System Preferences lets you change your alert sound, just as you have been able to do on Macs since time immemorial, or at least since 1985. But there's no setting that lets you pick a different sound to hear when you change the volume.

There is a way to change this setting—it's just a little trickier than using System Preferences. It's also not documented or supported, so be careful, and beware of unintended side effects. The sound is located in a file in the system folder. To change it, we're going to temporarily grant ourselves permission to mess with the file, rename it, replace it with another sound file, then put the permissions back the way they were.

To change the volume sound:

1. In the Finder, go to the following folder: `/System/Library/LoginPlugins/BezelServices.loginPlugin/Contents/Resources`.

2. Select the folder and choose File ⇨ Get Info.

3. In the Get Info window, find the "Ownership and Permissions" section and click the triangle next to "Details".

4. Click the padlock next to "Owner: system".

5. Click the popup that says "system" and choose your account. Leave the info window open—we'll need it again soon.

6. Locate another AIFF file that you want to use as the new volume sound. You can find some likely suspects in `/System/Library/Sounds`, where the alert sounds live.

7. Hold down Option and drag the chosen new sound to the Resources folder from step 1. By holding down Option, you should see a plus sign as you drag, indicating that you're making a copy of the file. Drop the file in that folder.

8. In the Resources folder, select the name of "volume.aiff", the current sound file. Rename it "old volume.aiff".

9. Now select the file you dropped in, the new sound, and rename it "volume.aiff".

10. Go back to the Info window from step 5, which you cleverly left open. Click the "owner" pop-up again and return ownership to the system. If you're asked for your password, go ahead and type it in to confirm the change. Click the padlock to lock the permissions. Now you can close the info window.

That's it! To hear your new volume sound, you have to log out and back in again, or log in as another user. This trick is cool, yet virtually useless—a true hack.

Hacking the Culture: Apple and HP

Apple is known for going its own way—"Think Different" was the company's ad slogan for several years. So the computer world was stunned early in 2004 when Apple and Hewlett-Packard announced that HP would license the iPod design from Apple, paint its iPods blue, and sell them as the HP Digital Music Player. Executives of both companies said this was the first time Apple had ever licensed a hardware product for sales by another company, but corporate memories are short.

A long time ago, when Apple was a tiny unknown startup company, a great big company named Bell & Howell was known for supplying audio-visual equipment to schools. Apple struck

Figure 9-6: The blue HP iPod is not the first Apple product to be recolored and produced by a different company. These black Apple II computers dotted schools in the late 1970s.

a deal with Bell & Howell to make Apple II computers in black cases instead of the familiar beige. The result was more Apple computers in schools, and Apple's first deal for letting somebody else make their stuff. Check out Figure 9-6 to see what a Bell & Howell Apple II looks like.

The black Apple II computers are collectors' items now. Will blue HP iPods end up the same way?

Get Music Out by Dragging

Most of the hacks in this chapter are about getting music out of iTunes by burning CDs. Here's a quick trick that provides another way for music to escape from iTunes: you can just drag it out of any song list, such as a playlist or the library. When you drag a song and drop it on the desktop or in a folder in the Finder or Windows Explorer, iTunes makes a copy of the song and puts it into the destination. Even though songs in playlists aren't the actual song files, iTunes is smart enough to track down the song file when you drag, and make a copy of it. The copy is in the same format as the original, so if you drag an MP3, you'll get an MP3, and so on.

Back Up Your Music

Do you back up your music? You have probably ripped dozens or even hundreds of CDs. You finally have all your favorite tunes on your computer. But to your computer, it's all just data, and it's only as permanent as your next catastrophic disk failure. Maybe you've even thought of that, and you figure you'll just use your CDs as backup—you can always restore from them in case something goes wrong with your ripped tunes.

There are a couple of flaws in the audio-CDs-as-backup strategy. First, and most obviously, it only covers music that came from CD in the first place. If you're a customer of the iTunes Music Store, you own music that was shipped to you on a wire, not a CD. And if you've read and used any of the fun music sources in Chapter 8, you have even more music that's not backed up anywhere. The second flaw in the strategy is assuming that you're actually going to invest the hundreds of hours you would need to rerip everything from CD again.

The quickest, easiest, and most expensive way to back up your music is to get an external hard disk that's big enough to hold all your tunes. You can now get very reliable external FireWire drives for about $1 per gigabyte: 300GB for around $300, for example. Add some high-quality backup software, such as Retrospect from Dantz, and you're all set.

If you want a lower cost technique, consider backing up onto data CDs or DVDs. The bigger your music library, the less interesting this technique becomes, because you'll need an enormous number of discs. A data CD can hold 650 Mb of stuff, and a DVD stores about 4.7GB.

To back up your music with CDs or DVDs, start by opening File ⇨ Preferences, going to the Burning tab, and choosing "Data CD or DVD". This format is the same as MP3 CD, except that it will include all songs in a list, while "MP3 CD" ignores anything that's not an MP3. After you're done in Preferences, just pick the playlist you want to back up. If you want to burn your whole library, make a new playlist and drag the Library icon to the icon for the new playlist, then burn from that mega-playlist.

Summary

You can't always be at your computer or iPod. Sometimes, it's useful to get music away from your digital devices and into the relatively old-fashioned formats of CD and DVD so you can listen in more places. Using the tricks in this chapter for burning CDs with iTunes, you can become a master of the burn and take your tunes with you to even more places.

Coming up in Chapter 10, we'll get into the iTunes music library to see what we can discover. I'll discuss playlists, file formats, album art, and more—see you there.

Music Library: Check it Out

The iTunes library is the repository for all your music. If your favorite symphony is not in the library, iTunes doesn't know about it, even if it's on your disk somewhere. That's why it's important to get full control over how you use your library. In this chapter, we'll go over some of the coolest tricks you can do with your library in iTunes.

Convert Between Audio Formats

iTunes knows about several different popular formats for digital music, including the legendary MP3, and Apple's favorite, AAC. When you import your music from CD, you get to choose which format you want iTunes to use for the songs. Most of the time, you'll pick MP3 or AAC. These formats save disk space by drastically reducing the size of music through compression. To keep full CD-quality fidelity, you can import your music in AIFF or WAV format, which simply copies the songs in their digital format from the CD to your hard disk. (For more about this topic, see *Keep Your Music CD Quality* in Chapter 8.)

Once you have imported your music, it's not necessarily stuck in that format forever. iTunes provides the means to help you transform songs from one format to another. The Convert Selection item in the Advanced menu grabs the selected track (or tracks) in iTunes and translates to whatever format you have chosen for importing music. You can explicitly see which format iTunes will convert to by pulling down the Advanced menu and looking at the Convert item (as shown in Figure 10-1). You can get the same effect by right-clicking the selection (or Control-clicking on a Mac if you don't have a multiple-button mouse).

You might remember that you can choose the current encoding format in Preferences, on the Importing page. So if you want to convert songs to AAC instead of MP3, open Preferences, go to Importing, and pick AAC from the Import Using list.

FIGURE **10-1: The Convert item in the Advanced menu tells you which format it will convert the selection to. You change this setting in Preferences.**

Conversions: Useful, possible, and otherwise

At first thought, this sounds like a terrific way to upgrade the quality of your music library simply by using more disk space: just choose a bunch of songs that you ripped as MP3s at 128K bits per second and convert to a higher bit rate, such as 192K bps. Unfortunately, it doesn't quite work that way. When you imported music at 128K bps, iTunes didn't keep the original data around when it was done compressing. Converting songs to 192K now won't bring back that lost data—the music won't sound any better, and it might sound worse, because it's going to be reencoded. The only way to get better quality is to go back to the source-your CD-and rerip.

If you can't use this feature to make your compressed music sound better, what can you do with it? The only scenario it's really useful for is converting from an uncompressed format (AIFF or WAV). You can go from AIFF to WAV or vice versa, which is useful for some programs that only understand one or the other. You can also convert from AIFF or WAV to one of the compressed formats, MP3 or AAC, if you want to create a copy of the song that will take up less disk space.

When you buy music from the iTunes Music Store, it comes in the Protected AAC format. You might think you could get your tunes out of Protected AAC jail by using this feature to convert them to free and unfettered MP3, but unfortunately, it doesn't work: Apple thought of that too. If you try to convert a music store song, iTunes informs you that you can't convert from a protected format. You can, however, burn Protected AAC songs to CD, then rip them back as unprotected MP3s.

The Convert feature has one more groovy hidden trick. If you hold down Option (on a Mac) or Shift (on Windows) while you choose the Convert menu item, iTunes will give you a box to choose a file on the disk to convert, rather than the selected song in iTunes. On the Macintosh, you can choose a folder if you want, and all music files in the folder will be converted.

Use a Cross-Platform Disk

As you discover the convenience of having all your CDs available in iTunes, your music library will grow like a monster and start to consume all available disk space in sight. If your home or office is cross-platform, you'll be very tempted to use both Macs and Windows machines for storing your tunes. When you have music stored on various computers, you can use iTunes' excellent music sharing feature to play songs from other machines. But iTunes sharing doesn't let you copy music from another computer: to do that, you actually have to delve into the Finder or Windows Explorer and copy the files themselves, or, if you get the music together in one library, use iTunes' "consolidate" feature, as described in *Get All Your Music Together in One Place* in Chapter 8.

For a greater degree of portability and flexibility, you might want to have a hard disk that you can transport from one computer to another. This technique is useful if you don't have a network that's fast or reliable. It's also handy for schlepping your music to a friend's house, to the office, or to a party, because external hard disks can provide far more capacity than iPods do.

The best part about using an external drive is that you can make the disk understandable by both Macs and PCs. Mac OS X will happily communicate with disks formatted for Windows. Your best bet is to use the FAT32 file system on external disks, which works fine with both Macs and PCs. You can format a disk as FAT32 on either a Mac or a PC, whichever suits you better.

Caution These instructions reformat a disk as FAT32, which erases the disk and destroys all the information on it. There are no steps here to preserve any data you might already have on the disk. If there's anything on the disk you want to keep, save it somewhere else first.

To use Mac OS X to format a disk as FAT32:

1. Start Disk Utility. This application is usually in Applications/Utilities.

2. In the column at the left, click to select the drive you want to format. Note: don't select the wrong drive! (Disk Utility won't let you erase your startup disk.)

3. In the "Volume Format" pop-up, select "MS-DOS File System". This really means FAT32, even though it doesn't say so. Maybe "FAT32" is not a posh enough term for Apple to use.

4. Click Erase to format the disk.

That's it. The disk will appear in the Finder, and you will be able to use it just like a Mac disk.

To use Windows XP to format the disk:

1. Click Start in the task bar.

2. Right-click My Computer and choose Manage from the shortcut menu.

3. In the Computer Management window, click Disk Management on the left (see Figure 10-2).

4. In the list on the upper-right, click the volume you want to format.

5. Choose Action ⇨ All Tasks ⇨ Format.

6. Pick FAT32 for the file system, then click OK. Click OK on the warning message that appears. Make sure you're erasing the right volume!

Once you have the disk formatted as FAT32, it will behave like any other disk on both Macs and Windows machines. You can use the disk to store individual MP3s, whole

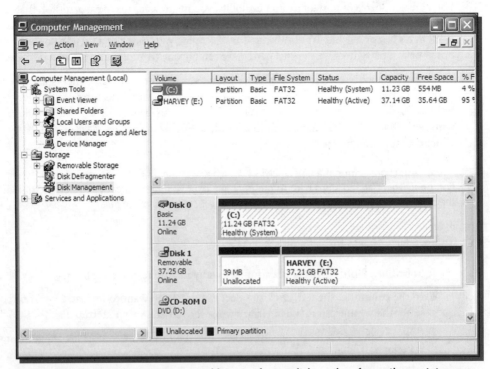

FIGURE 10-2: The Disk Management panel lets you format disks and perform other maintenance.

folders of music, or even entire music libraries. When you connect the disk to a Mac or PC, you'll have access to the tunes on that computer. Flexible!

Delete a Playlist and All Its Songs

Both the music library and your playlists are represented by icons in the source list. But the library and playlists are not equals. The library is special: it's the master playlist for all the music iTunes knows about, while playlists are simply lists of songs that are in the library. When you delete a tune from a playlist, you're telling iTunes you don't want that song on that list any more—the tune remains in the library. When you delete a song from the library, you're severing its connection from iTunes entirely, and iTunes even asks if you want to send the file to the Trash or Recycle Bin.

What about those times when you're looking at a song in a playlist and you want to remove it from the library entirely and throw it in the trash? iTunes provides a shortcut for that. Select a song in a playlist. If you hold down the Option key (on the Mac) or the Shift key (on Windows) while you press Delete, iTunes will take the song out of the playlist and the library, and even toss it in the trash if you say so. This one is handy, but be careful! Of course, if you happen to toss something you really wanted to keep, you can always drag it out of the bin.

Hacking the Culture: The iPod of Sauron

During the production of the epic *The Lord of the Rings* movies, director Peter Jackson found himself having to be in more than one place at a time. While the films' digital effects team was working in New Zealand, where the movies were filmed, Jackson was sometimes in England supervising the recording of the score. How could Jackson examine daily prints that were being produced in New Zealand?

Technology was the answer, with an iPod flavor. Every morning, new daily scenes of the movie were transferred over a secure (to prevent Orc mischief) network connection from New Zealand to the studio in London. But just as Sam and Frodo weren't quite finished when they got to Mount Doom, the dailies weren't done with their journey when they got to the studio: they still had to be transported to Jackson's home nearby. So, the dailies were downloaded to an iPod, which was then delivered to Jackson at home, where he watched the new stuff on a PowerBook G4 hooked up to external Apple Cinema Display.

Of course, the filmmakers could have accomplished the same scenario with any external FireWire disk. But somehow it must have just seemed cooler to use iPods for this task.

Listen to All the Music on Your Computer

Note This hack is Mac-only

If you have more than one computer running at home, or you're lucky enough to have access to an office or dorm full of music lovers, you are no doubt familiar with the wonderful music sharing feature in iTunes that lets you listen to your neighbors' songs. So it might seem completely heinous that if you take advantage of Mac OS X's multiple-user accounts, allowing your spouse, kids, or roommates to share your precious Mac, you don't have access to their music from your iTunes.

The reason you can't see or hear music that belongs to other user accounts on your computer is that each user's song files are stored inside separate folders. If you try to get to those folders, either from iTunes or the Finder, you'll discover that Mac OS X has set file permissions that prohibit you from getting inside. Try it and see. In the Finder, choose Go ⇨ Computer, click the hard disk, and click Users. Find the user whose library you want to explore and click the user folder. Double-click that user's Music folder. The Finder tells you don't have sufficient privileges to open the folder. That's not very nice!

If your account is part of the administrator group on your computer, you can get around this limitation by taking the following steps:

1. With the other user's Music folder selected, choose File ⇨ Get Info.

2. In the "Ownership and Permissions" section, click the triangle next to "Details".

3. Click the tiny lock next to the "Owner" pop-up (Figure 10-3).

4. Check the name in the "Owner" pop-up. You're going to change it, but you'll need it again for step 8. It's probably the same as the user's name. If your memory is as bad as mine, you might want to write it down.

5. Click the pop-up and choose your own account. Taking ownership will let you make changes to the folder's permissions.

6. Click the pop-up next to "Group" and choose "Staff".

7. Under "Group", click the "Access" pop-up and choose "Read Only". This change will give you access to the other user's music.

8. Go back to the "Owner" list and set it back the way it was before we started messing around.

9. Click the little lock to put things back the way they were.

10. Close the Music Info window.

FIGURE 10-3: Getting ready to change the owner of the Music folder.

Now that you have access to the music in the other account, you can get it into your library.

1. Start iTunes if it isn't already running.

2. Choose iTunes ⇨ Preferences and click the Advanced tab.

3. Make sure the item "Copy files to iTunes music folder when adding to library" is not checked, then click OK. This will prevent iTunes from making an extra copy of the other user's songs when you add them to your library.

4. Choose File ⇨ Add to Library and navigate to the other user's iTunes music folder. (It's in the hard disk at `/Users/<user name>/Music/iTunes/iTunes Music`.)

5. Click OK to add the music to your library.

Now you can listen to your kids' music—or your parents'. Try not to be too shocked!

FIGURE 10-4: For any song, you can find out which playlists it belongs to, then go to one of those playlists immediately.

Find All Playlists a Song Is On

As you build your music collection in iTunes, you'll add more playlists to control and manipulate your songs just the way you want. A cool tool hidden inside iTunes helps you find out which playlists contain any particular song.

To see this trick at work, locate any song in the library. When you see the song you want to check, right-click it (or command-click, if you're using a one-button mouse on a Mac). If the song is in any playlists, the menu that pops up includes an item named "Playlists" that tells you all the playlists the song belongs to, as shown in Figure 10-4. If you select a playlist from the menu, iTunes switches you to it, with the chosen song selected.

This handy feature also works if you right-click a song in a playlist, rather than in the library. In that case, the "Playlists" submenu only appears if the song is on at least one *other* playlist in addition to the one you're looking at. If it is, you can select it to switch there immediately.

Finetune the Music Library's Appearance

When you start iTunes for the first time, the music library presents a nice default appearance. But this book is not for people who like defaults. In this section, we'll talk about various ways you can tweak the way your music library appears until it's showing just the information you want, in just the way you want it.

Get rid of the "Genre" column

All iTunes tracks include a property called Genre. This is supposed to make it easier for you to figure out what category a particular song belongs to. But there is a serious flaw with the genre property. When you rip a CD, the information about the songs, such as the names of the artist and tracks, comes from GraceNote CDDB, a database of information that was built largely by user contributions. Despite the best efforts of GraceNote, this massive database is filled with errors, including misspelled names and transposed information (such as putting the artist name where the track should be, and vice versa). When it comes to genres, the problem is worse. There are no standards for what user contributors type into the genre field. For example, when I look through my iTunes library, I have genres (supplied by GraceNote CDDB) named Rock, Rock & Roll, and RockNRoll. Obviously, this makes it hard to rely on genre, unless you take the time to check your CDs after they're ripped and edit them to make sure you're using an orderly set of genres.

On the other hand, if most of your music comes from the iTunes Music Store, you're in better shape. The store seems to apply much better quality control to its genres. There is a well-defined set of genres (25 of them as of this writing), and all music in the iTunes Music Store is within one of those.

If you're down on genres, you might want to remove the "Genre" column that appears in the iTunes browser. To do this, go to Preferences on the iTunes menu (Mac) or the Edit menu (Windows), click General, and turn off the "Show genre while browsing" box. Just like that, the unwanted Genre column will go away. Note that it vanishes from the browser entirely, including when viewing playlists.

Bend columns with your bare hands

The initial appearance of your song lists in the library and playlists is just a suggestion. You have a great deal of power over how you want the columns of information to appear. The easiest way to choose the columns you want to see is by right-clicking any column title. You'll see a list of all possible columns, with check marks next to the ones that are displayed. Just check and uncheck column names to get the ones you want. If you prefer, you can make all your column on/off choices at once by choosing Edit ⇨ View Options (see Figure 10-5).

When you're seeing the columns you want, feel free to push them around. Grab any column's header and drag to move it to another position. (The exception is Song Name, which always insists on being the first column.) You can resize columns, too. Move the

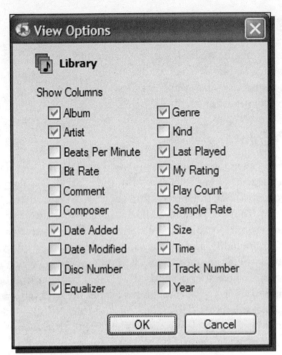

FIGURE 10-5: The View Options dialog box lets you choose the columns you want to display for the current song list.

mouse to the divider between any two columns. You'll notice it changes to a telltale double-arrow doohickey. Click and drag to make the column bigger or smaller.

You can also right-click a column header and choose Auto Size Column or Auto Size All Columns, but these options are less useful than they might seem. The Auto Size commands adjust the column to accommodate its longest item, which tends to make some columns, such as Song Name and Album, much wider than they need to be for most tracks.

One more tweak: you can display sources and songs in two different font sizes. By default, iTunes uses the smaller size. If you find this display too tiny, try the bigger text. Go to Preferences, click the General tab, and change Source Text and Song Text to Large. See if you like it better that way.

Be sure to check out the Equalizer column. This one is unique. When you add the Equalizer column, each song gets a little pop-up control that lets you choose its equalizer setting.

Separate and Not Equal

Each song list gets to have its own separate view settings. Notice how Figure 10-5 includes the word "Library" and its icon at the top? When you make changes to column settings, the settings stick with the library or the playlist you're looking at. This is very handy, because you will often want to look at different information for different playlists.

Fool with the browser

The list at the top that shows artists and albums (and optionally genres) is called the Browser. When you start iTunes, the Browser is hidden. You can display it for the library or for any playlists by choosing Edit ⇨ Show Browser. Like column settings, each song list keeps its own setting for whether the Browser is displayed.

You can also mess around with how much screen space the Browser gets. Click and drag the bar between the Browser and the songs to split the space between them. The dimple on the middle of the bar is a hint that tells you to drag the bar. You'll see another dimple like that on the bar at the left, which divides the source list from the rest of the window. Yep, you can drag that one, too.

Edit in place

Many of a song's properties are changeable: song name, album, comments, and so on. You can edit these by selecting the song and choosing File ⇨ Get Info to see a dialog box, or you can simply click the item in the list to modify it right there. The clicking process is a little tricky, but you'll get used to it. It's the same technique Apple uses to select text in the Finder. First, click to select the song you want to edit. Then, click again on the specific text you want to edit. You should see an editable text box appear around the words you clicked (Figure 10-6). Now you can just type whatever you want, and the entry is changed.

Playlists too

Remember, you can use these techniques on playlists as well as the library. They're all just lists of songs to iTunes.

See Album Art

You probably already know that iTunes can display the cover art from albums as the music plays. What, you didn't know that? Well, you should immediately go to the Edit menu and choose Show Artwork so you can join the rest of us here in the future.

FIGURE 10-6: Select and edit text right in a song list.

Sometimes you'll be clicking around various songs in your library, hoping to look at album art, but the image never changes. That's probably because the title above the album art says "Now Playing". If you want to see the art that goes with the songs you're looking at, click the words "Now Playing". The title will change to say "Selected Song", and now you'll get what you wanted.

Whenever you buy a song from the iTunes Music Store, you get the album art, free of charge. Unless most of your music came from the store, you have a lot of songs with no art. One way to change that is by following the advice you see in the empty art space: Drag Album Artwork Here. To take advantage of this feature, start by selecting the song or album you want to add art to. Then, using a Web browser that supports dragging images, such as Safari on the Mac, go to a CD listing in an online store, such as Amazon or Wal-Mart, and drag the album art into place in iTunes. Instant art! Getting album art this way for all your CDs would be pretty tedious, but clever people have invented tools that make the process much easier. See *Get Album Art* in Chapter 5 for the full story.

Art goes into iTunes, but it also comes out. You can get any album art image from the art space just by dragging it out and dropping it into another document. This is a great way to include your favorite album cover in your next family newsletter, school project, or parole report.

Size matters

Gee, that album art is awfully small, don't you think? Let's make it bigger. Grab the divider between the source list and the song list, and drag it to the right. The album art space starts growing as you drag. You can also make it smaller if you want.

For the maximum viewing effect, click the art image. It will open up into its own window, even larger than the biggest size you can get inside the regular iTunes window. You can open up as many of these as you want.

Summary

Take care of your music library, because that's where all the action is in iTunes. Using the hacks in this chapter, you can get rid of songs most efficiently, make the best use of cool album art, and even carry your tunes between Macs and PCs. And because the library is just another list of songs, many of the tricks we've talked about also work on playlists.

The next (and final) chapter is all about the iTunes Music Store, the revolutionary source of digital downloads that lets you legally acquire music online. Come along to Chapter 11 and find out what secret hacks lurk in the store.

iTunes Music Store

O n April 28, 2003, Apple opened its newest store: the iTunes
Music Store. This store instantly changed the rules of the legal
online music business forever. iTunes was the first music store
that thought about what customers wanted instead of what record companies demanded. For the first time, you could:

- Buy music online without having to pay obnoxious monthly
  membership fees.

- Move music between your computers and music players with
  reasonable freedom.

- Burn as many CDs as you wanted.

Since then, the store has been a huge hit, selling tens of millions of
songs to Mac and Windows users. Apple continues to expand the store,
adding artists and features.

In this chapter, we hack the store: we find the cool and little-known
ways to wander around, look in the basement and the back rooms (is
somebody smoking back there?) to find special stuff like music videos
and artist biographies, and learn how to discover what's new in the store
without even having to visit. Let's go shopping!

Get Around the Store

Shopping a virtual store like the iTunes Music Store is both better and
worse than going to a physical store. One of the main differences is the
way you get around the place. When you're there in person, there's one
method for exploring the store: you walk from one department to
another. In the iTunes Music Store, there are lots of ways to move
around and get what you need, find what you want, or discover cool new
things. In this section, we'll discuss some of the powerful and lesser-
known ways of exploring the store.

Use navigation tools

Apple's store is not a Web site, of course, but instead is an embedded
part of iTunes. This gives the company greater control over how the

FIGURE 11-1: iTunes Music Store home page.

store works, because it doesn't depend on which browser or even which operating system you're using. And Apple loves to control your experience. When you click Music Store in the sources list, iTunes shows you the store's home page, something like what you see in Figure 11-1.

Wow, it's so shiny! There's lots of cool stuff to see, and plenty to click. You can click the feature boxes at the top, any of the tiny album covers, or the items in the various lists, such as names of artists, albums, and songs. If you wonder whether some text on the screen is a link, just point the mouse at it. If you see an underline when the cursor is hovering, it's a link. The store's home page includes five small windows labeled New Releases, Exclusives, Pre-Releases, Just Added, and Staff Favorites. Each of these windows shows four albums, but they all scroll to reveal more when you click the arrows on the left or right. If you would rather all the albums in the window at once rather than watching them scroll past, click the See All link at the top right corner of the miniature window.

Take a look at the navigation controls at the top of the window. Use the cute little picture of a house to get back to the store's home page any time. The arrowheads pointing right and left are back and forward buttons for the store. They're pretty handy—use them the same way you do in a Web browser.

FIGURE 11-2: iTunes Music Store home page.

As you look at artists and albums, words that describe the item you're looking at appear next to the home button, as shown in Figure 11-2. These words form a sort of breadcrumb trail that shows how to get back from where you are. The words are actually buttons: click one to jump to any point in the hierarchy.

iTunes Music Store pages have zillions of arrows strewn about. For example, when you're looking at a list of songs resulting from a search, there are arrows next to each artist, album, genre, and composer name. You can click any of these arrows to go to a page all about that topic.

The store gives you ample opportunity to communicate with the outside world while you're shopping. Whenever you're looking at the page for an artist or album, you can click "Tell a friend" to send a cool e-mail postcard that includes links to the artist or album. When your friend (or other, non-friend recipient) gets the e-mail and clicks a link, iTunes goes to the store and shows the appropriate page. Apple is happy, apparently, to hear what you think of the iTunes Music Store. Click Requests & Feedback on the home page to get a form you can fill out to submit ideas about the store.

Narrow your search

The Search Music Store box at the top right corner of the screen is great for finding something in a hurry. If you're looking for *Black Friday* by Steely Dan, just click in the search box and type **Black Friday**, then press Return, and you'll quickly get a list that includes what you want. Sometimes the results from a quick search are a bit too broad to be useful. For example, let's say you're interested in collecting cover versions of the classic song "Yesterday" by Lennon & McCartney (although it's pretty well known that Paul wrote and recorded it mostly by himself). If you simply search for "Yesterday", you'll be inundated with too many results. "Yesterday" has been covered hundreds of times, but this search returns lots of songs that aren't the ones we want.

You can do a little better by clicking the magnifying glass in the search box and choosing Songs. This tells the store to look for the word "Yesterday" in song titles only, which eliminates a bunch of the results. But we're still getting songs that have "Yesterday" anywhere in the title. The best way to get what we want is Power Search. To use Power Search, click the magnifying glass and choose Power Search at the bottom of the menu.

Power Search lets you instruct the store to match information in specific tags. In this case, we can say we want to look for "Yesterday" in the song title and "McCartney" in the composer name. The result is a list of 10 songs that are much more likely to be what we're looking for.

FIGURE 11-3: iTunes Music Store music browser.

Use the browser to find music

If you come to the iTunes Music Store looking for a particular album, you'll probably go straight to the Search Music Store box and type in the name of the record you want. But if you're not there to buy anything in particular, and you have some time to kill and money to burn, check out the music browser. You can get the browser by clicking the Browse Music link on the home page, or poking the big eyeball at the top right corner of the iTunes window. The browser displays three columns—Genre, Artist, and Album—as shown in Figure 11-3.

To use the browser, click a Genre in the left column. iTunes then fills in the Artist column with a list of choices. When you pick an Artist, albums appear in the column on the right. Picking an album puts its songs in the song list at the bottom. You can also choose "All" in the Album column to see all the artist's songs at once. From the song list, you can double-click a song name to hear a 30-second preview, click an arrow to go that item's page, or even spend some money and buy the song.

The music browser includes one handy, hidden trick: double-click any item in the Genre, Artist, or Album columns to go directly to that item's page.

Tip   You can customize how you want the columns to appear in your iTunes Music Store browser, just as you can with any playlist. To change column widths, drag the divider line between columns. To move a column, grab the header and move it somewhere else. You can use the Edit ⇨ View Options command to decide which columns to display. For more on this, see *Bend Columns with Your Bare Hands* in Chapter 10.

Browse genre pages

One of the best-kept secrets in the iTunes Music Store is the existence of a home page for each genre. These pages look a lot like the store's home page, except that they're focused on one particular musical style. All the music on the home page—New Releases, Staff Favorites, Featured Artists, Today's Top Songs, and so on—is for that genre only. Most home pages have categories that are specific to that genre; for example, the New Age home page includes a set of Relaxing Ambient selections. Genre home pages provide a great way to find new music in a genre you're not very familiar with. So if you've loved classical music all your life, but now you suddenly want to try Hip Hop, this is a great way to do it.

You can get to a genre home page by clicking a genre link anywhere you see one, such as in a song list. You can also go directly to a genre home page by clicking the pop-up list that appears on the left side of any home page in the store.

Find all new music

The store's home page has a small New Releases box that shows you four new albums at a time. Four is not enough! You can see all the new releases by clicking See All at the top right corner of the New Releases box. When you do that, not only do you get a full list of the tunes added this week, but iTunes also shows you the new releases for each of the three previous weeks. This is handy for catching up on your new music purchases after you win the lottery.

Tip   You can subscribe to a very cool weekly e-mail newsletter that lets you know about all the new music added to the store. The e-mail, called *"New Music Tuesdays"*, comes with direct links to the store—just click in the e-mail and iTunes will take you to the album. To subscribe, go to `http://enews.apple.com/subscribe` and fill out the form, or change settings as described in *See Your Account Information* in this chapter. And yes, new music always comes out on Tuesdays, for some reason.

Browse music in charts

In its never ending quest to separate us from our money by providing great tunes, the iTunes Music Store offers a clever new way to browse: charts. So far, Apple provides two kinds of charts you can peruse: Billboard charts, which document the most popular songs, according to sales and radio airplay data; and radio charts, which show the tunes that are most played on particular radio stations. To use this feature, you click Billboard Charts or Radio Charts on the home page, or select one of the charts in the music browser.

Billboard charts

If you want to look at the Billboard charts, you'll get a choice: as of this writing, you can select Billboard Hot 100, Billboard Top R&B, or Billboard Top Country. Apple has said that others will be added.

The charts are organized by year, and they go all the way back to 1946, so if you've listened to popular music any time in the past 58 years or so, you have a good chance of finding something here you'll like. Browsing through a chart from your younger days brings a heavy dose of nostalgia, and you're likely to spend time listening to more than one 30-second preview. You also might spend money, of course. Sure, you have those songs on vinyl LP-ROM somewhere, but at 99 cents a pop, it's easy to justify buying them again so you can play them in iTunes and on your iPod.

The key limitation of this feature is that not all songs on the charts are available in the Store. For example, 74 of the Billboard Hot 100 for 1980 can be purchased in the Store, as can 53 of the Top Country 75 for 1998.

If you would rather save that 99 cents and digitize your LPs, be sure to check out "Get LPs into iTunes" in Chapter 8.

Radio charts

You'll love this feature if you like to listen to over-the-air radio when you're not grooving to iTunes and iPod music. The Music Store radio charts tell what's playing on more than 1000 radio stations in the United States, in over 200 cities and towns. So whether you like 107.7 The End in Seattle, or you're a Foghead fan of KFOG in San Francisco, you can see what they're playing and buy the tunes in the Store.

Buy Music at the Store

There are lots of ways to hack your buying experience at the iTunes Music Store to make it more comfortable. In this section, we'll discuss ways to get the most for your dollar (or 99 cents) as you add to your music collection.

Use the Shopping Cart

If you use Apple products a lot, you know that a big part of the company's genius lies in making products that are easy to use, not just more advanced technically. The 1-Click feature in the iTunes Music Store is a great example. 1-Click lets you buy a song just by clicking a button. Apple didn't even invent 1-Click—it's licensed from Amazon.com—but it's an important part of the store experience.

Even though 1-Click is very handy, sometimes it's better to turn it off. If you have a slow Internet connection and you're buying several songs, it can be a drag to have to wait while iTunes downloads each tune. You can turn off 1-Click and use a shopping cart instead, a feature that should be familiar if you spend any time buying stuff on the Internet.

When you use the cart, iTunes adds a Shopping Cart icon to the sources list, and all the "Buy" buttons in the store change to "Add". When you click one of these, the song or album goes into your shopping cart. Any time you want to review the contents of your cart, click its icon in the sources list and you'll see what's inside. In the cart, Apple thoughtfully includes a list of other songs you might like, based on what you have already picked up. You can click "BUY NOW" to download the songs you've selected, or "REMOVE" to change your mind about an album or track.

If you want to go on the cart, open iTunes Preferences and click the Store tab. In the dialog box, click "Buy using a shopping cart". Click OK, and your cart is ready. You can switch back to 1-Click any time you want.

See your account information

You have a trusted relationship with the iTunes Music Store. It knows important information like your name, address, and credit card number. You can review or change any of the info you've entrusted to the store by checking your account information. To see or change your account info:

1. Click Music Store on the sources list.

2. If you're not signed in, click the Sign In button and supply your account ID and password.

3. Once you're signed in, click your account ID in the sign-in box. You'll be asked for your password again. Type it in and click View Account.

After completing these steps, you'll see the Apple Account Information screen. From this screen, you can change your e-mail address, credit card, and password reset info. You can also buy or redeem a gift certificate, set up an iTunes allowance, or take a look at all the music you've bought from the store since the beginning of time (which as you know was on April 28, 2003). To look at your past purchases, click the Purchase History button. There you see it: your past comes back to haunt you. Note that Apple doesn't provide a total of all the money you've ever spent at the store. That would be too scary.

The store groups together all music purchases made in a single day. If you want more detail about a particularly fun day, click the arrow at the left of the purchase summary. There's an example in Figure 11-4.

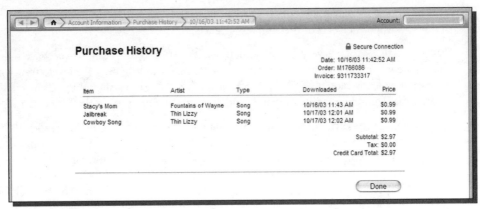

FIGURE 11-4: Music store purchase detail.

Caution

Apple warns you that once you've downloaded your music, you're responsible for backing it up —you can't download it again. This is an excellent reason to make sure you back up your purchased music after it's downloaded. If you fail to back up, and disaster strikes, you're in big trouble. You can contact customer service to plead for an exception so that you can download your music again—some iTunes Music Store customers posting on the Internet have reported success when doing that. But don't count on it: back up your tunes.

Wielding Your Authority

You probably already know that when you buy music from the Store, you can play it on five different computers. If you're about to get rid of a computer that you have used for playing tunes from the iTunes Music Store, make sure you deauthorize it before it leaves your possession. Here's how:

1. From the Advanced menu, choose Deauthorize Computer.

2. Make sure "Deauthorize Computer for Music Store Account" is selected (Figure 11-5).

3. Click OK.

4. Next, you'll be asked to supply your Store account password. This step makes sure that friends, children, and other souls can't cut your computer off from its music.

5. If all goes well, you'll see a message indicating that the computer has been deauthorized (Figure 11-6).

Once the computer is deauthorized, it won't be able to play music you bought from the Store, unless you re-authorize. If you decide you want to use this computer for Store-bought music again, just play a purchased song, then supply your password again. The computer will be back in the good graces of the Store.

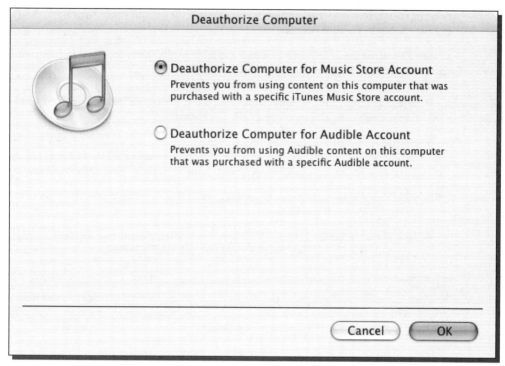

FIGURE 11-5: Deauthorizing your computer.

Check out iTunes essentials

When is an album not an album? When it's available from the iTunes Music Store. After all, when you buy an album from the store, you're not getting a physical object, just a bunch of bits that flow into your computer over an Internet connection. It didn't take long for Apple to figure out that as long as they were delivering virtual albums, they didn't have

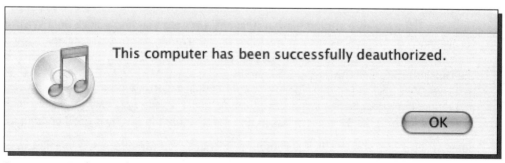

FIGURE 11-6: Confirming that your computer has been deauthorized.

to limit themselves to virtual copies of real albums: they could make their own. And that's the idea behind iTunes Essentials.

iTunes Essentials are collections of songs available at the store, arranged in lists that follow particular themes. Some examples of iTunes Essentials:

- *Break Up Songs*, a set of tunes about love gone wrong, including "I'll Never Fall in Love Again", "She's Gone", and "Ex-Girlfriend".

- *Soundtrack Classics* brings together a bunch of tunes that are best known for their connection to specific movies, such as "Raindrops Keep Falling on my Head" from *Butch Cassidy and the Sundance Kid* and "Mrs. Robinson" from *The Graduate*.

- *The Beauty of Opera* is a sort of "opera's greatest hits," with tracks from *Così Fan Tutte*, *Fidelio*, and *La Bohème*.

- *Hair Bands* is a collection of 1980s metal hits from groups like Twisted Sister, Def Leppard, and Quiet Riot (younger readers, ask your parents).

Each album in the iTunes Essentials collection comes with its own custom album cover. You can buy individual songs, or the whole list at once. To start playing around with this unique new way to acquire more music, click iTunes Essentials on the store's home page, on the left side near the bottom of the window.

Shopping the Competition

Articles in newspapers and magazines often mention the incompatibility between the iTunes Music Store and other online music outlets. The usual line is that you have two choices: Apple's store and an iPod, or any other store and any other portable music player. (If you have a Macintosh, you don't even have this choice, because only Apple's store supports Macs.) This is because Apple sells songs in Protected AAC format, which only iTunes and iPods know how to play, while other stores use a restricted version of Windows Media Audio (WMA), which Apple doesn't play in iTunes or iPod.

However, there is a way around these restrictions. Let's say you find a track on a WMA-based service, such as Napster, that's not available on the iTunes store. Assuming the store allows burning the track to CD, which is almost always the case, you can buy the song, burn it to CD, then rip it into a format iTunes and iPod understand, such as MP3 or AAC. Once it's in those formats, you'll be able to use it in iTunes and your iPod just like any other music file. The burning and reripping process causes some loss of clarity, but if it's the only way to get the tune, you might find it worth the 99 cents or less to find out whether the quality is good enough for you.

Some services give you WMA files without restrictions. You can also get WMA files when you rip CDs using Windows-based music players. Starting with iTunes version 4.5—the Windows

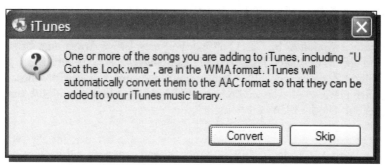

FIGURE **11-7: iTunes converts WMA files.**

version only—there's now an easy way to get unrestricted WMA files into iTunes and your iPod. Just drag one or more WMA files to the Library in the iTunes source list, and iTunes will show you a confirmation dialog (Figure 11-7) and then happily convert them to AAC format. The original WMA files aren't changed, and the new AAC files are fully compatible with iTunes.

See celebrity playlists

Here's another cool iTunes Music Store "virtual album" invention: the celebrity playlist. For this feature, Apple asks famous folks, like Tom Petty, Kevin Bacon, and Missy Elliott (older readers, ask your kids) to list their favorite songs. Apple then creates a playlist with the songs, plus a cool description of what makes the songs special to the person who put the list together. This is where you find out that Barry Manilow thinks Curtis Stigers is "the best kept secret in music", and Suzanne Vega has danced in front of the mirror to Duncan Sheik's "Barely Breathing". As with iTunes Essentials, you can buy individual songs or entire playlists.

Cross-Reference Want to feel like a celebrity? See *Make Your Own Celebrity Playlist* in this chapter to learn how to turn your favorite tunes into a crass selling tool.

Listen to audio books

Great music is not all there is to buy at the iTunes Music Store. If you think you've exhausted all the offerings at the store, check out the audio books section. You can start by choosing "Audiobooks" from the Genre pop-up on the store's home page. From this page, you can jump into audio book categories such as Sports, Self Development, and Classics. Download and listen to books by Neal Stephenson, George Carlin, Dan Brown, Stephen King, and hundreds of others.

The selection goes beyond books: the Periodicals category includes read-out-loud versions of *Scientific American*, the *Harvard Business Letter*, and *Fast Company*. You can find speeches and radio appearances by Dan Quayle, John Kerry, Lance Armstrong, Erin Brockovich, and dozens of others. The *National Lampoon Radio Hour* is here, as are *fully dramatized* Twilight Zone episodes. This is incredibly good stuff. Just as with songs, the store provides free previews of every audio book. The book samples last a minute and a half, three times the length of song previews.

Cross-Reference For information on how to buy audio books directly from `Audible.com`, see the section *Download Audio Books* in Chapter 2. `Audible.com` is worth checking out because prices there are sometimes cheaper than they are at the iTunes Music Store.

One thing to watch out for: abridged books. Reading books takes a long time—for example, Neal Stephenson's *The Diamond Age* is 512 pages long in paperback, and 18 1/2 hours on audio book. Because of this, many audio books are abridged: some stuff is left out. That makes them shorter and cheaper, but not the same as the paper book. Abridged audio books are always marked as such in the store.

But beware: unlike 99 cent songs, which you can grab like so many fun-size 3 Musketeers bars, most audio books are $10 or more, although some start at a couple of bucks. The audio books section of the store is an awesome way to blow through your credit card.

Champion Customer

When Steve Jobs delivered the keynote speech at Macworld Expo in January 2004, he described the success of the iTunes Music Store during its first 8 months in business. Jobs announced that the biggest store customer had spent more than $29,000. He went on to say that he couldn't give the name of the person who had spent that much so that the customer "wouldn't get in trouble with his parents."

Get More Free Stuff from the Store

We've discussed music, audio books, celebrity playlists, and other cool things you can find in the iTunes Music Store nooks and crannies. In this section, I'll point out more things you can do at the store that won't cost you anything. In fact, you don't even need to have a store account to use some of the features in this section. Have fun, you freeloader!

Listen to free previews

You probably know that you can get a free 30-second sample (also called a preview) of any song by double-clicking its title in a song list. You can also get a preview going by selecting a song and pressing Return or Enter. To preview another song, use the arrow keys to move the little speaker icon up and down the song list, then press the space bar to start listening. When a preview is finished, iTunes just stops—it doesn't go on to play the next one, as it does with a playlist. That's because if it just kept playing songs, it would be way too easy for folks to simply listen to dozens of song previews in a row, thus sucking down all the store's capacity and making things rotten for paying customers. So you have to start each preview manually.

If you have a slow connection, you might find your previews stuttering as the sample is loaded. You can fix this by asking iTunes to wait until the entire preview is downloaded before starting to play it. To do this, go to the Store tab in iTunes Preferences and check the box labeled "Load complete preview before playing". This setting will force you to wait a little longer before your preview starts, but you'll be able to get through the whole thing without the music stopping and restarting.

As You Wish

One of the coolest features of Amazon.com is the Wish List. This feature is promoted as a way to list your desires for other folks who are buying gifts for you, but the real value of the wish list is to keep track for *yourself* of what you want to buy someday. In iTunes 4.5, Apple introduced a similar ability to keep a list of tunes you'd like to purchase, just not right now. This feature works by allowing you to add iTunes Music Store previews to your playlists. You can try it out simply by dragging a song from the Store to a playlist in the source list.

Note that although you can keep as many previews as you want in a playlist, you still can't play a bunch of previews in a row automatically. When iTunes is playing a playlist and it encounters a preview, it will play that preview and then stop playing music until you start it again.

Get more artist information

The iTunes Music Store wants you to be an informed customer. Rather than just posting a bunch of albums and songs for you to buy, the store provides such features as 30-second previews and recommendations. In that spirit, you can use the store to find out cool stuff about your favorite artists. The key is to check out the artists' home pages in the iTunes Music Store. Let's take a look at some examples.

If you go to the Sheryl Crow page (Figure 11-8), you'll find links to an exclusive track, a celebrity playlist, her Web site, and even a video. Clicking the video link plays the music video right there in iTunes.

There are lots of other artists who get similar treatment in the iTunes Music Store, such as The Doors, Fischerspooner, They Might Be Giants, and Donna Summer. Not every artist has videos and Web links in the store, and the roster of those who do is always changing. Your best bet for finding the special ones is to look through the list of "Featured Artists" shown on the home page of the store and each genre.

FIGURE 11-8: Sheryl Crow page in iTunes Music Store.

Note You can see a complete list of music videos in the Store by clicking Music Videos on the Store's home page. For more about this, see the section *Watch videos and movie trailers* in this chapter.

You can get even more goodies for some artists. If you go to the page for John Coltrane, for example, you'll find links to a biography and discography, along with influencers, contemporaries, and "followers"—all with links to buy their music at the store, of course. Other artists that have biographies and influencers in the store include Eric Clapton (hey, I didn't know his real name was Eric Clapp), Bonnie Raitt, Moby, Aretha Franklin, Neil Young, Leonard Cohen, and dozens of others. Yes, Britney Spears too.

You can use the iTunes Music Store search feature to see what the store has to offer about your favorite artists.

1. Click the magnifying glass in the search box and choose Artists.

2. In the search box (which now says Search Artists under it), type the name of the artist you want to look for, and then press Return or Enter.

3. The top right corner of the window shows "Top Artists" that match your search. Click one to go to that artist's home page.

Try to do this only when you have some time to spare, because this is yet another way to pleasantly lose yourself inside the store for a long time.

Hacking the Culture: The Pepsi Analog Hack

Apple made a huge marketing splash early in 2004 by hooking up with Pepsi for a giveaway. Pepsi shipped *300 million* bottles of its products that advertised a chance to win a free song on the iTunes Music Store if there was a special code under the cap. One third of the caps were winners, while the other 200 million held only soda pop, not free music. (See Figure 11-9.)

A few weeks into the contest, somebody figured out a way to tell in advance if you were going to win. If you tilted the bottle at a 45-degree angle and looked hard through the plastic at the under-side of the cap, you could generally tell if the cap was a winner or not. With this hack, a diligent soft drink consumer could ensure that his bottle included a .99 musical prize before buying it. This is a great example of how hacking can expand beyond the limits of computers, digital devices, and high technology in general. And this hack is arguably ethical: the prizes were being given out any-way, and the hack simply improves the hacker's odds. Of course, the proprietor of your local store might disagree if you spend an hour hanging around and peering through his Pepsi products.

FIGURE 11-9: Pepsi iTunes giveaway redemption screen.
Used by permission of PepsiCo.

Use iTunes Music Store Links

When the music store first opened, clever shoppers soon discovered that Apple was using a system of Web-style URLs to refer to items in the store. By observing this URL system at work, you could decode what iTunes was doing and construct your own URLs that linked to songs, albums, and artists in the store. When you tried to open these links in a Web browser, iTunes would take control and go to the desired page. This was very cool. Later, Apple provided more information and features for using store links.

In this section, we'll discuss links to iTunes Music Store items and how to make them, share them, and have fun with them.

Get and share iTunes Music Store links

With iTunes 4.1 and later versions, Apple has made it incredibly easy for you to share a link to an item in the store. To grab the URL for any item, just right-click (or Control-click on a Mac) the item, then choose Copy iTunes Music Store URL from the menu. You're now loaded up with a link to the song, artist, or album that you can paste anywhere the text goes, such as in an e-mail or a Web article you're writing.

You can use drag and drop as a more direct way to get an item's link. Just drag a song or album cover and drop it into a target, such as a text document, and the store link travels along. Neat!

When you (or your e-mail recipient) click a link to a music store item, iTunes is summoned, connects to the music store, and displays the requested thing. Of course, once you're in the store, you can buy the song or album if you want, which is a big reason why Apple likes having these links.

Make Music Store URLs

You don't even have to be in iTunes to construct a link to a store item. Apple provides a cool Web page called iTunes Link Maker to help you out. This page, located at www.apple.com/itunes/linkmaker, lets you enter a song, album, or artist (or all of these), then automagically produces HTML containing a link to the item you want. You can then take the HTML and put it on your own Web site. Apple even provides a helpful badge and link that lets users download a free copy of iTunes if they don't have it. Figure 11-10 shows the page produced by the iTunes Link Maker.

Make your own celebrity playlists and iMixes

Why should celebrities have all the fun? Mac programming master John Vink has created the Celebrity Playlist Maker. This cool program lets you pick one of your playlists and

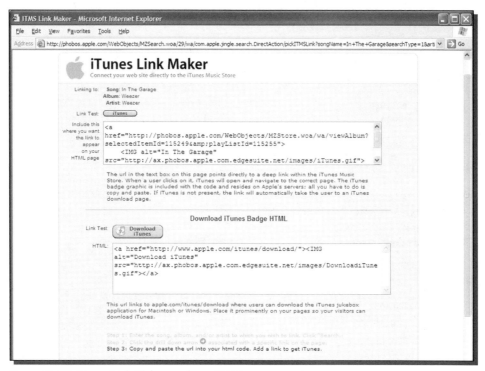

FIGURE 11-10: iTunes Link Maker produces HTML you can put on your pages.

turns it into a celebrity playlist, just like Beyoncé and Burt Bacharach get to have. You can even make insightful or silly comments about each song, just like the pros. And because Celebrity Playlist Maker generates real links to music store content, you can give your playlist to your friends, who can then click links so they can follow your impeccable taste in music and buy your recommendations. But please be careful: with great power comes great responsibility.

Figure 11-11 shows you the "pick a playlist" screen for Celebrity Playlist Maker. You'll find the Celebrity Playlist Maker on this book's companion Web site. Click the Hacking iPod link on the Extreme Tech Web site (www.wiley.com/compbooks/extremetech).

Another way to share your playlist is through Apple's iMix feature. With iMix, you can assemble your own playlist in iTunes, then publish it to the iTunes Music Store. You get to add your own comments for the whole mix, but not for individual songs. And, your audience gets to rate your iMix on a scale of one to five stars.

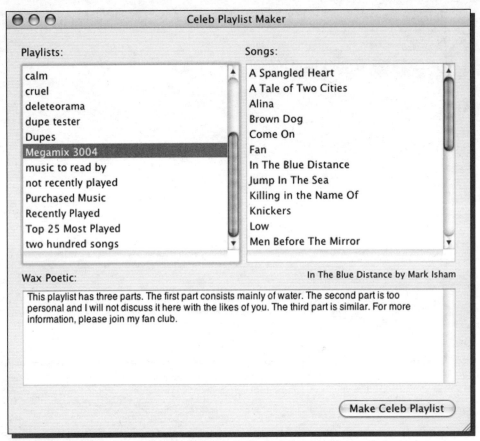

FIGURE 11-11: Make your own celebrity playlist.

Here's how to create your own iMix and put it on the iTunes Music Store for everyone's enjoyment:

1. Start with an existing playlist you already have in iTunes, or create a new one that holds the songs you want. You can use a conventional playlist or a smart playlist for this project.

2. Click the playlist to select its name in the iTunes source list.

3. You should see a right-pointing arrow next to the playlist name. Click that arrow. The first time you create an iMix, you'll see a dialog box explaining a little about how it works.

FIGURE 11-12: Publish your own iMix for fun and...well, for fun.

4. Next, the Music Store will ask you to sign in if you're not already connected. You can't publish an iMix unless you have a Music Store account, although publishing an iMix is free.

5. Once you're signed in, iTunes will confer with the Music Store and figure out which songs in your playlist are available in its virtual aisles. Then, it will create the iMix and ask you to name the iMix and enter its description (see Figure 11-12). After you click Publish, your iMix will be available on the store for all to see, buy, and rate. (You can find mine by going to your web browser and typing **http://tinyurl.com/39533.**)

Note   After you publish your iMix, iTunes displays a button you can click to tell your buddies about the iMix. If you click this button, iTunes e-mails a link that brings up your iMix. Once an iMix is published, it's not easy to find in the Music Store. The Store offers only two ways to view iMixes: top rated, and most recent. You can't search for an iMix by its name or by the name of the user who submitted it.

Miscellaneous Store Hacks

This section describes a few uncategorizable ways to have fun with the iTunes Music Store, from having the store send you reports of new releases to using the store to diagnose a bad Internet connection.

Get listings sent to you

As we've seen in this chapter, a big part of the fun of the iTunes Music Store is browsing. It's not hard to spend hours in the store just wandering around and enjoying the music. But you can also do the reverse: ask the store to send you highly focused information about what you want.

You can get information about iTunes Music Store content by subscribing to *RSS feeds* from Apple. RSS, which stands for Really Simple Syndication, is a file format that's designed to allow a Web site or other source to summarize information in an XML file and make it available for interested parties to read. Programs called RSS news readers grab RSS feeds and display them for you to read. When you subscribe to iTunes Music Store RSS feeds, your news reader gets new information when it's available. Instead of using iTunes to go through the store to find new stuff, the store delivers the news to you.

Apple publishes several RSS feeds for the store:

- Top Songs
- Top Albums
- New Releases
- Just Added
- Featured Albums & Exclusives

For example, if you subscribe to the Top Songs feed, you'll get a list of the hottest songs in the store delivered to your news reader every day. For each feed, you can choose to receive either 10 or 25 items. To subscribe to these feeds and to learn more about everything Apple does with RSS so you can spend even more of your time messing around with computer stuff, go to www.apple.com/rss. That page also provides links to a couple of RSS news readers, NetNewsWire for Macintosh and FeedDemon for Windows.

In addition to these standard feeds, Apple provides a way for you to construct your own custom RSS feeds that are narrowly focused on what you want. The custom feeds let you limit your news feeds to a particular genre or set of genres. You can also choose to receive fewer than 10 or more than 25 items at once. Use the page at phobos.apple.com/WebObjects/MZSearch.woa/wo/4.1 to generate your custom RSS feeds, as shown in Figure 11-13.

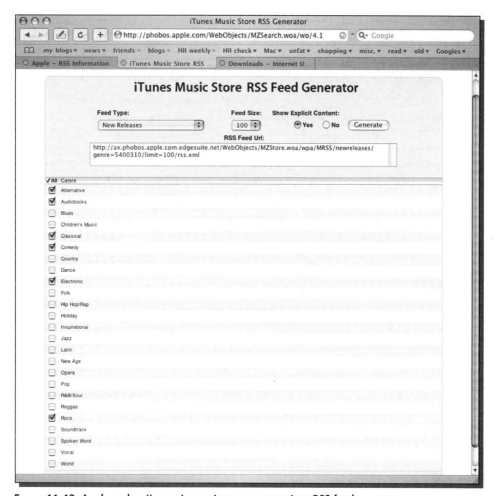

FIGURE 11-13: Apple makes it easy to create your own custom RSS feeds.

Watch videos and movie trailers

The iTunes Music Store isn't just for audio—you can also find some visual treats there. The Store includes more than 100 music videos for your amusement. You can't download them, but you can watch them in the Store. To check out the videos, just click "Music Videos" on the Store's home page.

The iTunes Music Store doesn't sell movies, but it offers a constantly updated collection of movie trailers for new releases and DVDs. As the originator of QuickTime technology, Apple has a long tradition of supplying movie trailers on the Internet. And the fact that Steve Jobs is a movie mogul himself—he's the chairman of animation studio Pixar—keeps

Apple interested in what's happening in the movie world. To see movie trailers, click the "Movie Trailers" link on the iTunes Music Store's home page.

Use iTunes Music Store to check your connection

iTunes has a Web browser buried inside it, and it uses that browser to connect to the store when you get the urge to do some shopping. The store and iTunes together form a very reliable pair. In fact, iTunes provides a great way to figure out if your Internet connection is working or not. If you're having trouble with your Web browser or e-mail program and you suspect your connection is flaky, click Music Store in the sources list. If you see the progress bar start to fill up and you're taken to the store, you know that your Internet connection is working OK, and the problem must lie somewhere else.

If you have recently been in the store, iTunes remembers the last page you looked at and shows you a cached version without actually connecting. To force a connection, just click any link on the page it's showing. Then watch the progress bar to see if your Internet connection is severed, or if you're just having trouble with an unreliable Web site or confused browser.

Rebuild "Purchased Music" playlist

As you buy tunes from the store, iTunes adds them to a special playlist it created for you called "Purchased Music". This playlist provides a handy reminder of what you've downloaded, so you can be sure to listen to your purchases. However, if you never use this playlist and you would rather not have it hanging around, you can delete it. If you do delete the "Purchased Music" list and you feel remorse later, you can get it back:

1. Choose Advanced ➪ Check for Purchased Music. You'll have to supply your account name and password.

2. iTunes will connect to the store and you'll most likely see a message that says "All purchased music has been downloaded for this account." As a side effect, the "Purchased Music" playlist is back—take a look at the sources list to confirm.

3. Although "Purchased Music" has been resurrected, it's blank. You have to find the songs yourself and add them to the list. To do this, select Library in the sources list.

4. Click in the Search box and type **Protected AAC**. This is the format for all music that the store sells, so it should find all the songs you've bought. Hey, that's a lot of songs!

5. Click anywhere in the song list to move the focus there, then choose Edit ➪ Select All.

6. With all your purchases now selected, drag them to "Purchased Music" and drop them there.

7. Now "Purchased Music" is back, and when you buy new tunes, they'll get added to the list.

Note If a song is downloading and something happens before it finishes—you quit iTunes, your network connection is lost, a bear steals your computer—you can still get the song you paid for. Just use the Check for Purchased Music item in the Advanced menu, and iTunes will automatically resume downloading any music that didn't quite get there previously.

Close the store

For our last trick, we present the ultimate anti-store hack: getting rid of it, at least in your copy of iTunes. If you find the store too tempting to have around, you can turn it off entirely. In iTunes Preferences, go to the Store tab, uncheck the "Show iTunes Music Store" box, and click OK. Poof, the store is gone from the sources list. Of course, if you ever want to bring it back, it's as simple as returning to Preferences and checking the box again.

Never Can Say Goodbye

Even if you have the store turned off in your copy of iTunes, clicking one of those links to content in the store (as described in *Use iTunes Music Store Links*) still takes you to the store. Unchecking the "Show iTunes Music Store" box in Preferences just removes the store icon from the sources list—it doesn't actually get you kicked out of the store.

Summary

The iTunes Music Store is a great place to spend a few hours or a few dollars. The store is just as cheap as you want it to be: you can browse for hours without spending a dime, get something great for 99 cents, or buy a few albums and audio books as you ring up a bill of $100 or more. It's very easy to get lost in the store even if you're not spending money. This chapter took longer to write than it should have because I couldn't resist stopping and listening to previews, sampling audio books, reading artist biographies, and taking Billboard-chart-induced nostalgia trips. Have a great time shopping in the store, and come on back for more hacky stuff next in the Appendices.

Appendices

part

iPod Note Reader

About iPod Note Reader

Apple shipped version 2.0 of the iPod software in 2003. This update expanded the iPod's repertoire to include a totally new category of information: notes. When you choose Extras from your iPod's main menu, you see the new Notes category, along with Contacts, Calendar, Clock, and Games. The Notes feature lets you create files of text on your computer that you can copy to your iPod and see on the screen.

iPod Note Reader is the software inside the iPod that deals with notes. Note Reader does a lot more than just show text files on the screen. It includes powerful features like a basic markup language for text formatting, a way to create hyperlinks to other notes, and even the ability to play songs from notes. Coolest of all, you can use Note Reader to hide the standard iPod main menu and provide your own custom user interface to notes and music.

In this appendix, we'll delve into the iPod Note Reader and learn about these and other neat things you can accomplish.

The cult of notes

Although Note Reader is one of the most powerful non-musical iPod features, it's vastly under-used. Apple devotes only a little space to Note Reader on the iPod part of its Web site, and there isn't a lot of non-Apple software that uses Notes. One key reason for this is that iPod 2.0 software, the version that includes Note Reader, doesn't work on the first two generations of iPods. Because of this, many shareware developers use the basic text displaying features of Contacts, available on all iPods, instead of taking advantage of cool Note Reader features.

The fact that Note Reader has unexploited cool features makes it a great candidate for hackery. I hope that reading this appendix will inspire you to create something cool for your iPod using Note Reader.

Getting notes onto your iPod

Loading notes onto your iPod is easy. Notes are simply text files, which you can create with virtually any editor or word processor on any computer. Using the Finder or Windows Explorer, put your wannabe notes inside the Notes folder when your iPod is connected to your computer. When you disconnect the iPod and choose Extras ⇨ Notes, all the items in the Notes folder appear. There's no syncing or other explicit process required.

Note When you create notes, make sure you save them as plain-text files. Word processors and text editors prefer to use file formats that also save information about fonts and other style elements, but these files won't look right in Notes. Almost every program has an option to allow you save as plain text, also called "text only".

Note Reader duplicates the hierarchy of notes and folders that you set up in the Finder or Windows Explorer. If you create subfolders inside the Notes folder, those subfolders will show up on your iPod. You can have folders nested as deeply as you want, and Note Reader will reflect your hierarchy.

Tip You can add the Notes command to your iPod's main menu, making it a little easier to get to. When you become a true Notes power user, you'll want this enhancement. To put Notes on your iPod's main menu:

1. From your iPod's main menu, choose Settings ⇨ Main Menu.

2. Scroll down under Extras to Notes.

3. Press *Select* to change the display to read "Notes On".

The next time you go back to the main menu, you'll see Notes in a much-deserved prominent position below Extras.

Note Reader Markup

In this section, we'll go over Note Reader's efficient markup language. Note Reader defines tags for various uses, including line breaks, links to other documents and songs, page titles, and more. If you've ever seen HTML, you should be able to figure out Note Reader's tags. Note Reader tags are enclosed between angle brackets, just as in many other markup languages. The text in Note Reader tags is case-insensitive, so <title> is just as good as <TITLE>.

Text

Note Reader defines a few tags for displaying text:

-
forces a new line. An actual carriage return in the file also forces a new line, although you can change that behavior by setting a preference.

- <P> and </P> can be used to enclose a line. Text following the </P> is displayed on a new line.

- <TITLE> and </TITLE> enclose the title of the note. This text is shown in the list of notes and is used as the note title, displayed at the top when the note is shown. Titles that are too long are truncated. If a note has no <TITLE>tag, its filename is used as the title.

The following are some examples of basic text tags:

```
Sedan delivery<BR>is a job I know I'll keep
```

Text starting with "is" is displayed on a new line.

```
<P>It was a dark and stormy night.</P> <P>At least my iPod was
well-protected from the elements.</P>
```

Starts a new line before "At least".

```
<TITLE>Not your father's note</TITLE>
```

Uses the text as the note's name in the Notes folder and at the top of the screen when the note is displayed.

Tips and ideas

- Because <BR> and <P> are used in HTML on Web sites, they can be handy when you're translating Web pages for a new life as iPod notes.

- You can use <BR> between items to force a new line without having to put each one on a separate line in your text file.

- When you use <TITLE>, remember that the note will be listed by its title when using the iPod software but it will appear under its filename when you look for it in the Finder or Windows Explorer.

Hyperlinks

Like any good hypertext language, Note Reader markup lets you link one document to another. Borrowing from HTML, Note Reader uses the A HREF tag. Start your linkage with <A HREF="filename"> and finish with </A>. Any text between the tags is a link, displayed on the iPod screen with an underline. If you highlight the link text and click the Select button, the linked note appears. You select links by scrolling the wheel. If there's only one link on the screen, it's always selected—scrolling the wheel doesn't do anything except provide finger exercise.

Absolute and relative references

Just as with HTML hyperlinks, Note Reader links can be relative or absolute. Relative links refer to files that are in the same folder as the note that contains the link. Absolute links let you refer to files outside the current folder.

Absolute links always start with a slash or other path delimiter; while relative links never start with a path delimiter. Absolute links start at the Notes folder, which is the base of the entire universe of notes when you use links. Use slash or another path delimiter to indicate that you're descending into a directory. For example,

```
See a <A HREF="/old map">map</A>.
```

links to a note named "old map" that's stored in the highest level of the Notes folder, while

```
Time for <a href="/recipes/cheesecake">dessert</a>
```

refers to a note named "cheesecake" in the "recipes" folder, which is in the Notes folder. Mmm...cheesecake.

Relative links start in the same folder as the current note, and never begin with a path delimiter. So, for example,

```
<A HREF="Danger Bird">Fly away</A>
```

links to a note in the same folder as the note containing the link. Here's another:

```
<A HREF="dogs/puppies">Puppy list</a>
```

This one finds a folder named "dogs" in the same folder as the current note, then gets a file named "puppies" in that folder.

If you want to impress officials of international standards bodies, you can use the standard URL syntax for a file when you create a link, which is to precede the filename with "FILE://". Using this syntax, our last example looks like this:

```
<A HREF="file://dogs/puppies">Puppy list</a>
```

The same syntax works for absolute references:

```
Time for <a href="file:///recipes/cheesecake">dessert</a>
```

As with tag names, references to filenames are always case-insensitive.

Note   When you create links to files, make sure you include any file extensions, such as .txt. Mac OS X and Windows often hide file extensions. In Mac OS X, you can see a file's full name, including any extension, by selecting the file in the Finder and choosing File ⇨ Get Info. In Windows, right-click the file and choose Open With. If you see a list of programs, pick Choose Program. The file's full name, including extension, will be shown at the top of the dialog box.

Cross-Reference See the section *"Path delimiters"* in this appendix for more information.

Linking to a folder

You can use a hyperlink to point to a whole folder of notes. If you click such a link, the list of notes in the folder appears on the screen. To point to a folder of notes, just link to the folder name. For example, if "spacecraft" is a folder of Notes, the following link:

```
<A HREF="spacecraft">The final frontier</A>
```

takes you to that folder. You can link to the Notes folder itself with various syntax forms, as in the following:

```
<A HREF="file://">Notes folder</A>

<A HREF="file:///">All my notes</A>

<A HREF="">Top level</A>

<A HREF="/">Take a look</A>
```

The ability to link to the Notes folder was added in iPod Software 2.1—it won't work in earlier versions.

Tips and ideas

- You can link to songs (see *"Links to songs"* in this chapter), but not to any other iPod information, such as Contacts.

- Linking files this way provides you with a solid basic hypertext system. You can use it to set up a web of linked information or even a simple database.

Note Reader's hyperlinks are ideal for adventure-style games. In fact, the original adventure game has been ported to the iPod. It's available for download at this book's companion Web site; click on the Hacking iPod link on the Extreme Tech Web site at www.wiley.com/compbooks/ extremetech. Other folks are getting into the act, too. *"The Rise of the Lost"* is a new notes-based iPod adventure game, available from XO Play at www.xoplay.com.

Links to songs

Your iPod is full of music, so it seems only natural that Note Reader lets you construct notes that link to songs. Hyperlinks to songs are a special kind of link, with following syntax:

```
<a href="ipod:music?song=optimistic">Big fish</a>
```

The "ipod:music" syntax tells the Note Reader that this is a song and not a note. Unlike links to notes, there's no folder hierarchy to specify. Clicking a song link starts playing the song. You can use various other values, called *filters*, instead of "song". Here's the full set of available filters:

- song
- artist
- album
- playlist
- genre
- composer

You can combine filters to distinguish between different songs with the same name:

```
<A HREF="ipod:music?song=Yesterday&artist="Bella
Cooperman">Classic version</A>
```

If you use a link that matches more than one song, all the matches are combined into a groovy temporary playlist. With judicious use of filters in song links, you can create playlists that even iTunes would envy. For example, you can grab a subset of an artist's music:

```
<a href="ipod:music?artist=Neil Young"&genre=rock">Rock out</a>
```

Because playing a single song is the most common use of this kind of link, it has a special shortcut syntax:

```
<a href="song=Disappointing Show">Play it</a>
```

When you click a song link, the iPod normally starts playing the song and goes to the Now Playing screen. You can keep the note on screen instead by using the "Now Playing" element in the tag:

```
<A HREF="ipod:music?song="Trancey"&NowPlaying=false">Listen</A>
```

Note Due to a bug, the nowPlaying tag is ignored in iPod Software 2.1 and iPod mini 1.0.

Tips and ideas

- Try using song links to make your own "*Name That Tune*" game. Use AppleScript or another automated tool on your computer to select some songs, then build a note with links to the songs.
- You can only specify one value for each filter, which means you can't create a playlist that combines multiple artists or albums, unfortunately.

■ See if you can construct a touch-tone generator with notes on your iPod. Get recordings of each of the tones a telephone can generate into iTunes. Then build a note containing numbers with links to their proper tones. For extra credit, read information from your iPod's Contacts and dial their numbers.

Referrer notes

Note Reader lets you create notes that hold no content of their own, but immediately open another note they point to. You can use this kind of note as a form of indirection. To do this, create a file that has one hyperlink in it, and give the file a name that ends in .link. When you open that file, you won't see its contents—instead, the linked file will open immediately. For example, create the following file:

```
<A HREF="camera"> </a>

<TITLE>My birthday present</TITLE>
```

Save the file as a note with the name `mylist.link`. Because the file ends with .link, when you select in the Notes folder, it will open the link it contains, which is the note called "camera". We've also given the note a title, "My birthday present", so that the ".link" name won't appear in the Notes folder.

The link can be to a song or playlist, too. If you link to music, the tunes will start playing when you open the note. This feature lets you create notes that play music as soon as they're opened, without having to select links.

Another Note Reader indirection trick lets you create a file that's a list of links to other notes. If you give this file a name ending with .linx, Note Reader will display it as if it were a folder of links instead of a note of links. So, for example, create a note with the following text:

```
<a href="Something Good">start</a>

<a href="Anything Can Happen">middle</a>

<a href="Trance Atlantic Flight">end</a>
```

Save the note in a file named `sample.linx`. When you go to Notes, you won't be able to open `sample.linx` directly. Instead, it will show up in Notes with an arrow after its name, as if it were a folder. Clicking the arrow shows the links in the folder, in the order they're listed in the file. If you then pick one of the links, you'll see the note it points to.

As with .link files, you can fill your .linx notes with musical hyperlinks. When you select one of those, a song starts to play. You can even mix notes with songs in the same .linx file.

Put a <TITLE> tag in the .linx folder to give it a different name when viewed in the Notes list.

Taking over the notes folder

You can gain control of the Notes folder by creating a file of hyperlinks, naming it `main.linx`, and putting it into the main Notes folder. When you go to Notes on the iPod, it lists the links from `main.linx` and totally ignores anything else in the Notes folder. You can even replace the word "Notes" that normally appears at the top of the screen by putting a <TITLE> tag in your main.linx file.

Take Complete Control of Your iPod

You can go one step farther and have Note Reader take over your iPod completely, forcing the iPod to start up into Notes mode and providing no way out. To find out more about this awesome trick, see the Preferences section in this appendix.

Tips and ideas

- Notes are alphabetized by title when you look at them on your iPod. Note Reader works this way in the Notes folder itself as well as any subfolder. But items in a .linx file appear in the same order in which they're listed in the file, alphabetical or otherwise. So, you can use a .linx file to provide an alternate ordering for notes in a folder. This can be useful for lessons, narrative text in chunks, or any other files that you want to force into a particular order.

Preferences

Note Reader defines preferences you can set by including preferences tags in your notes. You can set global preferences by including a file named "Preferences" or "Preferences.txt" in the Notes folder. Local preferences in the current note override corresponding global settings.

You can set turn each preference setting on or off by setting it to "true" or "false". Preferences tags look like this:

```
<meta name="SomePreference" content="true">
```

Here are the preferences you can set:

- NotesOnly. This preference lets you take complete control of the iPod. When the iPod starts up, it checks to see if NotesOnly is true. If so, the iPod bypasses the startup screen and goes directly to Notes instead, and there is no way out. If you turn this setting on and add a main.linx file, you can effectively create a custom user interface based on notes. You can only set NotesOnly in the global preferences file, not in individual notes.

French Heritage

This feature is nicknamed "museum mode" and reportedly was added to allow the Louvre in Paris to create an iPod-based audio tour.

- NowPlaying. When this is `true`, playing songs from Notes links will go to the Now Playing screen. Setting this to `false` will leave the note displayed when the music starts.

Note Due to a bug, the nowPlaying tag is ignored in iPod Software 2.1 and iPod mini 1.0.

- LineWrap. If this preference is `true`, Note Reader will ignore carriage returns in notes. Only <P> and <BR> tags will start a new line.

- ShowBodyOnly. This setting lets you put text in your notes that will never be displayed, such as comments. If this preference is `true`, only the text that lies between <BODY> and </BODY> tags is displayed. If those tags are not in the note, all the text is shown.

- HideAllTags. When this setting is `true`, text between the angle brackets is not displayed. This is useful for hiding stray HTML-style tags that aren't implemented by Note Reader.

The default value for NowPlaying is `"true"`; for all other preferences, the default is "`false`".

In addition to setting preferences, you can add a "<TITLE>" tag to the preferences file to specify a name that will appear at the top of the Notes screen in place of the usual "Notes".

If you put a <SHOWPREFERENCES> tag in any note, a list of the preferences and their settings will appear in its place when you look at the note.

Error Checking

When the iPod starts up, Note Reader scans all notes and checks them for various kinds of errors, including links to non-existent notes, syntax errors in tags, and other problems. If you open any note that includes an <ERRORS> tag, the list of all errors found is displayed instead of the contents of the note.

Note References to notes are checked to make sure the file actually exists, but links to songs are not checked.

Because all errors for all notes are reported together, you only need one note with the <ERRORS> tag. Just create a note with this tag and save it with the name "Errors". You can then use that note to check for any problems.

Limits and Other Issues

Each note can be up to 4Kb, and you can have up to 1,000 notes. Text beyond the 4K limit is ignored, as are notes past the first 1,000. Note Reader scans and reads notes in the background when the iPod starts up, loading up to 64K of notes at a time. If you go directly to Notes, and you have a lot of Notes, you might have to wait while the Note Reader finishes its work. But if you use a different feature right after starting up, you probably won't notice the iPod loading notes.

Path delimiters

You can use slash, backslash, or colon interchangeably to show descending directory levels when referring to a file. Here are some examples:

```
<a href="animals/dog">The dog goes woof</a>
```

```
<A HREF="radio:genre:deep house">play</A>
```

```
<a href="all\fewer\some\this one">Go for it</a>
```

You can't mix delimiters in a single file reference, so the following example will result in an error:

```
<a href="mark/my:words\this one">Go for it</a>
```

If a reference includes a file or directory that contains one of the delimiter characters in its filename, you should use a different delimiter when referring to it. For example, if a filename includes a slash, use a colon or backslash as the delimiter. In the unlikely case of a file reference that includes all three delimiters, use a backslash before the delimiters as an "escape" character. For example, to link to a file named *david/did\notes*: your link would look like this:

```
<A HREF="david\/did\\notes\:">Right here</A>
```

Note that a file with all three delimiters is even more unlikely than you might imagine, because colons are not allowed in file names in either HFS Extended or FAT32, the only file systems supported by iPod software. So our hypothetical file d*avid/did\notes*: would have to exist in some future file system that's neither HFS Extended nor FAT32.

Instructions tag

Any files that include an <INSTRUCTIONS> tag will be listed in the Notes with the name Instructions, no matter what its filename. When you open one of these notes, instructions for using the Notes feature will be displayed instead of the file's contents. The name "Instructions" and the contents are translated as appropriate to match the iPod's current language setting.

Text encodings

Note Reader supports various text encodings. If the iPod is set to use Japanese, Korean, or Chinese, Note Reader assumes notes are in the matching encoding. Otherwise, Note Reader assumes Latin-1 encoding on FAT32-formatted iPods and MacRoman on HFS-formatted iPods. You can tell Note Reader to use a non-default encoding for a file by including a tag like this:

```
<?xml encoding="MacJapanese"?>
```

Note reader supports the following encodings:

- Latin-1
- MacRoman
- MacJapanese
- Korean
- Simplified Chinese
- Traditional Chinese
- UTF8 Unicode
- UTF16 Unicode

If you have a note with an encoding tag, put the tag at the top of the file.

More Information

To get the full official story on Note Reader, see Apple's documentation, available at `developer.apple.com/hardware/ipod`. And if you create any Note Reader applications, let me know at `hackingipod@papercar.com`.

Where to Find More Information

iPods and iTunes are very popular, and as you might imagine, the Internet is filled with information about both. This appendix lists a bunch of the best sources of iPod knowledge.

General Information

- iPodlounge (`www.ipodlounge.com`) is probably the most popular and informative site. News, forums, downloads, and the famous "iPods around the world" gallery are cool sections. You can buy an iPodlounge t-shirt here.

- iPoding (`www.ipoding.com`) is another fun site filled with tips, discussions, and iPod stuff.

- iPod Hacks (`www.ipodhacks.com`) is an iPod news and community site with a slight techno-geeky bent, which is always nice.

- Meetup is a service for pushing folks away from their computers and into the real world, where they can get together in person. Find out about the iPod group at (`ipod.meetup.com.`)

iPod Accessories and Other Products

- Dr. Bott LLC (`www.drbott.com`) has a great collection of must-have and wanna-have iPod gear for sale.

- `www.everythingipod.com` sells stuff that ranges from color-coordinated iPod mini armbands to recordable CDs for iTunes.

- Apple's own online store carries a wide array of iPod accessories, and only the very best, of course. It's at `apple.com/store`.

- The big online retailers have plenty of iPod stuff as well. Search for iPod products at `shopping.yahoo.com`, `amazon.com`, and `froogle.com`.

Scripting, Programming, and Hacks

- Doug's AppleScripts for iTunes (`www.malcolmadams.com/itunes`) is indispensable for Mac iPod users who want to enhance their iTunes and iPod experiences.

- Explore the surprising depth and power of smart playlists at `smartplaylists.com`. Here you can find hints on making the most of your smart playlists and trade ideas with other iTunes fanatics.

- Visit `developer.apple.com/hardware/ipod` for advanced technical information on the iPod, including drawings and measurements to help you make cases and other accessories.

- If you're interested in programming your own plug-ins for the iTunes Visualizer, you'll need to visit `developer.apple.com/sdk/#iTunes` to get the tools and info.

- When you want to look for new shareware and utility programs for your iPod and iTunes, surf on over to `download.com`, `versiontracker.com`, and `macupdate.com`. These sites keep track of new software and provide links for downloading.

Apple and iPod News and Rumors

Apple gets a lot of press, especially now that it makes the world's most popular digital music player. There are many Web sites that deal in Apple news and rumors:

- Sources of Apple news include TidBITS (`www.tidbits.com`), MacNN (`www.macnn.com`), Macintouch (`www.macintouch.com`), and MacMinute (`www.macminute.com`). Read them every day before breakfast.

- For nerdier news and spirited discussions, see MacSlash (`macslash.org`) and SlashDot (`slashdot.org`).

- Many news sites allow you to create customized news by using queries or RSS feeds. For tons of iPod and iTunes news, try this at Wired (`wired.com`), Google News (`news.google.com`), CNET (`news.search.com`), and Yahoo News (`search.news.yahoo.com`).

- Get your salt shaker and check out Apple rumor sites, which are sometimes right but always fun, including SpyMac (`www.spymac.com`), Mac Rumors (`macrumors.com`), Think Secret (`thinksecret.com`), and the aptly named Crazy Apple Rumors (`www.crazyapplerumors.com`).

Official Apple Information

Go to the source for the definitive information.

- Visit `ipod.com` and `itunes.com` for the latest word from Apple on our favorite products.

- See `www.apple.com/support/ipod` to find out how to keep your iPod healthy, or make it better when it's not working well.

- Subscribe to RSS feeds from the iTunes Music Store by visiting `www.apple.com/rss`.

- In the unlikely, unhappy event your iPod needs service, visit `www.apple.com/support/ipod/service` to find out what you must do.

Everything Else

For new iPod and iTunes links, and for corrections and additions to this book, visit the book's companion Web site. Just go to the Extreme Tech Web site at `www.wiley.com/compbooks/extremetech` and click on the link to the *Hacking iPod* site.

iPod and iTunes Version History

About This Appendix

This appendix provides information about all versions of iPods, iPod software, and iTunes released by Apple.

Table C-1	iPod Models		
Generation	Intro date	Current software	Description
1	October 2001	1.3	The original iPod. 5GB capacity
	March 2002	1.3	10GB model
2	July 2002	1.3	Touch wheel. Thinner and lighter. Remote control. 10 and 20GB
3	April 2003	2.1	All touch controls. New control layout. Thinner and lighter. Backlit buttons. New connector and dock. 10, 15, and 30GB
	September 2003	2.1	20 and 40GB models
Mini	January 2004	Mini 1.0	Click wheel. 4GB. 5 colors

Table C-2   iPod Software Versions

Version	Intro date	New features
1.0	October 2001	First release
1.1	March 2002	Equalizer, shuffle by album, scrubbing, Contacts, Korean and Chinese languages
1.2 through 1.2.6	July 2002	Browse by album or genre, Calendar, clock, "OK to disconnect", audiobook support, sound check
1.3	April 2003	Backlight menu, AAC support
2.0 through 2.0.2	April 2003	On-The-Go playlist, reorganized clock menu, alarm clock, iCal to-do lists, Notes, new games, customizable main menu, backlight menu, update smart playlist info and rate songs on iPod, AAC support, museum mode
2.1	October 2003	Voice memo and photo storage support, On-The-Go playlist sync, music quiz
Mini 1.0	February 2004	First release

Table C-3   iTunes Versions

Version	Intro date	Description and new features
1	January 2001	First release. Rip, mix, burn!
2	October 2001	iPod support. Equalizer, crossfade, burn MP3 CDs. Last version for Mac OS 9
3	July 2002	Smart playlists, star ratings, sound check, join tracks, genres, keep music folder organized, copy to library on import, consolidate library
4	April 2003	iTunes Music Store and AAC support, music sharing, burn DVDs, album artwork.
		4.0.1: music sharing limited to local subnet only. Oops. 4.1: first Windows version. On-The-Go playlist sync, burn playlists that span discs, copy or drag links from iTunes Music Store, audiobooks in iTunes Music Store. 4.2: AOL accounts can be used in iTunes Music Store

If you're running Mac OS 9, you can download iTunes 2 at `docs.info.apple.com/article.html?artnum=120073`.

For More Information

If you're not sure which iPod model you have, check out the article at `docs.info.apple.com/article.html?artnum=61688`. To find out which software version your iPod is running, see `docs.info.apple.com/article.html?artnum=60984`.

iTunes Library XML Format

appendix D

Introduction

iTunes stores its music library using a structured format called XML. This appendix provides an overview of the iTunes library format.

You can find out where your Library file is located by opening iTunes Preferences and going to the Advanced tab. You can make a copy of your Library by choosing File ⇨ Export Library. Before you fool around with your Library file, make sure to create a copy by using this Export command.

Because XML files are just text, you can look at the Library using any text editor, or you can use an XML editor, such as Property List Editor in Mac OS X. Figure D-1 shows the first part of a Library file as displayed by Internet Explorer 6 for Windows. Figure D-2 shows the same information in Property List Editor on Mac OS X.

Header

The first few lines of the Library provide information about the XML document type:

```
<?xml version="1.0" encoding="UTF-8"?>
```

```
<!DOCTYPE plist PUBLIC "-//Apple
Computer//DTD PLIST 1.0//EN"
"http://www.apple.com/DTDs/PropertyList-
1.0.dtd">
```

```
<plist version="1.0">
```

The !DOCTYPE statement includes a link to Apple's document type definition (DTD) for its XML files.

The rest of the file is enclosed in <dict> tags.

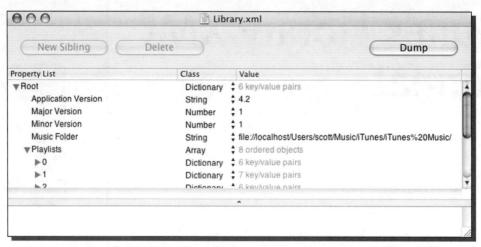

FIGURE D-1. Part of a Library displayed in Internet Explorer for Windows.

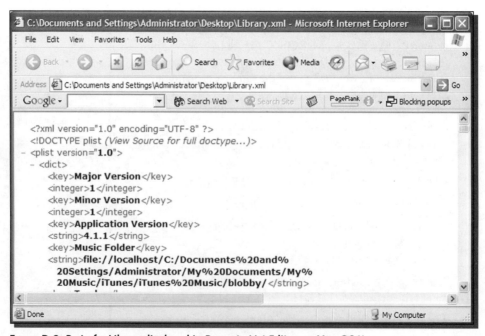

FIGURE D-2. Part of a Library displayed in Property List Editor on Mac OS X.

Creator and Library Info

The next section of the file contains keys that provide the version number of the iTunes application that's using the Library, and the location of the Library file:

```
<key>Major Version</key><integer>1</integer>

<key>Minor Version</key><integer>1</integer>

<key>Application Version</key><string>4.2</string>

<key>Music Folder</key>

<string>file://localhost/Users/scott/Music/iTunes/iTunes%20Music/</string>
```

Tracks and Playlists

The next section lists all the tracks in the Library. The entire section is enclosed in <dict> tags, as is each individual track. The information for each track starts with a key for its track ID and includes all other details about the track, as shown in the following example:

```
<key>Track ID</key><integer>1165</integer>

<key>Name</key><string>Born Fighter</string>

<key>Artist</key><string>Nick Lowe</string>

<key>Composer</key><string>Nick Lowe</string>

<key>Album</key><string>16 All-Time Lowes</string>

<key>Grouping</key><string>classics</string>

<key>Genre</key><string>Rock</string>

<key>Kind</key><string>MPEG audio file</string>

<key>Size</key><integer>3039019</integer>

<key>Total Time</key><integer>189779</integer>

<key>Start Time</key><integer>71000</integer>

<key>Stop Time</key><integer>142000</integer>

<key>Disc Number</key><integer>1</integer>

<key>Disc Count</key><integer>1</integer>

<key>Track Number</key><integer>1</integer>

<key>Track Count</key><integer>16</integer>

<key>BPM</key><integer>100</integer>

<key>Date Modified</key><date>2004-03-15T01:33:12Z</date>

<key>Date Added</key><date>2004-02-20T01:03:44Z</date>

<key>Bit Rate</key><integer>128</integer>

<key>Sample Rate</key><integer>44100</integer>

<key>Equalizer</key><string>Rock</string>

<key>Comments</key><string>Awesome liver version</string>
```

```
<key>Rating</key><integer>60</integer>

<key>Normalization</key><integer>1767</integer>

<key>Compilation</key><true/>

<key>File Type</key><integer>1297106739</integer>

<key>File Creator</key><integer>1397375309</integer>

<key>Location</key><string>file://localhost/Users/scott/Music/
iTunes/iTunes%20Music/Compilations/16%20All-Time%20Lowes/
01%20Born%20Fighter.mp3</string>

<key>File Folder Count</key><integer>4</integer>

<key>Library Folder Count</key><integer>1</integer>
```

Following the list of tracks, the playlists appear, enclosed in <dict> tags. The Library itself is listed in this section as a playlist. Each playlist includes an array of the tracks it contains. Here is an example of a regular playlist:

```
<key>Name</key><string>favorites</string>

<key>Playlist ID</key><integer>19338</integer>

<key>Playlist Persistent ID</key><string>F43F2BCA0A367E80</string>

<key>All Items</key><true/>

<key>Playlist Items</key>

<array>

    <dict>

    <key>Track ID</key><integer>1191</integer>

    <key>Track ID</key><integer>1230</integer>

    <key>Track ID</key><integer>1257</integer>

    <key>Track ID</key><integer>1380</integer>

    </dict>

</array>
```

Smart playlists include slightly different information, including encoded data for creating the playlist:

```
<key>Name</key><string>not recently played</string>

<key>Playlist ID</key><integer>12525</integer>

<key>Playlist Persistent ID</key><string>7E8BE57B647388FC</string>

<key>All Items</key><true/>

<key>Smart Info</key>

<data>

AQEAAwAAAIAAAAZAAAAAAAAAAAAAAAAAAAAAAAAAAAAAAAAAAAAAAAA

</data>
```

```
<key>Smart Criteria</key>
<data>
U0xzdAABAAEAAAABAAAAAAAAAAAAAAAAAAAAAAAAAAAAAAAAAAAA
</data>
<key>Playlist Items</key>
<array>
<dict>
<key>Track ID</key><integer>1165</integer>
</dict>
<dict>
<key>Track ID</key><integer>1167</integer>
</dict>
<dict>
<key>Track ID</key><integer>1169</integer>
</dict>
<dict>
<key>Track ID</key><integer>1171</integer>
</dict>
<dict>
<key>Track ID</key><integer>1180</integer>
</dict>
<dict>
<key>Track ID</key><integer>1182</integer>
</dict>
<dict>
<key>Track ID</key><integer>1184</integer>
</dict>
<dict>
<key>Track ID</key><integer>1192</integer>
</dict>
</array>
```

Computers are better at parsing XML files than are most humans. You can find a PHP script that converts an iTunes Library to an array at codetriangle.com/iTunesXmlParser. For another approach, and to find out more about PHP, see developer.apple.com/ internet/opensource/php.html. For more fun, check out www.itunesregistry .com, a place where iTunes users can use their Library files to report what they're listening to.

Index